Quick & Easy!

40-Minute Power Resume

The Only Resume You Will Ever Need!

The Complete Guide to Resume Development
for the unemployed, employed and underemployed.

Everything you need to know to...

- Write your winning resume in record time
  Use the *EXPRESS RESUME*...
  follow the ➔ for quick results!
- Beat out the competition through targeted job strategies
- Avoid 30 major job search eliminators
- Learn the magic of the Hill & Associates
  "Peanut Butter Principle"

by Beverly Hill

 Published by Renaissance Ink Press, 283 N. North Lake Boulevard, Suite 111, Altamonte Springs, FL 32701, First edition.

Library of Congress Cataloging-in-Publication Data
Hill, Beverly

The complete guide to resume writing. Everything you need to write a resume in 20 minutes to 2 hours and conduct a successful job search in record time.

Includes an index.
ISBN 0-9676906-0-9

HOW TO CONTACT THE AUTHOR

Beverly Hill provides career coaching, training, and development for private and corporate clients. Requests for information about these services, as well as inquiries about availability for coaching, resume development, career strategies, speeches, and seminars, should be directed to:

Hill & Associates, Inc.
283 N. North Lake Boulevard, Suite 111
Altamonte Springs, FL 32701-3437
(407) 767-8787 (407) 767-8801 Fax
Web site: www.JobAttack.com
Email: Bevrlyhill@aol.com

Acknowledgments

Thanks to our 11,000+ clients who have promoted the development of this book so it could be shared with others in hopes that other lives can be changed as theirs have.

Special thanks to...

Mari Yentzer, who shoved me out the door and said, "It is time to write the book!"

Bill and Cyndi Carroll, for being the first guinea-pigs to try it out.

To Robert Johnson who said we could do it in record time; Deborah Poulalion and Michele Randall who loaned their technical expertise through proofing, editing, and everything else that goes into putting a book together; and Karen Holland who was the wizard who kept things on track.

J.T. Shim, who was first a client and then a friend, who volunteered to review this book and did so in less than 24 hours!

To family and friends who put up with, "I can't. I am on a book deadline."

Greatest thanks goes to the Master Weaver, Who turned every down into an up and has molded me to give to others...who are stuck...just existing...and who forgot what they had...to see them bloom...and pass it on to others...that we all might smile because of our blessings. This is a beginning...

This book is dedicated to all those who are...
searching for their purpose
ready to take control
focused on achieving their career goal
willing to do what it takes
and ready to win
understanding all things are possible...

"As [a man] thinketh in his heart, so he is." Proverbs 23:7 (KJV)

About the Author

As a writer and member of the Professional Association of Resume Writers, National Resume Writers Association, Society for Human Resource Managers, Central Florida Employment Council and other groups, Beverly Hill brings writing expertise as well as the perspective of researcher, coach, corporate consultant, university faculty member and seminar presenter/ motivational speaker to this book. Her strengths in developing this book are twofold:

Solid professional credentials and practical experience.

"Ever since I was a kid" I didn't know what I wanted to be when I grew up, and my guidance counselor destined me for "maybe a nurse's aide or hairdresser." Totally discouraged and having nothing better to do, I decided to go to college with my best friend, ended up majoring in the easiest and most interesting topic I could find, and finally graduated with a BS in Psychology from Virginia Commonwealth University.

Not having a clue as to what I wanted to do with my life, I joined the U.S. Army to see the world. Instead of traveling, I was assigned to my college town to be a career counselor/Army recruiter. Thus my future was launched in career services.

Today I have more than 33 years experience, working both in the U.S. and international markets in career development, human resources, employee motivation, vocational and management training, curriculum development, outplacement, job coaching and writing.

I bring both perspectives to the job search field: *the frustrated, lost soul* and the *got-it-together* professional. Having also earned a Master's Degree in Health Care Management, I am a faculty member for the University of Phoenix and Stetson University.

Job coaching clients include: senior executives, middle managers, entry-level professionals, and university students. They come from such diverse fields as clerical support, health care, industrial, entertainment, financial, manufacturing, marketing and sales, and information specialists.

As you journey through this writing, you will find you are cast in the starring role! Have fun and enjoy! We guarantee you will be impressed with your resume! When it is done, review your resume and ask, "Would I hire this person?"

PREFACE

This book developed out of Job Attack Power seminars given since 1990. During those workshops I was barraged with questions, such as:

- How do I write a resume?
- How do I create quantifiable accomplishments?
- How do I know how to target a resume?

People who attended our seminars wanted a book they could give to friends or family members in other areas, as well as a written refresher for what they had learned.

The strategies used in this book have been researched through the personal lives of our clients—not in an academic setting. These tools work for everyone—from executive to student.

Where It All Started

After working 14 years in Saudi Arabia for a company that went through major downsizing—from 60,000 to 43,000 employees in 18 months—I became a pro at resume writing. Believing research is the key to a superior product, I created three different resumes and sent them to 100 Orlando companies, as I planned to relocate to Orlando one day. When companies called me in Saudi Arabia and paid three dollars a minute to talk with me, I asked, "What made you pick up the phone and call me?" Their response was always the same, "I didn't have to read your resume—everything I wanted to know jumped off the page." The *Power Resume* won every time!

When I returned to the U.S. in 1990, I started using the Job Attack Power Resume. One day I was being interviewed by a CEO who asked, "Who did your resume?" After working and living in a country that is quite different from the U.S., wearing funny clothes and being greatly concerned about my ability to meld back into the U.S. culture, I had an attack of low self-esteem and wondered, "What is wrong with my resume?" However, trying to call up all the confidence I could, I responded, "I did." The CEO said, "This is great! Could you do a resume for me? I need one for a prospectus." That momentous occasion resulted in more than 3,500 people being referred to my house and finally, in early 1995, I opened an office.

Today my company, Hill & Associates, has worked with more than 11,000 people who have found success with the resume, coaching and marketing tools.

Contents

Part IV Job Attack Power Builder Forms 213

Begin now! Take the mystery out of resume writing by using these quick and easy forms. It's the only shortcut to a powerful resume!

Introduction

Do You Need This Book?

Take a few minutes to see if this book is for you by completing the following. In the couple of minutes it will take to answer these questions you will find out if your resume strategies are working for you.

Test Your Resume IQ

Indicatc if thc following statements are **true** or **false**.
(The correct answers are on the next page.)

True	False		
❑	❑	1.	The smart way of doing a resume is to develop a generic resume that will cover all potential positions.
❑	❑	2.	A 10% to 15% response to resumes sent out is considered good.
❑	❑	3.	An employer prefers to hire a person who is already employed with another company.
❑	❑	4.	The average resume receives at least an initial 60-second review.
❑	❑	5.	It is important to include personal information in your resume—hobbies, family, health, interests, community activities, etc.
❑	❑	6.	The initial review of a resume is done by a knowledgeable person who selects those candidates that will be interviewed.
❑	❑	7.	Generic objectives on a resume get the best response from employers. In this way they can position you as they wish.
❑	❑	8.	Fancy fonts, colorful paper with artistic designs, and clip art is a great way to gain attention and get selected for the interview.
❑	❑	9.	The quality of your work should be presented in general statements referring to the project or task accomplished.
❑	❑	10.	If you answer an ad and you know the company name, but the ad doesn't give the name of a contact person, you should direct the resume to "To Whom it May Concern" or "Dear Sir/Madame."
❑	❑	11.	The best resumes are detailed histories written in the narrative.

Compare Your Answers

False 1. Every resume should **target the specific needs of the job** for which you are applying. Researching the company and position is essential in order to get the interview.

False 2. A resume should be targeted so the response is at least 50% or higher. Some of our clients receive as high as **95% return**.

True 3. An **employed person** is always more desirable. However, because of the reorganizations, mergers, etc., that have become commonplace today, the **unemployed** person is no longer viewed with great suspicion as once was the case.

False 4. We have studied hundreds of human resource managers and other hiring professionals and our results show the average resume receives a **2.9-second initial review**. How long would you spend if *you* had 500 resumes to review?

False 5. Including **personal information** on a resume can be costly. This information provides a good source of eliminators. Stick to the business of *what you can do for the company.*

False 6. The initial review of a resume can be done by an **optical scanner** (a computer that will quickly identify desired key words and determine whether the candidate is a good match), a **clerk** or some other designee who has the responsibility for screening resumes, or, if you are in luck, someone who has professional expertise and is the decision maker.

False 7. Generic objectives on a resume frequently become **eliminators** because the resume reviewer does not want to take the time to figure out if you are a fit for an open position.

False 8. Fancy fonts, colorful paper with artistic designs and clip art is a great way to impress the interviewer *at the time of the interview.* Unfortunately, these **gimmicks** sometimes cannot be read by scanners. Clip art and other graphics could also lead the person who opens the mail to classify the resume as a piece of advertising and it may be tossed. Avoid these potential **eliminators**.

False 9. The quality of your work should be presented in **quantitative terms** ($, %) whenever possible. The terms "awarded, recognized for, etc.," are also winners.

False 10. If you answer an ad and know the company name, but the ad doesn't give the name of a person to whom the resume should be directed, you should **do research** and then direct the resume to the **decision maker** or at least the director of human resources. Always go the extra mile. Addressing a specific person makes a difference.

False 11. The best resumes contain **easy-to-read bulleted key points.**

Congratulations if you scored 10! If not, continue on to find out...

Quick & Easy! 40-Minute Power Resume

How to Use This Book

To help you get your resume done in record time, we have made this the easiest "how to" book on resume writing. Here is how it works, step by step...

1. **A brief introduction** begins each chapter.
2. **Our Express Power Quick Tips** are in the front of each chapter and are referred to throughout the chapter.
   - Review the **Express Power Quick Tips** before reading the chapter.
   - They will give you an overview of key points that are important in developing your resume and may be all you need to complete your resume.
   - **Express Power Quick Tips** provide the formulas, do's/don'ts and introduce you to the **Action Steps**, that are marked by an ➔.
   - The ➔ indicates what you need to do to complete that step of the resume and where you need to do it.
3. **That's all there is!**
4. **Have fun and enjoy the results.** You are going to love your new resume and how easy it was to do!

Part I

Preparing for the Race: Learn the Facts

Before going on a trip or embarking on a new project, you have to get your act together: plan, prepare, and do your research. The same applies to your resume.

Part I makes it easy for you to "get it together" by briefly presenting:

Chapter 1 **Get Rid of Those Resume Eliminators**
Learn about the thirty common eliminators and how to overcome them. So often people just keep doing the same thing over and over and expect different results. Let's do something different!

Chapter 2 **How to Wow a Potential Employer**
Learn what the hiring manager wants and sell your matching skills so he/she can't wait to hire you!

Chapter 3 **Get Your Tools Together**
Learn the quick and easy steps for formatting your resume.

Power Tip

As you begin this journey into resume writing, ask yourself the question

What makes me the best candidate for the job?

This will be your focus, your niche, and will impact your success each step of the way.

Chapter 1

Get Rid of Those Resume Eliminators

- **Introducing the Obituary Resume.** (Exhibit 1-1)
  A *history* of what Roach *has done.*

- **Introducing the Power Resume.** (Exhibit 1-2)
  Presents *what Roach can do* for the specific position the company is advertising *based upon his past performance.*

- **Review 30 Resume Eliminators.** (Exhibit 1-3)
  The numbers on Roach's "Obituary" relate to the numbers on the Resume Eliminators Exhibit.

- **The Two Resumes Compared.** (Exhibit 1-4)

(17) (1)

BARRY M. ROACH
1979 Campbell Avenue
Daytona, FL 32720
(904) 734-1228

(2) OBJECTIVE (14)

(29) TO SECURE A CHALLENGING POSITION WITH A GROWING COMPANY THAT WILL UTILIZE MY KILLS AND EDUCATION.

SUMMARY (19)

ENTREPRENEUR WITH 20 YEARS MILITARY, 13 YEARS FILM PRODUCTION, 12 YEARS CONSTRUCTION, AND 1 YEAR OF SALES EXPERIENCE.

(26) EDUCATION

(9) (8) (21)

1961 GRADUATE DELAND HIGH SCHOOL
1961 U.S.M.C. COMMERCIAL FOOD SERVICE/COOK SCHOOL (FOUR-MONTH SCHOOL)
1982 COLLEGE CREDITS--UNIVERSITY OF MARYLAND
1986 HONORABLY DISCHARGED FROM U.S.M.C.
1985 HEVEIGNER SCHOOL OF REAL ESTATE
1986 HEALTH AND LIFE INSURANCE SCHOOL
1993 COLLEGE CREDITS--DAYTONA BEACH COMMUNITY COLLEGE

EXPERIENCE

(7) (16) (22) (13) (6) (4) (5)

1987-present	FOUNDED THE REMODELING COMPANY KNOWN FIRST AS RADIANT REDESIGNERS, WHICH LATER BECAME THE BARRY ROACH GROUP. THESE ENTERPRISES CONSIST OF REMODELING RENOVATION DIVISION AND MARINE ARTISAN CONTRACTING DIVISION, AFTER DOUBLING ACCOUNTS. SPECIALIZE IN MARKETING AND CONTRACT; COMMERCIAL, STRUCTURAL DESIGN, CONSTRUCTION & REMODELING. THE MARINE DIVISION CONDUCTS BUSINESS WITH THE RETAIL AND INSURANCE END OF COMPLETE REHAB. & RECONDITIONING OF ALL SIZES OF PERSONAL WATERCRAFT FROM TRAILERABLE TO 1OO'+ YACHT-SIZED VESSELS, AS WELL AS OTHER LUXURY VEHICLES SUCH AS RV'S, BUSES, AND AIRCRAFT.
1993-1995	SUCCESSFUL COORDINATION AND IMPLEMENTATION OF A MULTI-PHASE REMODELING SERVICE WITH THE HOME DEPOT, WHICH INCLUDES RESIDENTIAL AND COMMERCIAL REMODELING.
1986-present	FREELANCE STUDIO MECHANIC: MGM STUDIOS, TOUCHSTONE PICTURES, ORION PICTURES, ADIRONDAK SCENIC COMPANY, DISNEY. RESPONSIBILITIES INCLUDED THE UTILIZATION OF MECHANICAL, STRUCTURAL, ELECTRICAL, SOUND, LIGHTING, AND SET DRESSING AND DECORATING CRAFTS & TECHNOLOGIES. UNIVERSAL STUDIOS, IN PARTICULAR, USED TECHNICAL AND INDUSTRIAL TECHNIQUES NEVER BEFORE EMPLOYED. PAST MEMBER I.A.T.S.E.
1986	PROGRAM EXECUTIVE FOR PASSPORT INTERNATIONALE, DAYTONA BEACH, FL. COMPLETE DEVELOPMENT, COORDINATION, AND IMPLEMENTATION OF PROMOTIONAL & SALES PROGRAMS.
1964-1984	COMBAT/FIELD READINESS MAINTENANCE SUPERVISOR (USMC) RESPONSIBILITIES INCLUDED MAINTAINING THE REHABILITATION & PREPARATION OF FIRST STRIKE READINESS FOR FIELD SUPPORT EQUIPMT.

(23) (3) (27)

FEBRUARY 26, 1998

The "Obituary" Resume p 1
Exhibit 1-1

INTERESTS AND ACTIVITIES

(20) YOUNG LIFE YOUTH LEADER FROM 1992-PRESENT
YMCA COMMITTEE MEMBER & TECHNICAL MAINTENANCE CONSULTANT
FINANCIAL STEERING COMMITTEE MEMBER FOR TEEN CHALLENGE MINISTRY
MAINTENANCE CONSULTANT - ORLANDO TEEN CHALLENGE FACILITY
TRINITY HOME CHURCH MEN'S MAINTENANCE MINISTRY

PERSONAL

(24)

SSN:	222-22-2222
DOB:	4-04-43
MARRIED:	JOAN MACY ROACH
CHILDREN:	SCOTT (32)
	TINA (27)

REFERENCES

(10)

JOHN SEEBAUR	(555) 767-8892
CAPTAIN CHRIS CENNETE	(555) 663-9032
REV. DANIEL MAHER	(555) 455-7221

FEBRUARY 26, 1998

NOTE: The numbers on this resume correspond to the numbers on Resume Eliminations, Exhibit 1-3.

The "Obituary" Resume p 2
Exhibit1-1

BARRY M. ROACH

1979 Campbell Avenue • Daytona, Florida 32721 • (904) 734-1228

Qualified for:

 • **Director of Marketing and Business Development**

PROFESSIONAL PROFILE

- Dynamic professional employing more than 10 years of progressive accomplishments in marketing, business development, sales and project management.
- Results oriented organizer possessing analytical acumen, perception, judgement and energy.
- Resourceful and creative in pursuing unique methods to obtain goals and objectives.
- Positive self-starter with accelerated skills in organization and planning.
- Poised innovator with strong people skills and leadership ability.
- Proven team leader providing the momentum required to unite diverse groups toward achieving common goals.

AREAS OF EXPERTISE

• Outside Sales	• Team Building	• Contract Negotiations
• Business Plans	• Community Service	• Marketing
• Problem Solving	• Written Communications	• Key Account Sales
• Recruiting	• Oral Communications	• Presentations
• Client Retention	• Construction Supervision	• Prospecting
• Staff Development	• Project Management	• Liaison
• Remodeling	• Historic Renovations	• Customer Service
• Creative Design	• Trade Shows	• Supervision
• Consulting	• Interior Design	• Special Projects

PROFESSIONAL BACKGROUND

CLIENT RETENTION AND NEW BUSINESS DEVELOPMENT

Plan, organize and manage the overall client retention and new business development activities for various clients which include: evaluating client/project scope/requirements; coordinating professional consultants; and following client/project from inception to completion to ensure quality service and client retention.

Companies: Universal, Disney, MGM, Home Depot, Heilig Meyers, Orion Pictures, Bob Carr, First Union, Nations Bank, Massey Services and others.

- 20% increase in revenues through targeting high-end markets and streamlining expenses while ensuring quality.
- 120% increase in account sales through developing and implementing an aggressive yet client-centered sales strategy.
- 100% accomplishment of targeted goals and objectives on time and within budget through developing a strategic plan of action.
- Recognized for Quality Historical Renovations by media, contractors, and clients for dedication and commitment to excellence.
- Recognized for Innovative Interior Design Renovations for developing creative lighting, specialized cabinetry, and finishing accents.

The "Power" Resume p 1
Exhibit 1-2

EXPERIENCE

- Commercial Contractors, Orlando, FL — **Marketing & Business Development Director** — Oct 1997 - Present
  Key Accounts: Datametrix Corp, 4-C's Foundation, IPA, Taurus Investments & 30 Other Major Projects.
  Project Ranges: $500K - $5MM.
  Manage Two Divisions: Marketing & Collateral Administration Support; Business Development.
  Marketing to: Association Relations (NAIOP/SMPS), Institutional Clientele, End Users (Small Businesses) & Developers.

- Radiant Redesigners, Daytona, FL — **Renovation Design Manager** — Dec 1987 - Oct 1997
  Key Accounts: Home Depot, Heilig Meyers,
  Projects: Historical Renovation, Remodeling, Interior Design/ Lighting, New Construction,
  Project Ranges: $500 - 40K.
  Project Management, Key Account Sales, Operations, Scheduling, Staff Development, Sub-Contractor /Architect Liaison and Creative Design.

- IATSE, Orlando, FL — **Studio Design Mechanic** — Nov 1985- Nov 1987
  Key Accounts: MGM /Disney Studios, Universal, Adirondak, Scenic Corporation, Orion Pictures, Bob Carr Performing Arts Center, Melbourne Performing Arts Center,
  Projects: Lighting/Sound/Set/Electrics Design, Set Dressing, and Creative /Technical Projects.

- Passport Internationale, Daytona Beach, FL — **Special Program Consultant** — Jan 1984 - Oct 1985
  Special Promotion Development, Marketing/Advertising Design, and New Accounts.

- USMC, Jacksonville, NC — **Warehouse/Field Deployment Supervisor** — Jan 1981 - Jan 1984
  Staff: 10, Sq. Ft.: 50,000
  Inventory Control, Tracking, Equipment Maintenance, Shipping, Field Deployment Readiness, and Commander Liaison.

EDUCATION

- **University of Maryland,** USMC Educational System
  Major: Business Administration
- **Daytona Beach Community College**, Daytona Beach, Florida - Major: Business Administration
- **Continuing Education:** Dave Buster/Carl Mathews Contractor's School, State of Florida

---

BARRY M. ROACH

The "Power" Resume p 2
Exhibit 1-2

Power Tips:
Things to avoid in developing your resume.

Resume Eliminators

Note: The numbers on the Obituary Resume correspond to numbers on this list.

1. **Don't make your resume an obituary.** An *obituary* is a history of *what was,* not *what you can do for the company*. Focus on what the company wants: productivity, profitability, sales, cash flow, cost savings, and clients. Examples:
   Obituary: Supervised a team of teachers for a project.
   Power Approach: 100% compliance with project specifications through empowering a team of 14 teachers to...

2. **Don't use "generic objectives."** Generic objectives do not work. No one wants to take the time to figure out what you want to do. Be specific. Target a specific job!
   Power Approach: Sales Representative.

3. **Don't let "age" eliminate you:** "Of course there is no age discrimination." Wrong! The magic age seems to be 40. Limit your resume to no more than 15 years or 2 pages, whichever comes first. Exception: If you are an independent consultant, the more years, the better.
   Power Approach: Goal-directed professional with more than 15 years of progressive experience in...

4. **Don't write "wall-to-wall" paragraphs:** Hey, wake up! No one wants to read today. People are busy. Make it easy for the resume reviewer. Bullet key points. Reader-friendly resumes win!
   Power Approach:
   • Budgeting • Forecasting • Sales • Customer Service

5. **Don't tell more than they "need/want to know."** Being overqualified or too diverse can be an eliminator. Tell only what will sell you.

6. **Don't baffle them with words like "successful, terrific, etc.":** These are subjective/fictional words. Use objective/factual words.
   Power Approach: 250% increase in productivity through....

7. **Don't be mysterious by listing "years only" on your work history:** Technically, if you worked one day in the year 1999, you could put "1999," however this could be an eliminator. List the "month year" to the "month year" for *each* position. **Power Approach:** Jan 1996 - Feb 1999.

8. **Don't list every education program you have ever attended.** Only list those educational programs that support the job for which you are applying. Also, if you attended 20 schools before you obtained your degree, only list the school from which you graduated–otherwise, the reviewer may think you are unstable.

Exhibit 1-3 -1
Resume Eliminators

9. **Don't list dates of graduation.** Unless you are a recent graduate, leave them out. It doesn't take a rocket scientist to figure out how old you are by looking at graduation dates.

---

10. **Don't use references that have fired you or don't like you.** You do not have to use previous employers. Your references should be your professional fan club!

---

11. **Don't forget to ask your references if they will be references for you.** "Hi, I am calling for a reference on Dick Smith." Response from reference: "Gosh, I haven't seen Dick for 15 years. How is he, anyway?" This would not win you the job! You also should provide your references with a copy of your resume and *keep them informed* of what companies will be calling them and the job for which you are applying.

---

12. **Don't hope the resume reviewer will "read in between the lines" and know how wonderful you are.** On average, the person reviewing your resume will make a judgement in 2.9 seconds. This doesn't give them time to figure out what other things you might be able to do that relates to what they want. What they see is what they will react to. If you don't tell them quickly and concisely, they will never know!

---

13. **Don't use words like "tripled" in presenting your accomplishments.** They will never see the achievement as it blends in with other words. It is better to use numbers.
Power Approach: 300% increase in...
Put your numbers at the *beginning* of your accomplishments to draw attention.

---

14. **Don't hope a "generic" resume will work for all jobs for which you are apply ing.** It won't! The key is to develop a *generic* resume that will immediately be come a *targeted* resume by just changing the "job title" and a few "key words."

---

15. **Don't think the resume is "just a piece of paper to send out" with my work history on it.** The resume is a critical document that represents your entire life's work focused on what an employer wants. It is the key to opening the door. It is the key to the interview! Every word counts.

---

16. **Don't think *"what you have done"* is more important than *"what the company wants."*** If you don't focus on *what the company wants,* the company will not care about *what you have done,* and you will not get the interview.

---

17. **Don't use "fancy fonts, italics, graphics or all capitals" to get extra attention.** If the company is using a computer scanner to review the resumes for key words, there is a possibility your resume could be eliminated because the scanner can't read the font. Keep your resume simple and professional. If you are in a graphics/art field, take a portfolio of your work with you to the interview.

Exhibit 1-3-2
Resume Eliminators

18. Don't forget to take time to "research" the company and job. Not doing your research can be lethal! If they want an orange and you are providing an apple, do you think they will buy it? Would you? The more you know about a company, the better chance you have to create a match with your resume, letter, and interview.

---

19. Don't list the number of years of experience you have in diverse areas. Example: 10 years in accounting, 6 years in bookkeeping, 4 years in cost accounting, 5 years as office manager. It is human instinct to add it all up and what do you get? Wow—25 years! That would make the person over 45 and possibly eliminate them–even if the years of experience that were presented *overlapped* and they were only 35 years old!

---

20. Don't write the name of a company out "if it can eliminate you." Example: Bartenders School of America. Many companies may steer away from considering this resume. In this situation, it would be better to list the company as BSA. Many companies use initials as their name. This would at least provide the opportunity to get the interview.

---

21. Don't abbreviate professional titles, departments and so on and expect the reader to know what you are talking about. Example: ADA. That could stand for American Disabilities Act, American Dental Association, American Dietetics Association and many others. To prevent confusion, write it out.

---

22. Don't use "your name" as a company for which you have worked. This can alert a company that you are either an entrepreneur or covering a period of unemployment and may eliminate you from being considered. Entrepreneurs can be a threat to a company for fear the candidate may use the company's resources/clients to start another business. Entrepreneurs are also often stereotyped as freethinking troublemakers in the corporate structure.

---

23. Don't leave "unexplained" gaps of time in your resume. This creates a mystery. Develop your resume so there is no mystery. You can fill periods of unemployment gaps with "special projects/research/school" and other such headings.

---

24. Don't include "personal information" in your resume. Examples: date of birth, social security number, height, weight, marital status, children, hobbies, religious affiliation, political party, nonprofessional memberships and so on. These could all be used against you.

---

25. Don't forget to give yourself "credit for your accomplishments." Don't have an attack of "Aw, shucks, I can't say that about myself." If you don't tell it, who will? How will they know? Your accomplishments are the hook that will grab them!

Exhibit 1-3-3
Resume Eliminators

26. **Don't begin your resume with your "education."** While education is important, what *you can do for the company* and *how well* you can do it is more important, even if you are a new graduate.

---

27. **Don't give military titles if you are applying for a civilian position.** Not all companies want someone with a military background. This is a fact and may eliminate a person who is otherwise qualified. Unless you are applying for a position that is related to the Department of Defense or related contractor, civilianize your military job titles.
Power Approach: Change Battalion Commander to Operations Manager or another title, depending on responsibilities.

---

28. **Don't forget to demonstrate "progression in your field" from one position to another.** If you are in a career area that provides quantifiable measures of responsibility (annual budget, sales volume, staff, stores, seats, beds, etc.), make sure you list them consistently for each position presented to demonstrate growth.

---

29. **Don't forget to proofread your resume.** The company would interpret this as representing your professionalism. If you don't care how you represent yourself, they certainly will not want you representing them.

---

30. **Don't forget to keep your resume updated at all times**. You never know when your next job opportunity will come along.
Power Approach: Always have an updated resume in your glove compartment or nearby ready-to-go when an opportunity arises.

Exhibit 1-3-4
Resume Eliminators

Power Tips:
Things to use in developing your resume.

Overcoming Eliminators

As you review each resume, check off the "Obituary" or "Power" box. The resume which meets all these requirements is the winner! (Note that the letters on the Power Resume correspond to letters on this test.)

Obituary	Power		
❑	❑	A.	**Gives the EXACT JOB TITLE of the position for which Roach is applying?** **Power Tip!** Target the exact job title you want as reflected in the classified ad, the internet job listing, or a lead from a friend.
❑	❑	B.	**Describes Roach AS A PERSON.** **Power Tip!** In the Professional Profile section of your resume, target the personal characteristics that have been identified by the company's job requirements for the open position. Examples: results-oriented, resourceful, detail-oriented, etc.
❑	❑	C.	**Names at least 10 SKILLS/AREAS OF EXPERTISE Roach has.** **Power Tip!** Bullet your SKILLS, AREAS OF EXPERTISE and KNOWLEDGE focused on what thecompany wants. Example: Outside Sales, Team Building....
❑	❑	D.	**Tells what Roach does for an employer in quantitative terms, for example, increase productivity, profitability, clients, cost savings and so on..** **Power Tip!** Provide quantified data on how well you did your job. Also, put your numbers/awards and statistics at the beginning of the statement so they stick out like a light bulb saying, "Look at this!" Example: 20% increase in sales...
❑	❑	E.	**Gives the precise time frame Roach was in each job position and each company.** **Power Tip! Don't** use years only. Example: 1991 - present. **Don't** clump all the years together. Example: 1968 - 1991. This becomes a mystery and makes the reader wonder what a candidate is trying to hide. **Do** be specific. Include the month and year for start and finish of each position held. Example: Dec 1987 - Oct 1997.

Exhibit 1-4
Overcoming Eliminators

❑ ❑ F. **Gives only the important aspects of Roach's educational background.**

Power Tip! Only include education that is supportive to the job for which you are applying.

❑ ❑ G. **Provides information so clearly that you hardly had to read it?**

Power Tip! Don't provide wall-to-wall information—that is fill the page up—more is not necessarily better. This can overwhelm the reader.
Do be brief and to-the-point. Bullet key points.

❑ ❑ H. **Positions Roach so that he will not be eliminated based on age.**

Power Tip! Is there age discrimination? You bet there is! The magic number seems to be 40. As you get older, you acquire the disease of being overqualified, you cost too much or become a threat possibly to the person who is hiring you or someone else on staff. If they key in on the dates and figure out you are over 40, often times it is farewell to an opportunity for an interview. Positioning your age positively is critical.
Don't go back more than 15 years on your resume unless you are a consultant–then the older you are, the better you become at what you do!
Do highlight 15 years and focus on what the company wants. Example: Dynamic professional with more than 15 years of progressive accomplishments in...

❑ ❑ I. **Is easy to read, direct, to the point, and sells. It says...**

- This is the *job* I want.
- This is *who* I am as a person–at work, play, and socially.
- This is *what* I can do for you.
- This is *how well* I can do it.

Power Tip!
These are the critical points that should be presented in every resume.

Remember, the key to a resume reviewer's heart is to spoon-feed the information in such a way that the resume isn't a mystery and they get the information they need *immediately*.

Are you ready for the next lesson? Let's learn how to "Wow a Potential Employer!"

Exhibit 1-4
Overcoming Eliminators

Chapter 2

How to Wow A Potential Employer

Review these strategies and keep them in mind as you begin to develop your resume.

Introducing the 9 P's to wow employers. Exhibit 2-1.

The strategies presented in this book are prescriptions you can learn and use. You will experience the exhilarating personal growth that comes from identifying your skill set and transforming it into bottom line qualities.

Power Tip!

"Wowing"

a potential employer means letting them know what you can do that impacts the bottom line. This means an increase of...

- Productivity
- Profitability
- Sales
- Revenues
- Number of clients
- Retention
- Cost savings
- Quality

• Anything that contributes to $$$$$!!!! •

Power Tips:
Things to build into your resume. $$$$$$$

9 P's to Wow Employers

1. **Profitability**. Companies or organizations are in business to make money. It is a fact. Recognize and understand it.

   Key Point: How do you contribute to profitability?

2. **Productivity**. The only reason a company usually hires someone is because in some way they are going to impact the bottom line. Everyone does.

   Key Point*:* How have you contributed to increased productivity?

3. **Be Positive.** Choose your words carefully. Whether written or oral, your choice of words can sell or kill you.
   Negative words include: decrease, reduce, downsizing, fired, no, etc.
   Positive words include: increase, improve, rightsizing, streamlining, reorganization, yes, and other similar words.

   Key Point*:* Is what you are presenting **positive**? Can it be used against you?

4. **Be Proactive**. Go for it! Don't sit and wait for the telephone to ring. Don't wait for someone to offer you a job. Be so dynamic, solution-oriented, positive, and focused on what you want, that you create opportunities. You will get what you want if you plan your attack.

   Key Point: Are you proactive in all you do?

5. **Personality Wins.** You have heard the song, "You've got to have lots of personality..." and this is true in the resume as well. Let who you are shine through your resume. This can be done through the sections titled Professional Profile, Areas of Expertise, and Accomplishments/Awards.

   Key Point: Do you present a positive personality to everyone you meet?

6. **Persistence Pays Off.** Never quit or throw in the towel and just give up. Forge on to the end!

   Key Point: Are you persistent and follow through to a positive end?

7. **Performance Sells.** Wherever you go, whatever you do, whomever you interact with, you are on stage. People are constantly evaluating you and your resume, and many subconsciously ask, "Would you be a good fit for our company?"
   The goal is to position yourself so that everyone wants you.

   Key Point: Are you performing as well as you can to attract the good things you want personally, professionally and socially?

Exhibit 2-1
9 P's

---

8. **Presentation Is Everything.** In life there are many interviews. All must be won with flying colors! Professionalism and consistency are paramount to winning.

   The Resume: The first interview is what you put on paper, whether it is a resume, report, proposal, or some other document you have prepared. The critical elements include:

   - Readability: Is it simple, to the point, yet still powerful?
   - Are major points bulleted?
   - Is there a lot of white space? White space sells.
   - Do you focus on what you can do for the employer?
   - Do you document who you are, your credentials, and your work history to support the position you want?
   - Do you use the law of attraction in presenting your past performance record of productivity, profitability, cost savings, clients, sales, revenues, profit, and other things you can do for a company?
   - Does the document quickly illustrate (with little reading), this is who I am, what I can do for you, and how well?
   - Is the reader so excited that they can't wait to meet you?
   - Is your telephone ringing in response to your resume?

---

9. **Planning Results in Power**.
   If you make a plan and work your plan, your plan will work!

   Key Point: Do you have a plan for achieving your goals?

Remember, the only reason an employer is interested in a candidate is for what the potential employee can do for the company. Build this focus into your resume and also on the job wherever you are. This is a great way to get noticed and promoted!

You are now ready to get the tools together that will be necessary to complete your resume in record time!

Exhibit 2-1
9 P's

Chapter 3

Get Your Tools Together

- **Targeting Your Resume.** (Exhibit 3-1)
  1) Collect information about possibilities that interest you from the classifieds, internet, or any other job postings.
  2) You will need this information when you begin to develop the resume. It makes writing your resume quick and easy.
  3) This is how you "get the scoop" on what an employer wants.

- **Section Headings.** (Exhibit 3-2)
  1) We will focus on Recommended Headings and Optional Headings.
  2) Review Headings Not Recommended. These will be discussed further in a later chapter.

- **Resume Layout.** (Exhibit 3-3)
  The headings provide all the information an employer wants.
  1) Job you want (Objective).
  2) Who you are (Professional Profile).
  3) What you can do for the company (Areas of Expertise).
  4) Your work experience in a nutshell (Professional Background).
  5) How well you have done your job (Accomplish ments).
  6) Your work history (Experience).
  7) Credentials (Education, Affiliations, Licensure, Certification, Memberships, etc.).

- **The Facts About Yourself.** (Exhibit 3-4)
  If you gather these facts before you start typing your resume, you will be able to do it in record time.

Keys to Targeting Your Resume

(The Lazy Way to Success)

- Divide your paper into 3 columns and follow steps 1-3.

Step #1	Step #2	Step #3
• Classified Ads: Newspaper. Clip ads that interest you and tape them in the left hand column. • Internet Ads. Make a copy and number them. They are usually too large to tape to your data sheet. • Leads from Friends. Try to get the same info an add may have and include it on your sheet.	Write the EXACT JOB TITLE from the ad.	Extract verbatim from the ad and list: • Characteristics • Skills/Expertise • Experience/Years • Qualifications/Licensure/ Certifications
Classified Ad Clipping DIRECTOR OF PROCUREMENT Exciting Full Time Opportunity in the Central Florida Area. An established Florida Company needs an individual with a Strong Balance of Computer and People Skills. Fast-Paced Facility. Analytical Planner. ISO-9000, JIT, Vendor Relations, Quality Control, Database Coordination, Contracts, Negotiations, Facility Management, Materials Management. Full Benefits, including Medical, Dental, Life, STD, LTD & 401K, Personal Days & Vacation after 6 months. Fax resume to 407-XXX-XXXX.	Director of Procurement	• strong computer skills • strong people skills • fast-paced facility • analytical planner • ISO-9000 • JIT • vendor relations • quality control • data base coordination • contracts • negotiations • facility management • materials management

Keys to Targeting Your Resume
Exhibit 3-1

Power Resume Builder Section Headings

Headings

Check off the headings you feel are critical to present your resume so it sells you.

A. Recommended Headings

These headings promote the job you want, who you are, what you can do for the company, and how well. That is what a company wants to know. The key to the resume is attracting their interest. During the interview you can share other significant experience, stories, etc.

- ❑ Objective/Qualified for
- ❑ Professional/Executive Profile
- ❑ Areas of Expertise/Skills/Knowledge
- ❑ Professional Background/Experience
- ❑ Experience/Experience While Working Way Through School/Work History
- ❑ Education

B. Optional Headings as Applicable

- ❑ Affiliations/Memberships
- ❑ Certification/Licensure
- ❑ Publications/Articles
- ❑ Projects

C. Headings Not Recommended

These headings should rarely be used because the Job Attack Power Resume covers these under the above headings. Occasionally, another heading needs to be included to meet a particular need requested by the hiring company.

	Heading	Where Included in Job Attack Power Resume
❑	Community Activities	Experience, Accomplishments
❑	Interests/Special Interests/Hobbies	Save it for the interview unless requested
❑	References	Never include. Provide when requested
❑	Equipment	Areas of Expertise
❑	Computer Experience	Areas of Expertise
❑	Recent Work	Experience
❑	Career Achievements	Accomplishments
❑	Relevant Competencies	Areas of Expertise, Accomplishments
❑	Management Experience	Areas of Expertise, Experience
❑	Languages	Areas of Expertise
❑	Awards	Accomplishments, Experience
❑	Volunteer Activities	Areas of Expertise, Experience. When requested.
❑	Skills Summary	Areas of Expertise
❑	Certificates of Completion	Certification/Licensure
❑	Current Position	Experience
❑	Highlights	Professional/Executive Profile
❑	Military Experience	Experience/Downplay the military unless it specifically sells to the job.

Headings: Samples
Exhibit 3-2

	Name
	Street • City, State Zip • (XXX) xxx-xxxx • Email abc@xyz.net
	Qualified for/Objective
Job I want ➔	Exact Job Title
	PROFESSIONAL PROFILE
Who I am ➔	• Your whole life in one sentence focused on your next job • 5 statements of who you are as a person • Self-starter... • Analytical planner... • Team player, etc...
What I can do for you ➔	**AREAS OF EXPERTISE** (Approximately 24 - 33 bulleted skills) • Budgeting • Finance • Taxes • • • • • • • • •
	PROFESSIONAL BACKGROUND
My work experience in a nutshell ➔	**FUNCTIONAL AREA YOU ARE FOCUSING ON** Plan, organize and manage the overall activities of____which include: evaluating _______; providing _______; and ensuring compliance with _____________.
Accomplishments ➔	• (List 5 major accomplishments following the Peanut Butter Principle See page 71.) • 100% compliance with... • 250% increase in productivity... • 150% increase in revenues/sales/profitability... • Awarded/Ranked/Recognized for...
Work History ➔	**EXPERIENCE** • Company, City, ST — **Job Title**, Key Word Duties. Accomplishment — Mo/19XX-Mo/19XX
Credentials➔	**EDUCATION** • Degree in ____, School, City, State **AFFILIATIONS/MEMBERSHIPS/LICENSURE/CERTIFICATION** • Name of Group/Certification, Organization/Licensing Body

Exhibit 3-3 - Headings: Sample Layout

Power Tips:
Things to remember...

Get Your Tools Together

Now that you are learning about the Power Resume strategies, you are that much closer to achieving your goal. A little research beforehand will get you an interview every time unless:

- You don't meet the qualifications.
- There is not a vacant position.
- There is an available position but an internal candidate has been positioned for promotion or someone who knows someone will be filling the position, and they just collect resumes because of required regulations (EEOC).

Targeting Your Resume

Don't:
1. Develop your resume without research.
2. Assume the resume reviewer will read between the lines.

Do:
1. Research what the company wants through the classifieds, job postings, the internet and people who provide leads to you.
2. Ensure your resume is an exact match with the company's advertised/ unadvertised position description.
3. ➔ Identify the exact job title for the position you want and transfer it to Power Resume Builder Exhibit 1-B.

Are You Ready to Do Your Resume in Record Time?

Great! Before we begin, review the following checklist to make sure you have everything you need:

1. **Data to Support Your Background and Experience**
   - ❑ Work history
   - ❑ List of accomplishments
   - ❑ List of educational experiences
   - ❑ Qualifications
2. **Data from Potential Employers/Classifieds/Internet Postings/etc. identifying the qualifications for the job listing**
   - ❑ Fill out form in Exhibit 3-1.

Great–let's begin. Start your timer! See if you can beat the 20-minute record while maintaining quality.

Part II

Blast Off!
Write Your Resume NOW!

This is where the action is. In just nine simple steps your resume will be done!

Step 1	**The Heading**: Put your name in lights.
Step 2	**The Objective**: Go for the Bull's-eye.
Step 3	**The Professional Profile**: Tell them who you are to get them excited.
Step 4	**Areas of Expertise**: Wow them with your knowledge and skills.
Step 5	**Professional Background**: Let them know in one sentence what you have done in a lifetime as it relates to what you want to do.
Step 6	**Accomplishments**: Advertise what you can do for them in quantitative terms.
Step 7	**Work Experience**: Translate it so it sells.
Step 8	**Education**: Share the qualifications that make you the best candidate.
Step 9	**Professional Affiliations, Certifications, Licensure, Publications, Projects**: Tell what sells.

In each section, remember to:

1. Review the Express Power Quick Tips.
2. Follow the ➔ and complete the action on the Resume Builder Forms.

Step 1

The Heading: Put Your Name in Lights

So often job seekers forget that the resume is their unique, personalized marketing tool. Most resume headings don't do their job. Look at the 7 sample headings on the following page. Which one is easiest to read, stands out and gets your attention?

The Power Heading (example #1) wins the prize because you can't miss the name. It is large and positioned in the upper right-hand corner.

- Research has shown that this is the highest paid advertising space– other than the front and back cover of a publication.
- The name is underlined with two lines (bold and thin) to get the reader's attention.
- A thin line under the address completes the heading and separates it from the body of the resume.
- The address is presented on one line, separated by bullets (•) to present a more professional appearance.

Express Power Quick Tips: The Heading

Don't:

1. Use fancy fonts.
2. Use italics.
3. Use all TALL capitals.

Do:

1. Put YOUR NAME in a 24- to 30-point font. Use Times, Garamond, Americana, Palatino, Helvetica, Bookman, or other simple, easy-to-read standard font.
2. Right justify your name and address.
3. Put the address, phone number, fax number, pager number, email address, and other essential information on the second line.
4. Use bullets (•) to separate address, phone number, etc.
5. Use your resume heading as your personal stationery for all other job search correspondence.
6. ➔ Input your header information on Power Resume Builder, Form 1-A.

CARSTON C. WYLAND

1111 Winfred Lake Circle • Palm Springs, Florida 39888 • (555) 498-2654

1

CARSTON C. WYLAND
1111 Winfred Lake Circle
Palm Springs, FL 39888
(555) 498-2654

2

CARSTON C. WYLAND
1111 Winfred Lake Circle
Palm Springs, FL 39888
(555) 498-2654

3

CARSTON C. WYLAND

1111 Winfred Lake Circle
Palm Springs, FL 39888

home (555) 498-2654
work (555) 498-7656

4

CARSTON C. WYLAND

1111 Winfred Lake Circle, Palm Springs, FL 39888, (555) 498-2654

5

C A R S T O N C. W Y L A N D
1111 Winfred Lake Circle * Palm Springs, FL 39888 * (555) 498-2654

6

Carston C. Wyland
1111 Winfred Lake Circle
Palm Springs, FL 39888
(555) 498-2654

7

Heading
Exhibit Step 1 -1

Step 2

The Objective: Go for the Bull's-eye!

Target the EXACT JOB you want.

Before you can begin to go after a job, you have to determine the job you want. This is the most important step when generic resumes are sent out with the wishful hope that they will find the right destination, job seekers set themselves up for failure. The key for a successful job search is to plan and target what you are doing.

Remember the saying: "When in doubt, throw it out!" And that is what happens to many resumes because they are not targeted. The reader is not going to take the time to figure out what you want to do and whether or not you fit into their organization. They are busy.

Express Power Quick Tips: The Job Objective

Don't:

1. Make your resume a generic, cover-all-my-bases solution to your job search.
2. Depend on the reviewer to know everything about you.

Do:

1. Get the reader's attention at first glance. Your resume needs to jump off the page and say, "I am the best thing since peanut butter, and this is what I can do for you!" Generate the reader's excitement so they can't wait to interview you.
2. Target the resume to the specific job for which you are applying.
3. Do your research before submitting your resume: Preparation ensures success!
4. Create a reader friendly objective!
5. ➔ Input your EXACT JOB TITLE for which you are applying on Power Resume Builder, Form 1-B.

Now, that was easy! On to Step 3...

Keys to Targeting Your Resume

(*The Lazy Way to Success*)

- Divide your paper into 3 columns and follow steps 1-3.

Step #1

- Classified Ads: Newspaper.
  Clip ads that interest you and tape them in the left hand column.
- Internet Ads.
  Make a copy and number them. They are usually too large to tape to your data sheet.
- Leads from Friends.
  Try to get the same info an add may have and include it on your sheet.

Classified Ad Clipping

DIRECTOR OF PROCUREMENT
Exciting Full Time Opportunity in the Central Florida Area. An established Florida Company needs an individual with a Strong Balance of Computer and People Skills. Fast-Paced Facility. Analytical Planner. ISO-9000, JIT, Vendor Relations, Quality Control, Database Coordination, Contracts, Negotiations, Facility Management, Materials Management. Full Benefits, including Medical, Dental, Life, STD, LTD & 401K, Personal Days & Vacation after 6 months. Fax resume to 407-XXX-XXXX.

Step #2

Write the EXACT JOB TITLE from the ad.

Director of Procurement

Step #3

Extract verbatim from the ad and list:

- Characteristics
- Skills/Expertise
- Experience/Years
- Qualifications/Licensure/Certifications

- strong computer skills
- strong people skills
- fast-paced facility
- analytical planner
- ISO-9000
- JIT
- vendor relations
- quality control
- data base coordination
- contracts
- negotiations
- facility management
- materials management

Keys to Targeting Your Resume
Exhibit 3-1

Step 3

The Professional Profile:

Tell them who you are to get them excited!

Your professional profile will provide 6 brief statements describing who you are as a person at work, home and play. Strategies and formulas for creating a unique and proven professional profile include:

1. **First Statement:** Focuses on your world of work (page 36).
2. **Statements 2-5:** Focus on who you are as a person (pages 37-39).
3. **Sample Professional Profile Statements:** provide a listing of profile statements which have been researched through classifieds, job descriptions, and other resources (Exhibit 3-1). You may select the ones you like or create your own.
4. **Create Your Professional Profile Worksheet:** (Exhibit 3-2)

Express Power Quick Tips: Professional Profile

Don't:

1. List the number of years spent in each career area, (For example, 10 years accounting, 4 years payroll and so on).
2. Present in paragraph format.

Do:

1. Focus your profile on the *position you want.*
2. Make sure your focus meets the *company's need.*
3. Learn how to sell yourself so they see you as fitting in with their organization in *values, flexibility, goals and objectives.*
4. Learn how to sell *who you are* while eliminating possible discrimination due to the age factor.
5. Use descriptive words to describe your personal characteristics.
6. ➔ Create your personal profile by referring to Sample Professional Profile Statements (Exhibit 3-1) and create your Professional Profile Statements (Exhibit 3-2).
7. ➔ Create your Professional Profile statements and transfer this information to Power Resume Builder Form 1 - C.

Now you know how to focus your professional profile on who you are, what you want and what the company is looking for. The next step is #4, where it is time to tell the company what you can do for them.

First Statement Focused on Career | **Power Resume Builder**

The Professional Profile: First Statement. The first statement focuses on your world of work as it relates to the *job* for which you are applying.

Example: (A) **Dedicated** (B) **professional** with more than (C) **15** years of progressive accomplishments in (D) **accounting and administrative support.**

Professional Profile Formula.

(A) **(Descriptive characteristic)**
(B) **(Professional/recent college graduate/employee)** with more than
(C) (**Number of years of experience**) years of progressive accomplishments in
(D) **(Desired field**).

1. **Descriptive Characteristic**. If you had to describe yourself professionally (in the world of work) in one or two words what would you choose?

❑ Dynamic
❑ Goal-driven
❑ Dedicated
❑ Results-oriented
❑ Focused
❑ Other____________________
❑ Hard-working
❑ Visionary

➔ Transfer this information to Power Resume Builder Form 1-C.

2. **Professional**. Which word best describes your work experience? Replace the word professional if you are a recent college graduate or an entry level employee as follows:

❑ If you have graduated within one year use recent college graduate.
❑ If you are just beginning to work or have an entry-level position, use employee.
❑ Most all others will use professional.

➔ Transfer this information to Power Resume Builder Form 1-C.

3. **Number of Years of Experience.** Never put over 15 years of experience UNLESS you are an independent consultant.

How many years of experience do you have in your desired field?_______

➔ Transfer this information to Power Resume Builder Form 1-C.

4. **Desired Field.** One of the major problems with many resumes today is the fact that they do not focus specifically on *what the company wants.* Here are some ideas that will help you focus on your area of interest.

Check off the focus area which applies to you or create your own in the space provided.

❑ sales, marketing, and customer service
❑ project administration and production management
❑ creative design, promotions, and advertising
❑ warehousing, purchasing, and distribution systems
❑ customer service and medical sales
❑ software design, development, and maintenance
❑ materials management and quality control
❑ financial management, investments, and loan management
❑ training, development, and curriculum design
❑ human resources, benefits, and compensation
❑ banking and financial affairs
❑ in and outpatient services
❑ administrative support services and special events
❑ public relations, promotions, and media relations
❑ construction and project management
❑ mergers, acquisitions, and new business development
❑ (Your statement)____

On what (job) field are you focusing this resume?

➔ Transfer this information to Power Resume Builder Form 1-C.

The Professional Profile: Five Subsequent Statements.

- The remaining 5 statements represent who you are at home, work and play.
- It is the generic you.
- Key words in this section should include team player, team builder, leader, self-starter–all roles you play on the job.
- It is important to promote yourself as someone who can get the job done, is fun to be around, great with all types of people and focused on the bottom line.
- On page 38 are sample Professional Profile Statements, Exhibit 3-1, and on page 39 is a guide to create your professional profile statements, Exhibit 3-2.
- ➔ Create your professional profile statements and transfer this information to Power Resume Builder Exhibit Form 1-C.

Sample Professional Profile Statements — Power Resume Builder

A. Select 5 profile professional profile sample statements below that best represent you OR
B. Select 5 from each column on the next page and mix/match/create your own professional profile.
C. Transfer your professional profile statements to the Power Resume Builder Form 1-C.

- ❑ Analytical planner, able to take complex and unrelated information and organize them into workable terms.
- ❑ Catalytic problem solving leader, who thinks logically, values creativity, and cares about people.
- ❑ Creative and open-minded, deadline oriented.
- ❑ Creative promoter, able to work independently and in a group setting.
- ❑ Dedicated to excellence in service and in building relationships.
- ❑ Dependable, always gets the job done.
- ❑ Dedicated team player, employing strong communication skills with diverse groups.
- ❑ Diplomatic leader, able to motivate diverse groups.
- ❑ Disciplined self-starter, with the unique ability to comprehend complex, unrelated information and digest it into workable terms.
- ❑ Diverse achiever, able to interpret task directions and provide solutions in a timely manner.
- ❑ Eager to learn, meet new challenges, and assimilate new concepts and ideas quickly.
- ❑ Effective achiever, able to meet all goals while staying within budgetary constraints.
- ❑ Enthusiastic self-starter, able to "get the job done."
- ❑ Flexible, always willing to help out wherever needed.
- ❑ Hard-working and goal-oriented individual, employing strong organizational skills and attention to detail.
- ❑ Highly energetic and open-minded.
- ❑ Highly motivated individual with cogent communication skills in diverse settings.
- ❑ Inspiring self-starter, able to organize resources to achieve goals.
- ❑ Innovative, diverse and industrious achiever, with a highly creative and open mind.
- ❑ Levelheaded individual, respectful of others, and able to work with all types of people.
- ❑ Loyal and dedicated team player, exercising strong organizational skills and attention to detail.
- ❑ Loyal and dedicated individual, demonstrating integrity in achieving all goals and objectives.
- ❑ Loyal and dedicated individual, employing strong communication skills with diverse groups.
- ❑ Motivated achiever, able to work with diverse populations.
- ❑ Motivated achiever, able to implement workable solutions to diverse situations.
- ❑ Motivated self-starter, exhibiting high ethics, hard work, dedication, competence and confidence, underscored by a personal commitment to outstanding professional performance.
- ❑ Motivated team leader, demonstrating effective communication skills in working with diverse groups.
- ❑ Personable, able to make clients happy.
- ❑ Personable individual with outstanding analytical skills and attention to detail.
- ❑ Poised innovator, with strong people skills and leadership ability.
- ❑ Positive self-starter with accelerated skills in organization and planning.
- ❑ Positive motivator, able to work with diverse populations.
- ❑ Proven leader, providing the momentum required to unite diverse groups toward a common goal.
- ❑ Respected team builder, able to empower others to achieve common goals.
- ❑ Results-oriented self-starter, able to achieve all goals and objectives.
- ❑ Results-oriented organizer, possessing analytical acumen, perception, judgment and energy.
- ❑ Resourceful and creative in pursing unique methods to attain goals and objectives.
- ❑ Resourceful self-starter, with the outstanding ability to gather, comprehend and convey information.
- ❑ Resourceful problem-solver, who thrives on translating complex and unrelated information into understandable terms.
- ❑ Self-starter with exceptional analytical, financial, and organizational skills.
- ❑ Detail-oriented team player, able to plan, organize, and complete projects on-time and within budget.

Sample Professional Profile Statements
Exhibit Step 3-1

Create Your Professional Profile Statements

Power Resume Builder

A. Select 5 from each column below and mix/match/create your own professional profile. OR,
B. Select 5 profile professional profile sample statements on page 38 that best represent you.
C. Transfer your Professional Profile statements to the Power Resume Builder Form 1-C.

Characteristic

- ❑ Analytical
- ❑ Catalytic problem solving
- ❑ Creative
- ❑ Dedicated
- ❑ Dependable
- ❑ Diplomatic
- ❑ Disciplined
- ❑ Diverse
- ❑ Energetic
- ❑ Enthusiastic
- ❑ Effective
- ❑ Goal-oriented
- ❑ Hardworking
- ❑ Industrious
- ❑ Innovative
- ❑ Inspiring
- ❑ Levelheaded
- ❑ Loyal
- ❑ Motivated
- ❑ Personable
- ❑ Poised
- ❑ Productive
- ❑ Proven
- ❑ Resourceful
- ❑ Respected
- ❑ Results-oriented
- ❑ Other

____

____

____

Role

- ❑ Achiever
- ❑ Innovator
- ❑ Leader
- ❑ Motivator
- ❑ Organizer
- ❑ Planner
- ❑ Promoter
- ❑ Self-starter
- ❑ Team builder
- ❑ Team leader
- ❑ Team player
- ❑ Visionary
- ❑ Other

____

____

____

____

____

____

____

____

____

____

____

Description of how I work.

- ❑ able to implement workable solutions to diverse situations.
- ❑ exhibiting high ethics, hard work, dedication, competence and confidence, underscored by a personal commitment to outstanding professional performance.
- ❑ demonstrating effective communication skills in working with diverse groups.
- ❑ able to make clients happy.
- ❑ with outstanding analytical skills and attention to detail.
- ❑ with strong people skills and leadership ability.
- ❑ with accelerated skills in organization and planning.
- ❑ providing the momentum required to unite all diverse groups toward a common goal.
- ❑ able to empower others to achieve common goals.
- ❑ able to achieve all goals and objectives.
- ❑ possessing analytical acumen, perception, judgement and energy.
- ❑ resourceful and creative in pursuing unique methods to attain goals and objectives.
- ❑ with the outstanding ability to gather, comprehend and convey information.
- ❑ who thrives on translating complex and unrelated information into understandable terms.
- ❑ with exceptional analytical, financial and organizational skills.
- ❑ able to plan, organize and complete projects on time and within budget.
- ❑ able to take complex and unrelated information and organize it into workable terms.
- ❑ who thinks logically, values creativity and cares about people.
- ❑ deadline oriented.
- ❑ able to work independently and in a group setting.
- ❑ dedicated to excellence in service and in building relationships.
- ❑ dependable, always gets the job done.
- ❑ exhibiting effective communication skills with diverse populations.
- ❑ able to motivate diverse groups.
- ❑ with the unique ability to comprehend complex, unrelated information and digest it into workable terms.
- ❑ able to interpret task directions and provide solutions in a timely manner.
- ❑ eager to learn, meet new challenges and assimilate new concepts and ideas quickly.
- ❑ able to meet all goals while staying within budgetary constraints.
- ❑ able to "get the job done."
- ❑ flexible, always willing to help out wherever needed.
- ❑ with cogent communicative skills in diverse settings.
- ❑ able to organize resources to achieve goals.
- ❑ respectful of others and able to work with all types of people.
- ❑ exercising strong organizational skills and attention to detail.
- ❑ demonstrating integrity in achieving all goals and objectives.
- ❑ able to work independently or with a group to achieve targeted goals.

Step 4

Areas of Expertise

Wow Them With Your Knowledge and Skills

A detailed listing of skills according to profession is provided for your easy reference and use. Remember it is critical to identify what you can offer a company through the use of *key words*. Only then will you receive the attention you deserve.

The following keyword lists for selected professions are provided for your reference in identifying words to include on your resume. The lists provided are not all-inclusive.

Exhibits

4-1	Administrative/Clerical	4-11	Insurance
4-2	Advertising/Public Relations	4-12	Management/Business/International
4-3	Architecture/Drafting/Design	4-13	Materials Management/Warehousing/Distribution
4-4	Creative Arts	4-14	Manufacturing
4-5	Education	4-15	Operations Management
4-6	Engineering	4-16	Real Estate
4-7	Finance/Banking/Accounting	4-17	Sales & Marketing
4-8	Healthcare/Medical	4-18	Sciences (Environmental/Laboratory)
4-9	Hospitality	4-19	Security/Loss Prevention/Law Enforcement
4-10	Human Resources/Social Services	4-20	Technical/Computer

Express Power Quick Tips: Areas of Expertise

Don't:

1. Write your skills in lengthy paragraph form.

Do:

1. Identify and bullet your expertise/knowledge areas.
2. Use one to two words to represent a skill.
3. Target the skill set the company wants.
4. Select the exhibits which relate best to your career field.
5. Check off the words which apply to your field and the position for which you are applying.
6. Add any additional words which you have identified as important based upon your classified ads and research.
7. ➔ Transfer your selected key words to Power Resume Builder Form 2.

In this chapter, you learned how to identify what you can do for a company through promoting bulleted key words on your resume. In the next chapter, we will continue to build your exciting resume with Step 5–Your Professional Background.

Power Resume Builder
Areas of Expertise/Skills/Knowledge

Administrative/ Clerical

❑ Accounting	❑ Accounts Payable	❑ Accounts Receivable
❑ Advertising Strategies	❑ Appointment Setting	❑ Bookkeeping
❑ Business Operations	❑ Business Plans	❑ Client Relations
❑ Cost Reductions	❑ Customer Service	❑ Dictation
❑ Drafting Correspondence	❑ Expense Reports	❑ Internet & Email
❑ Interviewing	❑ Inventory Control	❑ Liaison
❑ Lotus 1-2-3	❑ Management Support	❑ Marketing Materials
❑ Medical Terminology	❑ Meeting Planning	❑ MS Access
❑ MS Excel	❑ MS PowerPoint	❑ MS Publisher
❑ MS Windows	❑ MS Word	❑ Multi-Faceted Tasks
❑ Office Equipment	❑ Office Layout	❑ Office Management
❑ Oral Communications	❑ Policies & Procedures	❑ Presentations
❑ Planning & Organizing	❑ Problem Solving	❑ Proposals
❑ Purchasing	❑ Quality Assurance	❑ Reports
❑ Scheduling	❑ Special Events	❑ Special Projects
❑ Speedwriting	❑ Supervision	❑ Team Building
❑ Time Management	❑ Training	❑ Travel Coordination
❑ Written Communications	❑ Typing: ___WPM	❑ WordPerfect
❑ Reception	❑ Guest Relations	❑ Customer Relations
❑ ________________	❑ ________________	❑ ________________
❑ ________________	❑ ________________	❑ ________________
❑ ________________	❑ ________________	❑ ________________
❑ ________________	❑ ________________	❑ ________________

Express Power Quick Tips

In the AREA OF EXPERTISE/SKILLS/KNOWLEDGE:

1. This section represents what you can do for a company.
2. This list is not all inclusive.
3. Add additional areas of expertise/skills/knowledge that represent your background.
4. Be sure to include all the skills you have that match those identified in the classified ad, job posting or other available information collected. See Keys to Targeting Your Resume Exhibit 1-4.
5. Remember, if you don't tell them what you can do, they will never know!
6. ➔ Check off the areas of expertise that you have and transfer them to the Power Resume Builder Form 2.

Administrative/Clerical Exhibit 4-1

Power Resume Builder
Areas of Expertise/Skills/Knowledge

Advertising/Public Relations

- ❑ Advertising Campaigns
- ❑ Agency/Client Liaison
- ❑ Bilingual: German
- ❑ Broadcast Media
- ❑ Cable Media
- ❑ Computer Proficient
- ❑ Consumer Goods
- ❑ Creative Programs
- ❑ Cross-Product Partnerships
- ❑ Departmental Liaison
- ❑ Direct Mail
- ❑ Feature/Article Writing
- ❑ Image Building
- ❑ Media Negotiations
- ❑ Manuscript Development
- ❑ Multi-Media Presentations
- ❑ New Business Development
- ❑ Planning & Organization
- ❑ Photographic Techniques
- ❑ Photography/Design Liaison
- ❑ Production/Print Processes
- ❑ Proposal/Contract Writing
- ❑ Publicity
- ❑ Scheduling
- ❑ Strategic Marketing
- ❑ Tour Coordination
- ❑ Training & Development
- ❑ Trend Analysis & Tracking
- ❑ ____________________
- ❑ Advertising Strategies
- ❑ Bilingual: _____
- ❑ Bilingual: Spanish
- ❑ Budgeting
- ❑ Client Relations
- ❑ Conceptualization
- ❑ Content/Copy Editing
- ❑ Creative Strategies
- ❑ Customer Briefings
- ❑ Desktop Publishing
- ❑ Editing
- ❑ Focus Groups
- ❑ In-House Style Manual
- ❑ Media Placement
- ❑ Negotiations
- ❑ Outdoor Media
- ❑ Presentations
- ❑ Press Releases
- ❑ Product Development
- ❑ Project Management
- ❑ Proofreading
- ❑ Public Awareness
- ❑ Publicity Campaigns
- ❑ Special Events
- ❑ Strategic Thinking
- ❑ Trade Shows
- ❑ Value-Added Programs
- ❑ ____________________
- ❑ ____________________
- ❑ Agency Liaison
- ❑ Bilingual: French
- ❑ Brand Marketing
- ❑ Business Plans
- ❑ Communications
- ❑ Conference Marketing
- ❑ Creative Problem Solving
- ❑ Database Marketing
- ❑ Development & Review
- ❑ Fact Checking
- ❑ Free-lance Resources
- ❑ International Campaigns
- ❑ Merchandising Displays
- ❑ News Releases
- ❑ Page Layout
- ❑ Press Inquiries
- ❑ Print Media
- ❑ Project Coordination
- ❑ Promotions
- ❑ Prospecting
- ❑ Public Relations
- ❑ Publishing
- ❑ Speech Development
- ❑ Team Building
- ❑ TV/Print Production
- ❑ Vendor Relations
- ❑ ____________________
- ❑ ____________________

Express Power Quick Tips

In the AREA OF EXPERTISE/SKILLS/KNOWLEDGE:

1. This section represents what you can do for a company.
2. This list is not all inclusive.
3. Add additional areas of expertise/skills/knowledge that represents your background.
4. Ensure the skills that you have that match those identified in the classified ad, job posting or other available information collected, are included under this heading. See Keys to Targeting Your Resume Exhibit 1-4.
5. Remember, if you don't tell them what you can do, they will never know!
6. ➔ Check off the areas of expertise that you have and transfer them to the Power Resume Form #2.

Power Resume Builder
Areas of Expertise/Skills/Knowledge

Architecture/ Drafting/Design

❑ Accessories/Artwork	❑ Architecture	❑ Auto CADD
❑ Bilingual: _____	❑ Bilingual: French	❑ Bilingual: German
❑ Bilingual: Spanish	❑ Blueprints	❑ Budgeting
❑ CADD	❑ Client Relations	❑ Color Schemes
❑ Commercial & Residential	❑ Conceptual Drawings	❑ Contract Liaison
❑ Construction Coordination	❑ Contractor Liaison	❑ Consulting
❑ Creative Strategies	❑ Engineering	❑ Engineering Liaison
❑ Environmental Issues	❑ Faux Finishes	❑ Floor Plans/Elevations
❑ Furniture Plan/Procurement	❑ Historical Renovations	❑ Interior Design
❑ Materials & Resources	❑ Problem Solving	❑ Project Management
❑ Public Relations	❑ Quality Assurance	❑ Remodeling
❑ Renderings	❑ Research	❑ Residential & Industrial
❑ Scheduling	❑ Space Planning	❑ Specifications
❑ Walls/Floors	❑ Window Treatments	❑ Working Drawings
❑ __________	❑ __________	❑ __________
❑ __________	❑ __________	❑ __________
❑ __________	❑ __________	❑ __________
❑ __________	❑ __________	❑ __________
❑ __________	❑ __________	❑ __________
❑ __________	❑ __________	❑ __________
❑ __________	❑ __________	❑ __________
❑ __________	❑ __________	❑ __________

Express Power Quick Tips

In the AREA OF EXPERTISE/SKILLS/KNOWLEDGE:

1. This section represents what you can do for a company.
2. This list is not all inclusive.
3. Add additional areas of expertise/skills/knowledge that represents your background.
4. Ensure the skills that you have that match those identified in the classified ad, job posting or other available information collected, are included under this heading. See Keys to Targeting Your Resume Exhibit 1-4.
5. Remember, if you don't tell them what you can do, they will never know!
6. ➔ Check off the areas of expertise that you have and transfer them to the Power Resume Builder Form #2.

Architecture/Drafting/Design Exhibit 4-3

Power Resume Builder
Areas of Expertise/Skills/Knowledge

Creative Arts

- ❑ Acting
- ❑ Bookings
- ❑ Budgeting
- ❑ Clay Modeling
- ❑ Commercials
- ❑ Community Involvement
- ❑ Editing
- ❑ Fashion Design
- ❑ Graphics
- ❑ Illustrator
- ❑ Lotus 1-2-3
- ❑ Menu Development
- ❑ MS Excel
- ❑ MS Publisher
- ❑ On-Camera/Air Personality
- ❑ Painting
- ❑ Photoshop
- ❑ Problem Solving
- ❑ Prop Management
- ❑ Purchasing
- ❑ Set Design
- ❑ Training
- ❑ TV/Film Extra
- ❑ ________________
- ❑ ________________
- ❑ ________________
- ❑ Advertising
- ❑ Broadcasting
- ❑ Charitable Events
- ❑ Comedy
- ❑ Comps
- ❑ Creative Strategies
- ❑ Entertainment
- ❑ Fine Arts
- ❑ HTML
- ❑ Internet & www
- ❑ Master of Ceremony
- ❑ Modeling
- ❑ MS Office
- ❑ MS Word
- ❑ Package Design
- ❑ Paste Up
- ❑ Presentations
- ❑ Production Scheduling
- ❑ Public Relations
- ❑ Quark Express
- ❑ Sound Dubbing
- ❑ Trend Analysis
- ❑ WordPerfect
- ❑ ________________
- ❑ ________________
- ❑ ________________
- ❑ Agency Liaison
- ❑ Brochures
- ❑ Claris Works
- ❑ Commercial Art
- ❑ Costume Design
- ❑ Customer Relations
- ❑ Event Planning
- ❑ Forecasting
- ❑ Host
- ❑ Layout & Design
- ❑ Media Relations
- ❑ MS Access
- ❑ MS PowerPoint
- ❑ Newsletters
- ❑ Pagemaker
- ❑ Photography
- ❑ Press Events
- ❑ Promotions
- ❑ Publications
- ❑ Sculpting
- ❑ Special Events
- ❑ TV/Video Production
- ❑ Writing
- ❑ ________________
- ❑ ________________
- ❑ ________________

Express Power Quick Tips

In the AREA OF EXPERTISE/SKILLS/KNOWLEDGE:

1. This section represents what you can do for a company.
2. This list is not all inclusive.
3. Add additional areas of expertise/skills/knowledge that represents your background.
4. Ensure the skills that you have that match those identified in the classified ad, job posting or other available information collected, are included under this heading. See Keys to Targeting Your Resume Exhibit 1-4.
5. Remember, if you don't tell them what you can do, they will never know!
6. ➔ Check off the areas of expertise that you have and transfer them to the Power Resume Builder Form #2.

Power Resume Builder
Areas of Expertise/Skills/Knowledge

Education

- ❑ Academics
- ❑ Assessments
- ❑ French
- ❑ Child Care
- ❑ Computerized Learning
- ❑ Crisis Intervention
- ❑ Diagnosing
- ❑ First Aid/CPR
- ❑ Growth & Development
- ❑ Interpersonal Relations
- ❑ Mathematics
- ❑ Multi-Task Management
- ❑ Parental Administrative Liaison
- ❑ Planning & Organization
- ❑ Programs
- ❑ Public Relations
- ❑ Safety
- ❑ Sign Language
- ❑ Special Activities
- ❑ Student Development
- ❑ Supervision
- ❑ Time Management
- ❑ Volunteer Coordination
- ❑ Annual Reviews
- ❑ Band
- ❑ German
- ❑ Community Programs
- ❑ Cost Controls
- ❑ Curriculum
- ❑ Documentation
- ❑ Fundraising
- ❑ History
- ❑ Lesson Plans
- ❑ Mentoring
- ❑ Music
- ❑ Photography
- ❑ Policies & Procedures
- ❑ Progress Reports
- ❑ Reading
- ❑ Scheduling
- ❑ Social/Life Skills
- ❑ Special Education
- ❑ Student Relations
- ❑ Supply Ordering
- ❑ Training
- ❑ Writing
- ❑ Art
- ❑ Behavior Modification
- ❑ Spanish
- ❑ Computer Proficient
- ❑ Creative Learning
- ❑ Development
- ❑ English
- ❑ General Education
- ❑ IEP's
- ❑ Liaison
- ❑ Motivation
- ❑ Oral Communication
- ❑ Physical Education
- ❑ Problem Solving
- ❑ Psychology
- ❑ Report Writing
- ❑ Science
- ❑ Social Studies
- ❑ Special Projects
- ❑ Study Skills
- ❑ Teaching
- ❑ Tutoring
- ❑ Written Communication

❑ ____________ ❑ ____________ ❑ ____________

❑ ____________ ❑ ____________ ❑ ____________

❑ ____________ ❑ ____________ ❑ ____________

Express Power Quick Tips

In the AREA OF EXPERTISE/SKILLS/KNOWLEDGE:

1. This section represents what you can do for a company.
2. This list is not all inclusive.
3. Add additional areas of expertise/skills/knowledge that represents your background.
4. Ensure the skills that you have that match those identified in the classified ad, job posting or other available information collected, are included under this heading. See Keys to Targeting Your Resume Exhibit 1-4.
5. Remember, if you don't tell them what you can do, they will never know!
6. ➔ Check off the areas of expertise that you have and transfer them to the Power Resume Builder Form #2.

Power Resume Builder
Areas of Expertise/Skills/Knowledge

Engineering

❑ Auto CADD	❑ Budgeting	❑ Business Operations
❑ CADD	❑ CALS	❑ Client Relations
❑ Creative Design	❑ Compliance Issues	❑ Continuous Improvement
❑ Customer Service	❑ Design	❑ Drafting
❑ Documentation	❑ Formulation	❑ Governmental Regulations
❑ ISO-9000	❑ Lotus 1-2-3	❑ Mainframe
❑ Manufacturing	❑ Mathematical Analysis	❑ Mechanical Engineering
❑ MS Access	❑ MS Excel	❑ MS Word
❑ Multi-Task Management	❑ Oral Communications	❑ Planning & Organization
❑ Policies & Procedures	❑ Problem Solving	❑ Process Improvements
❑ Production Engineering	❑ Project Management	❑ Quality Assurance
❑ Quality Engineering	❑ Research & Development	❑ Security Clearance
❑ Specifications	❑ Strategic Planning	❑ Team Leader
❑ Technical Reports	❑ Technical Sales	❑ Tests & Measurements
❑ TQM	❑ Training	❑ Trend Analysis
❑ Trouble Shooting	❑ Word Perfect	❑ Workstations
❑ Written Communications	❑ Vendor Relations	
❑ ________________	❑ ________________	❑ ________________
❑ ________________	❑ ________________	❑ ________________
❑ ________________	❑ ________________	❑ ________________
❑ ________________	❑ ________________	❑ ________________
❑ ________________	❑ ________________	❑ ________________
❑ ________________	❑ ________________	❑ ________________
❑ ________________	❑ ________________	❑ ________________

Express Power Quick Tips

In the AREA OF EXPERTISE/SKILLS/KNOWLEDGE:

1. This section represents what you can do for a company.
2. This list is not all inclusive.
3. Add additional areas of expertise/skills/knowledge that represents your background.
4. Ensure the skills that you have that match those identified in the classified ad, job posting or other available information collected, are included under this heading. See Keys to Targeting Your Resume Exhibit 1-4.
5. Remember, if you don't tell them what you can do, they will never know!
6. ➔ Check off the areas of expertise that you have and transfer them to the Power Resume Builder Form #2.

Power Resume Builder
Areas of Expertise/Skills/Knowledge

Finance/Banking/Accounting

- ❏ Accounting
- ❏ Auditing
- ❏ Banking Regulations
- ❏ Bilingual: French
- ❏ Bonds
- ❏ Budgeting
- ❏ Closing
- ❏ Compliance Issues
- ❏ Credit Analysis
- ❏ Deposits
- ❏ Financial Analysis
- ❏ Financial Statements
- ❏ Foreign Currency
- ❏ Investments
- ❏ Loan Underwriting
- ❏ Payment Disputes
- ❏ Portfolio Management
- ❏ Reconciliation
- ❏ Retail Lending
- ❏ SEC Regulations
- ❏ Stocks
- ❏ Taxes
- ❏ Withdrawals
- ❏ Accounts Payable
- ❏ Background Checks
- ❏ Banking Transactions
- ❏ Bilingual: German
- ❏ Bookkeeping
- ❏ Business Development
- ❏ Collateral Review
- ❏ Consumer Loans
- ❏ Credit Checks
- ❏ Diversified Lending
- ❏ Financial Planning
- ❏ Financing
- ❏ General Ledger
- ❏ Loan Applications
- ❏ MIS
- ❏ Operations Management
- ❏ Post-Closing
- ❏ Referral Programs
- ❏ Risk Rating
- ❏ Staff Development
- ❏ Strategic Planning
- ❏ Training
- ❏ Accounts Receivable
- ❏ Balancing
- ❏ Bilingual: _____
- ❏ Bilingual: Spanish
- ❏ Branch Operations
- ❏ Cash Handling
- ❏ Collections
- ❏ Cost Accounting
- ❏ Customer Relations
- ❏ Feasibility
- ❏ Financial Reporting
- ❏ Forecasting
- ❏ International Banking
- ❏ Loan Origination
- ❏ Mutual Funds
- ❏ P&L
- ❏ Processing
- ❏ Registration
- ❏ Sales & Marketing
- ❏ Statement Analysis
- ❏ Tactical Planning
- ❏ Traveler's Checks

❏ ____________________ ❏ ____________________ ❏ ____________________

❏ ____________________ ❏ ____________________ ❏ ____________________

❏ ____________________ ❏ ____________________ ❏ ____________________

Express Power Quick Tips

In the AREA OF EXPERTISE/SKILLS/KNOWLEDGE:

1. This section represents what you can do for a company.
2. This list is not all inclusive.
3. Add additional areas of expertise/skills/knowledge that represents your background.
4. Ensure the skills that you have that match those identified in the classified ad, job posting or other available information collected, are included under this heading. See Keys to Targeting Your Resume Exhibit 1-4.
5. Remember, if you don't tell them what you can do, they will never know!
6. ➔ Check off the areas of expertise that you have and transfer them to the Power Resume Builder Form #2.

Power Resume Builder
Areas of Expertise/Skills/Knowledge

Healthcare/Medical

❑ Admitting
❑ Blood Testing
❑ Case Management
❑ Compliance
❑ Crisis Intervention
❑ Dental Hygiene
❑ Disease Prevention
❑ Facility Operations
❑ Grants
❑ Health Education
❑ Home Health Care
❑ Insurance
❑ Medical Records
❑ Medicare
❑ Monitoring Equipment
❑ Obstetrics
❑ Operating Room
❑ OSHA/Safety
❑ Patient Histories
❑ Pharmaceuticals
❑ Podiatry
❑ Problem Solving
❑ Public Health
❑ Radiology
❑ Reports
❑ Staff Development
❑ Technician
❑ Unit Start-ups

❑ ____________________

❑ ____________________

❑ Advocacy
❑ Cardiology
❑ Central Supply
❑ Continuing Education
❑ Cytotechnology
❑ Dental Technician
❑ Engineering
❑ First Aid/CPR
❑ HAZMAT
❑ Histology
❑ ICU/CCU/PCU
❑ JCAHO
❑ Medical Terminology
❑ Medications
❑ Nuclear Medicine
❑ Occupational Therapy
❑ Optometry
❑ Outpatient
❑ Patient Relations
❑ Physical Therapy
❑ Practice Management
❑ Program Development
❑ Public Relations
❑ Records Review
❑ Respiratory Therapy
❑ Statistical Analysis
❑ Transitional Care
❑ Utilization Review

❑ ____________________

❑ ____________________

❑ Assessments
❑ Care Planning
❑ Claims Management
❑ Counseling
❑ Dentistry
❑ Dietetics
❑ Environmental Services
❑ Geriatrics
❑ Health Risk Assessments
❑ HMO/PPO
❑ Inpatient
❑ Lab Work
❑ Medical/Surgical
❑ Mental Health
❑ Nursing
❑ Oncology
❑ Orthopedics
❑ Patient Care
❑ Pediatrics
❑ Physician Recruitment
❑ Primary Care
❑ Psychiatry
❑ Quality Assurance
❑ Referrals
❑ Social Services
❑ Surveys
❑ Treatment Plans
❑ Volunteer Coordination

❑ ____________________

❑ ____________________

Express Power Quick Tips

In the AREA OF EXPERTISE/SKILLS/KNOWLEDGE:

1. This section represents what you can do for a company.
2. This list is not all inclusive.
3. Add additional areas of expertise/skills/knowledge that represents your background.
4. Ensure the skills that you have that match those identified in the classified ad, job posting or other available information collected, are included under this heading. See Keys to Targeting Your Resume Exhibit 1-4.
5. Remember, if you don't tell them what you can do, they will never know!
6. ➔ Check off the areas of expertise that you have and transfer them to the Power Resume Builder Form #2.

Power Resume Builder
Areas of Expertise/Skills/Knowledge

Hospitality

- ❑ Accounting
- ❑ Bilingual: French
- ❑ Budgeting
- ❑ Communication Skills
- ❑ Computer Proficient
- ❑ Corporate Liaison
- ❑ Creative Displays
- ❑ Customer/Guest Service
- ❑ Forecasting
- ❑ Housekeeping
- ❑ Multi-Task Management
- ❑ Operations Management
- ❑ Oral Communications
- ❑ MS PowerPoint
- ❑ Presentations
- ❑ Property Management
- ❑ Recruiting & Staffing
- ❑ Restaurants
- ❑ Scheduling
- ❑ Special Projects
- ❑ Strategic Planning
- ❑ Time Management
- ❑ Travel
- ❑ ________________
- ❑ ________________
- ❑ ________________
- ❑ ________________

- ❑ Advertising Strategies
- ❑ Bilingual: German
- ❑ Business Plans
- ❑ Community Services
- ❑ Concierge
- ❑ Cost Controls
- ❑ Creative Solutions
- ❑ Employee Relations
- ❑ Grand Openings
- ❑ International Marketing
- ❑ Inventory Control
- ❑ Maintenance
- ❑ MS Excel
- ❑ MS Word
- ❑ Problem Solving
- ❑ Public Relations
- ❑ Referral Programs
- ❑ Safety/OSHA
- ❑ Security
- ❑ Special Promotions
- ❑ Supervision
- ❑ Training
- ❑ Written Communications
- ❑ ________________
- ❑ ________________
- ❑ ________________
- ❑ ________________

- ❑ Bilingual: _____
- ❑ Bilingual: Spanish
- ❑ Catering
- ❑ Computer Literate
- ❑ Contract Negotiations
- ❑ Creative Design
- ❑ Creative Strategies
- ❑ Food & Beverage
- ❑ Guest Relations
- ❑ Interpersonal Relations
- ❑ Liaison
- ❑ Marketing Strategies
- ❑ MS Office
- ❑ Planning & Organization
- ❑ Promotional Materials
- ❑ Quality Assurance
- ❑ Reservations
- ❑ Sales & Marketing
- ❑ Special Events
- ❑ Staff Development
- ❑ Team Building
- ❑ Translations
- ❑ www/Internet
- ❑ ________________
- ❑ ________________
- ❑ ________________
- ❑ ________________

Express Power Quick Tips

In the AREA OF EXPERTISE/SKILLS/KNOWLEDGE:

1. This section represents what you can do for a company.
2. This list is not all inclusive.
3. Add additional areas of expertise/skills/knowledge that represents your background.
4. Ensure the skills that you have that match those identified in the classified ad, job posting or other available information collected, are included under this heading. See Keys to Targeting Your Resume Exhibit 1-4.
5. Remember, if you don't tell them what you can do, they will never know!
6. ➔ Check off the areas of expertise that you have and transfer them to the Power Resume Builder Form #2.

Hospitality Exhibit 4-9

Power Resume Builder
Areas of Expertise/Skills/Knowledge

Human Resources Social Services

- ❑ ADA Implementation
- ❑ Benefits Administration
- ❑ Case Management
- ❑ Compensation
- ❑ Counseling
- ❑ Curriculum Development
- ❑ Departmental Restructuring
- ❑ Employee Handbooks
- ❑ Empowerment Programs
- ❑ Governmental Compliance
- ❑ Internal Auditing
- ❑ Job Description Development
- ❑ Leadership Development
- ❑ Life Transitions
- ❑ Multi-Task Management
- ❑ Organizational Development
- ❑ OSHA/Safety
- ❑ PC: IBM
- ❑ Planning & Organization
- ❑ Quality Assurance
- ❑ Recruiting
- ❑ Relationship Building
- ❑ Scheduling
- ❑ Sexual Harassment
- ❑ Staffing
- ❑ Team Leader
- ❑ Transfers & Relocations
- ❑ Written Communications
- ❑ Affirmative Action
- ❑ Budgeting
- ❑ Client Advocacy
- ❑ Compliance
- ❑ Crisis Management
- ❑ Discharge Planning
- ❑ Drug Testing
- ❑ Employee Relations
- ❑ Forecasting
- ❑ Hiring
- ❑ Internal Investigations
- ❑ Interviewing
- ❑ Labor Relations
- ❑ Management Liaison
- ❑ Mentoring
- ❑ Oral Communications
- ❑ P&L
- ❑ Performance Reviews
- ❑ Presentations
- ❑ Recognition Programs
- ❑ Reference Checks
- ❑ Risk Management
- ❑ Screening
- ❑ Special Projects
- ❑ Strategic Planning
- ❑ Training
- ❑ Unemployment
- ❑ Women's Issues
- ❑ Assessments
- ❑ Career Counseling
- ❑ Community Relations
- ❑ Conflict Resolution
- ❑ Customer Service
- ❑ Diversity Programs
- ❑ EEOC
- ❑ Facilitator
- ❑ Groups/Individuals
- ❑ HRIS
- ❑ Interpersonal Relations
- ❑ Job Fairs
- ❑ Liaison
- ❑ Mediations
- ❑ Operations
- ❑ Orientation
- ❑ Payroll Administration
- ❑ Policies & Procedures
- ❑ Problem Solving
- ❑ Records Retention
- ❑ Relationship Abuse
- ❑ Salary Negotiations
- ❑ Seminars
- ❑ Staff Development
- ❑ Team Building
- ❑ Train-the-Trainer
- ❑ Wage & Hour Law
- ❑ Workers' Compensation
- ❑ ____________________
- ❑ ____________________
- ❑ ____________________
- ❑ ____________________
- ❑ ____________________
- ❑ ____________________

Express Power Quick Tips

In the AREA OF EXPERTISE/SKILLS/KNOWLEDGE:

1. This section represents what you can do for a company.
2. This list is not all inclusive.
3. Add additional areas of expertise/skills/knowledge that represents your background.
4. Ensure the skills that you have that match those identified in the classified ad, job posting or other available information collected, are included under this heading. See Keys to Targeting Your Resume Exhibit 1-4.
5. Remember, if you don't tell them what you can do, they will never know!
6. ➔ Check off the areas of expertise that you have and transfer them to the Power Resume Builder Form #2.

Power Resume Builder
Areas of Expertise/Skills/Knowledge

Insurance

- ❑ Adjustments
- ❑ Bilingual: French
- ❑ Case Management
- ❑ Client Relations
- ❑ Compliance Issues
- ❑ Corporate Leasing
- ❑ Customer Service
- ❑ First Reports
- ❑ Insurance Claims
- ❑ Legal Documents
- ❑ Medical
- ❑ New Construction
- ❑ Planning & Organization
- ❑ Problem Solving
- ❑ Public Relations
- ❑ Relocations
- ❑ Resales
- ❑ Scheduling
- ❑ Supervision
- ❑ Training
- ❑ Bodily Injury Claims
- ❑ ________________
- ❑ ________________
- ❑ ________________
- ❑ ________________
- ❑ ________________
- ❑ ________________

- ❑ All-Lines License
- ❑ Bilingual: German
- ❑ Claim Verification
- ❑ Commercial Lines
- ❑ Computer Proficient
- ❑ Cost Controls
- ❑ Disability
- ❑ Foreclosures
- ❑ Interpersonal Relations
- ❑ Liability Claims
- ❑ Mitigating Damages
- ❑ Oral Communications
- ❑ Personal Lines
- ❑ Product Education
- ❑ Quality Assurance
- ❑ Report Writing
- ❑ Research
- ❑ Special Projects
- ❑ Team Leader
- ❑ Travel
- ❑ Subrogation
- ❑ ________________
- ❑ ________________
- ❑ ________________
- ❑ ________________
- ❑ ________________
- ❑ ________________

- ❑ Auto Claims
- ❑ Bilingual: Spanish
- ❑ Claims Management
- ❑ Community Programs
- ❑ Conflict Resolution
- ❑ Coverages
- ❑ Documentation
- ❑ Home Owners/Catastrophe
- ❑ Jewelry Claims
- ❑ Liaison
- ❑ Multi-Task Management
- ❑ Payout & Denial
- ❑ Policies & Procedures
- ❑ Property
- ❑ Record Keeping
- ❑ Reports
- ❑ Sales & Marketing
- ❑ Specialty Lines
- ❑ Time Management
- ❑ Workers Compensation
- ❑ Written Communications
- ❑ ________________
- ❑ ________________
- ❑ ________________
- ❑ ________________
- ❑ ________________
- ❑ ________________

Express Power Quick Tips

In the AREA OF EXPERTISE/SKILLS/KNOWLEDGE:

1. This section represents what you can do for a company.
2. This list is not all inclusive.
3. Add additional areas of expertise/skills/knowledge that represents your background.
4. Ensure the skills that you have that match those identified in the classified ad, job posting or other available information collected, are included under this heading. See Keys to Targeting Your Resume Exhibit 1-4.
5. Remember, if you don't tell them what you can do, they will never know!
6. ➔ Check off the areas of expertise that you have and transfer them to the Power Resume Builder Form #2.

Insurance Exhibit 4-11

Power Resume Builder
Areas of Expertise/Skills/Knowledge

Management/Business International

- ❑ Bilingual: ____
- ❑ Client Relations
- ❑ Cost Controls
- ❑ Employee Relations
- ❑ Financial Analysis
- ❑ Hiring
- ❑ International Markets
- ❑ ISO-9000
- ❑ Leadership
- ❑ Mentoring & Coaching
- ❑ MS PowerPoint
- ❑ MS Word
- ❑ New/Key Accounts
- ❑ OSHA & Safety
- ❑ P&L Management
- ❑ Problem Solving
- ❑ Planning & Organization
- ❑ Promotional Materials
- ❑ Recruiting
- ❑ Sales: Outside/Inside
- ❑ SPC Standards
- ❑ Strategic Planning
- ❑ Technical Presentations
- ❑ Travel
- ❑ ____________________
- ❑ ____________________
- ❑ ____________________
- ❑ ____________________
- ❑ Business Operations
- ❑ Compliance Issues
- ❑ Customer Service
- ❑ Executive Boards
- ❑ Forecasting
- ❑ Human Resources
- ❑ Interviewing
- ❑ JIT
- ❑ Liaison
- ❑ MS Access
- ❑ MS Publisher
- ❑ Multi-Task Management
- ❑ New Business Development
- ❑ Operations Management
- ❑ Performance Improvement
- ❑ Product Development
- ❑ Project Management
- ❑ Policy & Procedure Manuals
- ❑ Safety Compliance
- ❑ Scheduling
- ❑ Staff Development
- ❑ Target Marketing
- ❑ Time Management
- ❑ Warehouse Management
- ❑ ____________________
- ❑ ____________________
- ❑ ____________________
- ❑ ____________________
- ❑ Budgeting
- ❑ Computer Proficient
- ❑ Decision Making
- ❑ Facility/Equipment Maintenance
- ❑ Internal Controls
- ❑ Inventory Management
- ❑ Labor Relations
- ❑ Manufacturing
- ❑ MS Excel
- ❑ MS Windows
- ❑ Negotiations
- ❑ Process Improvement
- ❑ Oral Communications
- ❑ Presentations
- ❑ Procurement
- ❑ Performance Evaluations
- ❑ Quality Assurance
- ❑ Sales & Marketing
- ❑ Shipping & Receiving
- ❑ Start-Up Operations
- ❑ Team Building
- ❑ Training
- ❑ Written Communications
- ❑ ____________________
- ❑ ____________________
- ❑ ____________________
- ❑ ____________________

Express Power Quick Tips

In the AREA OF EXPERTISE/SKILLS/KNOWLEDGE:

1. This section represents what you can do for a company.
2. This list is not all inclusive.
3. Add additional areas of expertise/skills/knowledge that represents your background.
4. Ensure the skills that you have that match those identified in the classified ad, job posting or other available information collected, are included under this heading. See Keys to Targeting Your Resume Exhibit 1-4.
5. Remember, if you don't tell them what you can do, they will never know!
6. ➔ Check off the areas of expertise that you have and transfer them to the Power Resume Builder Form #2.

Management/Business/International Exhibit 4-12

Power Resume Builder
Areas of Expertise/Skills/Knowledge

Materials Management
Warehousing/Distribution

- ❑ Auditing
- ❑ Bilingual: French
- ❑ Budgeting
- ❑ Compliance Issues
- ❑ Costing
- ❑ Customs
- ❑ Domestic & International
- ❑ Forecasting
- ❑ Inventory Control
- ❑ JIT
- ❑ Lotus 1-2-3
- ❑ MS Access
- ❑ MS Word
- ❑ New Product Development
- ❑ Problem Solving
- ❑ Product Development
- ❑ Purchasing
- ❑ Reorders
- ❑ Road/Rail/Air/Pipeline
- ❑ Shipping & Receiving
- ❑ Special Promotions
- ❑ Strategic Planning
- ❑ Training
- ❑ Trouble Shooting
- ❑ Warehouse Management
- ❑ FIFO
- ❑ ________________
- ❑ ________________
- ❑ Bid Preparation
- ❑ Bilingual: German
- ❑ Business Operations
- ❑ Contract Management
- ❑ CPM
- ❑ Database Development
- ❑ Facility Management
- ❑ Imports/Exports
- ❑ Inventory Management
- ❑ Liaison
- ❑ Manufacturing & Production
- ❑ MS Excel
- ❑ Multi-Task Management
- ❑ New Product Selection
- ❑ Procedures
- ❑ Product Research
- ❑ Quality Assurance
- ❑ Resource Allocation
- ❑ Scheduling
- ❑ Sourcing
- ❑ Specifications
- ❑ Supplier Evaluation
- ❑ Transportation
- ❑ Vendor Consolidation
- ❑ Word Perfect
- ❑ ________________
- ❑ ________________
- ❑ ________________
- ❑ Bilingual: _____
- ❑ Bilingual: Spanish
- ❑ Business Plans
- ❑ Cost Reductions
- ❑ Customer Service
- ❑ Distribution
- ❑ Financial Analysis
- ❑ Internal Controls
- ❑ ISO-9000
- ❑ Logistics
- ❑ Materials Management
- ❑ MS PowerPoint
- ❑ Negotiations
- ❑ Pricing Strategies
- ❑ Procurement
- ❑ Proposals
- ❑ Regulatory Guidelines
- ❑ Sales & Marketing
- ❑ Selection
- ❑ Supplier Development
- ❑ Staff Development
- ❑ TQM
- ❑ Trend/Buying Analysis
- ❑ Vendor Relations
- ❑ Workflow Analysis
- ❑ ________________
- ❑ ________________
- ❑ ________________

Express Power Quick Tips

In the AREA OF EXPERTISE/SKILLS/KNOWLEDGE:

1. This section represents what you can do for a company.
2. This list is not all inclusive.
3. Add additional areas of expertise/skills/knowledge that represents your background.
4. Ensure the skills that you have that match those identified in the classified ad, job posting or other available information collected, are included under this heading. See Keys to Targeting Your Resume Exhibit 1-4.
5. Remember, if you don't tell them what you can do, they will never know!
6. ➔ Check off the areas of expertise that you have and transfer them to the Power Resume Builder Form #2.

Materials Management/Warehousing/Distribution Exhibit 4-13

Power Resume Builder
Areas of Expertise/Skills/Knowledge

Manufacturing

❑ Auditing
❑ Business Operations
❑ Computer Proficient
❑ Decision Making
❑ Equipment Maintenance
❑ Final Testing
❑ Hiring
❑ Internal Controls
❑ ISO-9000
❑ Laboratory Testing
❑ Manufacturing Engineering
❑ MS Access
❑ MS Publisher
❑ Multi-Task Management
❑ New Business Development
❑ Operations Management
❑ Written Communications
❑ Planning & Organization
❑ Operations Management
❑ Performance Evaluations
❑ Production Engineering
❑ Production Management
❑ Quality Assurance
❑ Recycling Programs
❑ Research & Development
❑ Scheduling
❑ SPC Standards
❑ Strategic Planning
❑ Technical Presentations
❑ Tests & Measurements
❑ Warehouse Management
❑ ____________________

❑ Bilingual: ____
❑ Client Relations
❑ Cost Controls
❑ Departmental Interface
❑ Facility Maintenance
❑ Finished Goods
❑ Human Resources
❑ Interviewing
❑ JIT
❑ Leadership
❑ Manufacturing
❑ MS Excel
❑ MS Windows
❑ Negotiations
❑ P&L Management
❑ Oral Communications
❑ Presentations
❑ Problem Solving
❑ Procurement
❑ Product Development
❑ Production Planning
❑ Promotional Materials
❑ Raw Materials
❑ Reports
❑ Safety/OSHA
❑ Shipping & Receiving
❑ Staff Development
❑ Supervision
❑ Team Building
❑ Time Management
❑ Training
❑ ____________________

❑ Budgeting
❑ Compliance Issues
❑ Customer Service
❑ Employee Relations
❑ FIFO
❑ Forecasting
❑ Inspection
❑ Inventory Management
❑ Labor Relations
❑ Liaison
❑ Mentoring & Coaching
❑ MS PowerPoint
❑ MS Word
❑ New/Key Accounts
❑ OSHA & Safety
❑ Packing & Shipping
❑ Policies & Procedures
❑ Process Engineering
❑ Production Control
❑ Process Improvements
❑ Project Management
❑ Purchasing
❑ Recruiting
❑ Safety Compliance
❑ Sales & Marketing
❑ Soldering
❑ Start-Up Operations
❑ Target Marketing
❑ Technical Support
❑ TQM
❑ Travel
❑ ____________________

Express Power Quick Tips

In the AREA OF EXPERTISE/SKILLS/KNOWLEDGE:

1. This section represents what you can do for a company.
2. This list is not all inclusive.
3. Add additional areas of expertise/skills/knowledge that represents your background.
4. Ensure the skills that you have that match those identified in the classified ad, job posting or other available information collected, are included under this heading. See Keys to Targeting Your Resume Exhibit 1-4.
5. Remember, if you don't tell them what you can do, they will never know!
6. ➔ Check off the areas of expertise that you have and transfer them to the Power Resume Builder Form #2.

Power Resume Builder
Areas of Expertise/Skills/Knowledge

Operations Management

- ❑ Bilingual: ____
- ❑ Client Relations
- ❑ Cost Controls
- ❑ Facility/Equipment Maintenance
- ❑ Human Resources
- ❑ Interviewing
- ❑ JIT
- ❑ Mentoring & Coaching
- ❑ MS PowerPoint/Publisher
- ❑ Multi-Task Management
- ❑ New Business Development
- ❑ Operations Management
- ❑ Performance Evaluations
- ❑ Written Communications
- ❑ Planning & Organizing
- ❑ Policy & Procedure Manuals
- ❑ Safety Compliance
- ❑ Scheduling
- ❑ Staff Development
- ❑ Target Marketing
- ❑ Technical Presentations
- ❑ Warehouse Management
- ❑ ____________
- ❑ ____________
- ❑ ____________
- ❑ Business Operations
- ❑ Compliance Issues
- ❑ Customer Service
- ❑ Employee Relations
- ❑ Forecasting
- ❑ Internal Controls
- ❑ Inventory Management
- ❑ Labor Relations
- ❑ MS Access
- ❑ MS Windows
- ❑ Negotiations
- ❑ OSHA & Safety
- ❑ P&L Management
- ❑ Problem Solving
- ❑ Oral Communications
- ❑ Project Management
- ❑ Quality Assurance
- ❑ Sales & Marketing
- ❑ Shipping & Receiving
- ❑ Start-Up Operations
- ❑ Team Building
- ❑ Time Management
- ❑ Travel
- ❑ ____________
- ❑ ____________
- ❑ ____________
- ❑ Budgeting
- ❑ Computer Proficient
- ❑ Decision Making
- ❑ Financial Analysis
- ❑ Hiring
- ❑ International Markets
- ❑ ISO-9000
- ❑ Manufacturing
- ❑ MS Excel
- ❑ MS Word
- ❑ New/Key Accounts
- ❑ HAZMAT
- ❑ Presentations
- ❑ Procurement
- ❑ Product Development
- ❑ Promotional Materials
- ❑ Recruiting
- ❑ Sales: Outside/Inside
- ❑ SPC Standards
- ❑ Strategic Planning
- ❑ Team Leader
- ❑ Training
- ❑ ____________
- ❑ ____________
- ❑ ____________
- ❑ ____________

Express Power Quick Tips

In the AREA OF EXPERTISE/SKILLS/KNOWLEDGE:

1. This section represents what you can do for a company.
2. This list is not all inclusive.
3. Add additional areas of expertise/skills/knowledge that represents your background.
4. Ensure the skills that you have that match those identified in the classified ad, job posting or other available information collected, are included under this heading. See Keys to Targeting Your Resume Exhibit 1-4.
5. Remember, if you don't tell them what you can do, they will never know!
6. ➔ Check off the areas of expertise that you have and transfer them to the Power Resume Builder Form #2.

Operations/Management Exhibit 4-15

Power Resume Builder
Areas of Expertise/Skills/Knowledge

Real Estate

- ❑ Acquisitions
- ❑ Advertising Campaigns
- ❑ Bilingual: German
- ❑ Bursements
- ❑ Communication Skills
- ❑ Cost Controls
- ❑ Escrow
- ❑ Follow-Up
- ❑ Judgment Searches
- ❑ Legal Contracts
- ❑ Loan Processing
- ❑ Multi-Site Supervision
- ❑ Project Management
- ❑ Public Records
- ❑ Refinancing
- ❑ Repair & Maintenance
- ❑ Residential & Commercial
- ❑ Underwriting
- ❑ ____________
- ❑ ____________
- ❑ ____________
- ❑ ____________
- ❑ ____________
- ❑ ____________

- ❑ Appraisals
- ❑ Bilingual: _____
- ❑ Bilingual: Spanish
- ❑ Cash-Flow Analysis
- ❑ Construction Practices
- ❑ Debt Consolidation
- ❑ Feasibility Studies
- ❑ Forecasting
- ❑ Leases
- ❑ Lien Waivers
- ❑ Market Analysis
- ❑ Negotiations
- ❑ Property Management
- ❑ Purchase & Lease
- ❑ Regulations
- ❑ Resident Interface
- ❑ Special Projects
- ❑ Valuations
- ❑ ____________
- ❑ ____________
- ❑ ____________
- ❑ ____________
- ❑ ____________
- ❑ ____________

- ❑ Bidding Contracts
- ❑ Bilingual: French
- ❑ Building Operations
- ❑ Closings
- ❑ Contract Preparation
- ❑ Development
- ❑ Financial Modeling
- ❑ HUD Programs
- ❑ Leasing Strategies
- ❑ Listings
- ❑ Multi-Family
- ❑ On-Line Transactions
- ❑ Proposals
- ❑ Real Estate Law
- ❑ Rent Rolls
- ❑ Sales & Marketing
- ❑ Tax Credit Programs
- ❑ Zoning & Permits
- ❑ ____________
- ❑ ____________
- ❑ ____________
- ❑ ____________
- ❑ ____________
- ❑ ____________

Express Power Quick Tips

In the AREA OF EXPERTISE/SKILLS/KNOWLEDGE:

1. This section represents what you can do for a company.
2. This list is not all inclusive.
3. Add additional areas of expertise/skills/knowledge that represents your background.
4. Ensure the skills that you have that match those identified in the classified ad, job posting or other available information collected, are included under this heading. See Keys to Targeting Your Resume Exhibit 1-4.
5. Remember, if you don't tell them what you can do, they will never know!
6. ➔ Check off the areas of expertise that you have and transfer them to the Power Resume Builder Form #2.

Power Resume Builder
Areas of Expertise/Skills/Knowledge

Sales & Marketing

❑ Acquisitions
❑ Bilingual: _____
❑ Bilingual: Spanish
❑ Budgeting & Controls
❑ Chemical
❑ Communication Skills
❑ Computer Proficient
❑ Corporate Liaison
❑ Cross-Product Partnerships
❑ Database Marketing
❑ Forecasting
❑ International Campaigns
❑ Interpersonal Relations
❑ Management Decisions
❑ Merchandising Displays
❑ Multi-Task Management
❑ Multi-Media Presentations
❑ Operations Management
❑ New Business Development
❑ Pharmaceutical/Medical
❑ Photography/Design Liaison
❑ Planning & Organization
❑ Professional Networking
❑ Publicity Campaigns
❑ Quality Assurance
❑ Sales & Marketing
❑ Special Events
❑ Staff Development
❑ Supervision
❑ Technical Sales
❑ Trade Shows
❑ Travel
❑ Trend Analysis & Tracking
❑ Written Communications

❑ Advertising Strategies
❑ Bilingual: French
❑ Brand Development
❑ Business Plans
❑ Client Relations
❑ Community Services
❑ Consumer Goods
❑ Creative Design
❑ Creative Strategies
❑ Financial Analysis
❑ Hospitality
❑ Inside Sales
❑ Inventory Control
❑ Market Analysis
❑ MS Excel
❑ MS PowerPoint
❑ Oral Communications
❑ Outside Sales
❑ Pricing
❑ Product Development
❑ Product Research
❑ Promotional Materials
❑ Prospecting
❑ Publishing
❑ Recruiting & Staffing
❑ Scheduling
❑ Special Projects
❑ Strategic Marketing
❑ Target Marketing
❑ Territory Management
❑ Training
❑ Trend Analysis
❑ Value-Added Programs
❑ Wholesale Distribution

❑ Agency/Client Liaison
❑ Bilingual: German
❑ Brand Marketing
❑ Business Solutions
❑ Collections
❑ Computer Literate
❑ Contract Negotiations
❑ Creative Displays
❑ Customer Service
❑ Focus Groups
❑ Industrial
❑ International Marketing
❑ Key Accounts
❑ Marketing Strategies
❑ MS Office
❑ MS Word
❑ Order Fulfillment
❑ Presentations
❑ Problem Solving
❑ Product Marketing
❑ Promotions
❑ Proposals
❑ Public Relations
❑ Purchasing
❑ Retail
❑ Seminars
❑ Special Promotions
❑ Strategic Planning
❑ Team Building
❑ Time Management
❑ Translations
❑ TV/Print Production
❑ Vendor Relations
❑ www/Internet

Express Power Quick Tips

In the AREA OF EXPERTISE/SKILLS/KNOWLEDGE:

1. This section represents what you can do for a company.
2. This list is not all inclusive.
3. Add additional areas of expertise/skills/knowledge that represents your background.
4. Ensure the skills that you have that match those identified in the classified ad, job posting or other available information collected, are included under this heading. See Keys to Targeting Your Resume Exhibit 1-4.
5. Remember, if you don't tell them what you can do, they will never know!
6. ➔ Check off the areas of expertise that you have and transfer them to the Power Resume Builder Form #2.

Sales & Marketing Exhibit 4-17

Power Resume Builder
Areas of Expertise/Skills/Knowledge

Sciences
Environmental/Laboratory

- ❑ Sciences
- ❑ Biology
- ❑ Data Collection
- ❑ Environmental Science
- ❑ Field Projects
- ❑ Geotstatistics/Kriging
- ❑ Lab Analysis
- ❑ Marine Biology
- ❑ Oral Communications
- ❑ Policies & procedures
- ❑ Report Writing
- ❑ RO Desalinization
- ❑ Seismic Surveying
- ❑ Supervision
- ❑ Veterinary Sciences
- ❑ Watershed Runoff
- ❑ Written Communications
- ❑ ________________
- ❑ ________________
- ❑ ________________
- ❑ ________________
- ❑ ________________

- ❑ Animal Handling
- ❑ Botany
- ❑ Documentation
- ❑ Field Engineering
- ❑ Filtration
- ❑ Hydrology
- ❑ Laboratory Testing
- ❑ Mathematical Analysis
- ❑ Ornithology
- ❑ Problem Solving
- ❑ Research
- ❑ Safety/OSHA
- ❑ Sonic Well Logging
- ❑ Tissue Samples
- ❑ Water Quality
- ❑ Zoology
- ❑ ________________
- ❑ ________________
- ❑ ________________
- ❑ ________________
- ❑ ________________
- ❑ ________________

- ❑ Bilingual: ____
- ❑ Computer Proficient
- ❑ Engineering
- ❑ Field Observation
- ❑ Geohydrology
- ❑ Interpersonal Relations
- ❑ Lab Equipment
- ❑ Matlab
- ❑ Plant Handling
- ❑ Processing Modflow
- ❑ Resources
- ❑ Scientific Collection
- ❑ Statistical Analysis
- ❑ VAX
- ❑ Waste Water Treatment
- ❑ HAZMAT
- ❑ ________________
- ❑ ________________
- ❑ ________________
- ❑ ________________
- ❑ ________________
- ❑ ________________

Express Power Quick Tips

In the AREA OF EXPERTISE/SKILLS/KNOWLEDGE:

1. This section represents what you can do for a company.
2. This list is not all inclusive.
3. Add additional areas of expertise/skills/knowledge that represents your background.
4. Ensure the skills that you have that match those identified in the classified ad, job posting or other available information collected, are included under this heading. See Keys to Targeting Your Resume Exhibit 1-4.
5. Remember, if you don't tell them what you can do, they will never know!
6. ➔ Check off the areas of expertise that you have and transfer them to the Power Resume Builder Form #2.

Sciences/Environmental/Laboratory Exhibit 4-18

Power Resume Builder Areas of Expertise/Skills/Knowledge — Security/Loss Prevention/Law Enforcement

❑ ADA Implementation
❑ Benefits Administration
❑ Case Management
❑ Compensation
❑ Counseling
❑ Curriculum Development
❑ Departmental Restructuring
❑ Employee Handbooks
❑ Empowerment Programs
❑ Governmental Compliance
❑ Internal Auditing
❑ Job Description Development
❑ Intelligence
❑ Life Transitions
❑ Mass Disaster
❑ Organizational Development
❑ OSHA/Safety
❑ PC: IBM
❑ Planning & Organization
❑ Quality Assurance
❑ Recruiting
❑ Security Clearances
❑ Scheduling
❑ Sexual Harassment
❑ Staffing
❑ Team Leader
❑ Transfers & Relocations
❑ Written Communications
❑ Affirmative Action
❑ Budgeting
❑ Client Advocacy
❑ Compliance
❑ Crisis Management
❑ Discharge Planning
❑ Drug Testing
❑ Employee Relations
❑ Forecasting
❑ Hiring
❑ Internal Investigations
❑ Interviewing
❑ Labor Relations
❑ Management Liaison
❑ Mentoring
❑ Oral Communications
❑ P&L
❑ Performance Reviews
❑ Presentations
❑ Recognition Programs
❑ Reference Checks
❑ Risk Management
❑ Screening
❑ Special Projects
❑ Strategic Planning
❑ Training
❑ Unemployment
❑ Women's Issues
❑ Assessments
❑ Career Counseling
❑ Community Relations
❑ Conflict Resolution
❑ Customer Service
❑ Diversity Programs
❑ EEOC
❑ Facilitator
❑ Groups/Individuals
❑ HRIS
❑ Interpersonal Relations
❑ Job Fairs
❑ Liaison
❑ Mediations
❑ Operations
❑ Orientation
❑ SWAT
❑ Policies & Procedures
❑ Problem Solving
❑ Records Retention
❑ Relationship Abuse
❑ Salary Negotiations
❑ Seminars
❑ Staff Development
❑ Team Building
❑ Train-the-Trainer
❑ Wage & Hour Law
❑ Workers Comp

❑ ________________ ❑ ________________ ❑ ________________

❑ ________________ ❑ ________________ ❑ ________________

Express Power Quick Tips

In the AREA OF EXPERTISE/SKILLS/KNOWLEDGE:

1. This section represents what you can do for a company.
2. This list is not all inclusive.
3. Add additional areas of expertise/skills/knowledge that represents your background.
4. Ensure the skills that you have that match those identified in the classified ad, job posting or other available information collected, are included under this heading. See Keys to Targeting Your Resume Exhibit 1-4.
5. Remember, if you don't tell them what you can do, they will never know!
6. ➔ Check off the areas of expertise that you have and transfer them to the Power Resume Builder Form #2.

Security/Loss Prevention/Law Enforcement Exhibit 4-19

Power Resume Builder
Areas of Expertise/Skills/Knowledge

Technical/Computer

- ❑ Application Development
- ❑ Bilingual: _____
- ❑ Bilingual: Spanish
- ❑ Client-Server Technology
- ❑ Configuration & Installation
- ❑ Customer Service
- ❑ Data Conversion
- ❑ Debugging
- ❑ Electronics Hardware Design
- ❑ End-User Training
- ❑ Hardware/Software Groups
- ❑ Installation/Maintenance
- ❑ Layered Network Architecture
- ❑ Mainframe programming
- ❑ Microprocessor Programming
- ❑ MS Windows 3.1
- ❑ Multi-Task Environments
- ❑ New Technology
- ❑ Oracle Database
- ❑ Planning & Organization
- ❑ Preventative Maintenance
- ❑ Real-Time Development
- ❑ Replicated Environments
- ❑ Security/Access
- ❑ Software Porting
- ❑ System Integration
- ❑ Technical Support
- ❑ Trouble Shooting
- ❑ Video Conferencing
- ❑ Written Communications
- ❑ CNE
- ❑ __________________
- ❑ __________________
- ❑ Analysis
- ❑ Bilingual: French
- ❑ Cabling Topologies
- ❑ Capability Studies
- ❑ Conflict Resolution
- ❑ Data Acquisition
- ❑ Database Management
- ❑ Design
- ❑ Electrical Design
- ❑ Error Resolution
- ❑ Frame Relay
- ❑ Interface Engines
- ❑ Interpersonal Relations
- ❑ Lotus 1-2-3
- ❑ MS Access
- ❑ MS Windows 95
- ❑ Negotiations
- ❑ Novell
- ❑ Oral Communication
- ❑ Peripheral Devices
- ❑ Project Coordination
- ❑ Relational Databases
- ❑ Sales Support
- ❑ Signal Processing
- ❑ Specifications
- ❑ Systems Design
- ❑ Test & Measurement
- ❑ UNIX
- ❑ Visual Applications
- ❑ Windows NT
- ❑ COBOL
- ❑ __________________
- ❑ __________________
- ❑ Backup/Recovery
- ❑ Bilingual: German
- ❑ Call Center Operations
- ❑ Computer Graphics
- ❑ Cross-Platforms
- ❑ Data Architecture
- ❑ Database Tuning
- ❑ DOS
- ❑ Embedded Controls
- ❑ File Server Maintenance
- ❑ Industry Trends
- ❑ International Markets
- ❑ Liaison
- ❑ Modifications
- ❑ MS Excel
- ❑ MS Word
- ❑ Networking
- ❑ Operating Systems
- ❑ PC Based Tool
- ❑ Problem Solving
- ❑ Quality Assurance
- ❑ Research
- ❑ Security Administration
- ❑ Software Integration
- ❑ SQL/SQL* Plus
- ❑ Tape Libraries
- ❑ Training & Education
- ❑ User Interface Design
- ❑ WAN/LAN
- ❑ Workstations
- ❑ MCSE
- ❑ Macintosh
- ❑ __________________

Express Power Quick Tips

In the AREA OF EXPERTISE/SKILLS/KNOWLEDGE:

1. This section represents what you can do for a company.
2. This list is not all inclusive.
3. Add additional areas of expertise/skills/knowledge that represents your background.
4. Ensure the skills that you have that match those identified in the classified ad, job posting or other available information collected, are included under this heading. See Keys to Targeting Your Resume Exhibit 1-4.
5. Remember, if you don't tell them what you can do, they will never know!
6. ➔ Check off the areas of expertise that you have and transfer them to the Power Resume Builder Form #2.

Step 5

Professional Background

Tell Your Life's Work History in One Easy Sentence

Understanding how to strategically present your experience by focusing on *the* functional area in which you want to work is one of the Power Resume's secrets to success. Remember, "What you focus on is what you get." Well, when it comes to your resume, this is particularly important. Not only will you learn how to focus your resume, but you will also get tips on using what we fondly refer to as *name droppers*. These are tidbits of information which will strongly sell you to a particular company or assist you in overcoming an obstacle.

Introducing strategies for presenting your functional work experience:

- Professional Background Overview (Exhibit 5-1).
- Professional Background Formula (Exhibit 5-2).
- Professional Background Sample (Exhibits 5-3).
- Name Droppers (Exhibit 5-4).

Express Power Quick Tips: Professional Background

Don't:

1. Tell too much or be too wordy.
2. Use more than four lines.

Do:

1. Represent what you have done during your entire world of work in one sentence that is focused toward what the company wants.
2. Only use one sentence.
3. Follow the rule of three: Verb, Verb, and Verb (Exhibit 5-1).
4. Refer to examples according to profession in (Exhibit 5-3). Select the example which best represents your profession and modify it as necessary.
6. Use name droppers when applicable (Exhibit 5-4).
7. ➔ Complete the Power Resume Builder Form 3.

Now that we have focused your resume on who you are and what you can do for a potential employer in Step 5. Let's take a look at *how well* you can do it in Step 6.

Power Resume Builder - Rule of 3 | **Professional Background Overview**

Purpose: • Provides a statement of the overall duties of your employment.

Format:

FUNCTIONAL FOCUS ON THE AREA YOU WANT TO WORK IN

Formula: **Verb***, **verb** and **verb** the overall activities of **department/unit/organization/assigned projects/region/the area for which they are responsible** which include: **verbing**; **verbing**; and **verbing**.

* Recommend first verb be the word "plan." Everyone must plan their work before they begin. Planners are achievers.

Example:

ACCOUNTING/FINANCE

Plan, organize and manage the overall accounting activities for various organizations which include: coordinating accounts payable/receivable; preparing required financial reports and other documents; and ensuring compliance with corporate standards for fiscal affairs.

Power Resume Builder

Professional Background Formula

Understanding how to strategically present your experience by focusing on *the* functional area in which you want to work is one of the Power Resume's secrets to success.

What is the formula for developing the Professional Background?

The professional background formula has been strategically developed so it is easy to *read* and *retain,* and it *relates* to the job for which you are applying. As a result of our research, we have identified the following rules which apply to the professional background:

1. **Rule of 3**. From the time you are a kid, you learn by threes—A, B, C, and 1, 2, 3. Even advertisers form their jingles around a cadence of three. Job descriptions often follow this pattern as well. They begin with:

    - Plan, control, and direct
    - Plan, coordinate, and manage
    - Analyze, design, and produce, and so on.

    Therefore, practice the *Rule of 3.*

2. **Rule of One Sentence**. When it comes to reading a sentence, most people are obsessive-compulsive and will rush to finish the sentence before they stop. The period(.) gives them permission to stop. We have, therefore, constructed the professional profile so it is one sentence. If they begin to read this statement, they most likely will finish it. It is user friendly and is more in concert with how their job descriptions are written.

3. **Rule: Use the Global Statement**. Focus on *what the company wants.* The longer you work, the more skills you have. This is where you run into the danger of being classified as *overqualified* by telling too much. So be smart:

    - *Identify what the company wants.*
    - *Take everything you have done from your entire work history that applies to the job, and sell it.*

    The Professional Background, therefore, is a global statement which encompasses all your experience in a particular function in one sentence. This skill is also very useful in proposal development once you arrive at your new position.

ACCOUNTING/FINANCE

Plan, organize, and manage the overall accounting activities for various organizations which include: coordinating accounts payable/receivable; preparing required financial reports and other documents; and ensuring compliance with corporate standards for fiscal affairs.

ADVERTISING

Plan, organize, and manage advertising and marketing activities for various companies which include: evaluating promotional strategies and client needs; providing services, solutions and marketing programs; and ensuring quality customer service in compliance with corporate goals and objectives.

COMPUTER SOFTWARE DESIGN

Plan, organize, and manage overall software design and development for various companies which include: identifying project goals and objectives; directing the refining process with client technical resources and establishing checkpoints; and ensuring compliance with established contract specifications.

CUSTOMER SERVICE

Plan, organize, and manage the overall customer service activities for various companies which include: evaluating client needs; providing support and timely solutions; and ensuring goals and objectives are met while maintaining quality service.

CONSULTING

Plan, organize, and manage the overall consulting activities for various organizations which includes: assessing client goals and objectives; developing strategies and solutions; and monitoring client/project from inception to completion to ensure quality service.

CREATIVE ARTS

Plan, rehearse, and perform as a television personality, actor/actress, singer, model, master of ceremonies, etc., which include: performing at productions, benefits, stage performances, etc.; representing various organizations at special functions; and ensuring quality performances in accordance with contract specifications.

Sample Statements for Accounting/Finance, Advertising, Computer Software Design, Customer Service, Consulting, Creative Arts - Exhibit 5-3

EDUCATION

Plan, organize, and manage assigned educational activities which include: evaluating and designing curriculum; motivating and mentoring students; and monitoring student progress to ensure compliance with educational standards.

ENGINEERING

Plan, organize, and manage the assigned engineering activities for various projects, which include: evaluating technical needs; creating innovative plans and solutions; and monitoring the project to ensure compliance with goals and objectives.

HEALTHCARE

Plan, organize, and manage the overall healthcare activities for various organizations, which include: evaluating patient and physician needs; implementing healthcare plans and programs; and ensuring compliance with targeted goals, JCAHO and other medical/professional regulatory entities.

HOSPITALITY

Plan, organize, and manage the overall hospitality duties, which include: determining guest needs; developing and implementing quality service programs, referrals and events; and monitoring guests to ensure complete satisfaction.

HUMAN RESOURCES

Plan, organize, and manage the overall human resource responsibilities, which include: assessing manpower requirements and programs; developing and implementing change programs and organizational solutions; and monitoring projects to ensure compliance with targeted goals and federal/state regulations.

INSURANCE

Plan, organize, and manage assigned insurance functions, which include: evaluating client/organizational needs; providing services and solutions; and ensuring quality customer service in accordance with regulatory standards and corporate objectives.

MAINTENANCE

Plan, organize, and manage the overall activities for the mechanical maintenance department, which include: supervising and training staff; inspecting and maintaining equipment; and ensuring all corporate goals and objectives were met.

Sample Statements for Education, Engineering, Healthcare, Hospitality, Human Resources, Insurance, Maintenance - Exhibit 5-3

MANUFACTURING

Plan, organize, and manage the overall manufacturing operations which include: determining customer/plant/staff requirements; hiring, scheduling, and training staff; and monitoring production/customers/staff to achieve targeted goals, budgets, and deadlines.

OFFICE SUPPORT/ADMINISTRATION

Plan, organize, and manage the overall office/administrative support functions for various companies which include: identifying management needs/concerns; providing timely support and solutions; and ensuring compliance with departmental/corporate goals and objectives.

OPERATIONS MANAGEMENT

Plan, control, and direct the total operations for various companies which include: evaluating operational requirements (manpower, resources, projects); developing and implementing tactical and strategic plans; and ensuring compliance with corporate goals and objectives.

PUBLIC RELATIONS

Plan, organize, and coordinate the overall public relations activities for various companies which include: evaluating corporate image and desired impact; developing innovative promotions and positive media relations to increase recognition and credibility; and monitor process to ensure compliance with identified goals and objectives.

PURCHASING

Plan, organize, and manage purchasing activities which include: evaluating organizational requirements (equipment, supplies); coordinating bidding, contract negotiations and vendor relations; and ensuring quality products are provided in a timely manner in support of corporate objectives.

REAL ESTATE

Plan, organize and manage the overall real estate sales program which include: analyzing property values and developing marketing proposals; targeting clients and meeting client needs; and ensuring appropriate documents and contracts are processed.

RESTAURANT MANAGEMENT

Plan, organize and manage the overall restaurant operations for various companies which include: evaluating store/client requirements; developing budgets, strategies and creative menus; and monitoring to ensure compliance with goals and objectives while enhancing quality service.

Sample Statements for Manufacturing, Office Support/Administration,Operations Management, Public Relations, Purchasing, Real Estate, Restaurant Management - Exhibit 5-3

SALES & MARKETING

Plan, organize, and manage sales and marketing activities which include: developing innovative marketing strategies and training staff; promoting quality products, services, and solutions; and ensuring achievement of targeted goals and objectives.

SCIENCES

Plan, organize, and complete assigned scientific research activities which include: assessing research project/laboratory needs; collecting and testing samples; and reporting findings in a timely fashion, while complying with safety, OSHA, and environmental regulations.

SECURITY/LAW ENFORCEMENT

Plan, organize, and complete security/law enforcement activities which include: determining safety/security needs; proactively monitoring typical activity and responding to unusual activity; and reporting findings in compliance with laws and regulations.

WAREHOUSE MANAGEMENT

Plan, organize, and manage the overall warehousing activities for the company which include: evaluating shipping and receiving operational and support requirements; providing organizational guidelines, inventory control programs, and resource distribution as required; and ensuring compliance with OSHA standards and operational objectives.

Power Resume Builder | **Professional Background: Name Droppers**

NAME DROPPING SECTION (Insert after *Professional Background* paragraph.)

Purpose: To provide a brief history of clients/companies/industries/projects worked with.

Ask: What name dropping can I do that will sell me the most? Select from examples.

- **Key Accounts**: AT&T, Disney, Coca-Cola, Gooding's Supermarkets, Kroger Company, Wal-Mart, Car Stop, REMAX, and others

  OR

- **Clients**: Residential, Commercial, Municipal, and others

  OR

- **Publications**: Software Manuals, Training Journals, and Video Training.

  OR

- **Companies**: Corporate, Construction, Medical, Associations

  OR

- **Industries**: Art Galleries, Educational Institutions, Restaurants, Offices, Wholesale, Distribution, and Retail

  OR

- **Facilities**: Sheraton Savannah Inn & Country Club, Holiday Inn, Miracle Mile Resort, Walt Disney Swan, and others

  OR

- **Projects**: Residential Facilities, Multi-Purpose Family Life Center, Volunteer Recruitment, Major Gift Development, and Industry Magazines

  OR

- **Products**: Medical, Technical, Educational, Electrical, Automobile, and others

Sample "Name Droppers" - Exhibit 5-4

Step 6

Accomplishments

Sell What You Can Do in Quantitative Terms

Review the results-oriented tools for quantifying accomplishments, using the following Exhibits.

- Accomplishments: Ideas to Get You Thinking (Exhibit 6-1).
- "Peanut Butter Principle" Formula for Quantification (Exhibit 6-2).
- Accomplishments: How to Figure Percents (Exhibit 6-3).
- Quantification Steps 1-4 (Exhibit 6-4).
- Accomplishments Samples (Exhibit 6-5).
- My Starter List for Building Accomplishments (Exhibit 6-6).
- Accomplishments: A - Z (Exhibit 6-7).

Express Power Quick Tips: Accomplishments

Don't:

1. Use *subjective* words such as successful, terrific, wonderful, etc.
2. Write accomplishments expressed as duties in job descriptions.
3. Type more than 2 1/2 lines of copy for each accomplishment.

Do:

1. Quantify your accomplishments using the Hill & Associates "Peanut Butter Principle" discussed on page 73.
2. Place your percentage or number as the *first word* in your sentence.
3. Quantify everything you do so you will become a natural at focusing on the *bottom line*.
4. Remember, companies are in business to make a profit—and the only reason they need employees is to increase the bottom line.
5. ➔ Create at least 15 accomplishments so you have a resource of goodies from which to draw significant bits of trivia to sell yourself.
6. ➔ Insert the accomplishments you develop on Power Resume Builder Form 4.
7. Once you arrive at your perfect job, continue to apply the Peanut Butter Principle to everything you do. This fosters job security!

In this chapter you'll learn that the "Peanut Butter Principle" causes a paradigm shift in most people's thinking, to consider not only *what* they have done, but *how well*. Employers then can't wait to meet the job seeker to see if he/she might have the capacity to do the same for their companies. Once you learn how terrific you are in Step 6, the next step will be how to present your work history in Step 7.

Accomplishments:
Ideas to Get You Thinking

- ***Have you done anything in your work that allows things to get done faster? And with less people?***

  Examples:
  - ❑ Mary Ellen rearranged the paper flow.
  - ❑ Jim computerized the accounting process.
  - ❑ Alice rearranged the office saving steps.
  - ❑ Michael consolidated 8 forms into 1 form.

- ***Have you increased dollars in any way?***

  Examples:
  - ❑ Sandra sold twice as many computer units.
  - ❑ Randy sold old clients additional services.
  - ❑ Martha raised twice as much in a fundraising event.
  - ❑ Dick increased the average sale per client.

- ***Have you saved the company any money?***

  Examples:
  - ❑ Bill saved money through negotiating contracts.
  - ❑ Sarah saved money through avoiding spoilage.
  - ❑ Betty saved money through identifying a safety hazard.
  - ❑ Cal saved money through developing a recycling program.

- ***Have you increased the number of clients?***

  Examples:
  - ❑ Darryl developed a follow-up system for referrals.
  - ❑ Evelyn developed a targeted marketing program.
  - ❑ Francine created a client incentive program for new referrals.

- ***Have you been recognized for anything?***

  Examples:
  - ❑ George received an Outstanding Customer Service award.
  - ❑ Harriett was #1 sales person.
  - ❑ Ike was Employee of the Month.

- ***Have you done 100% of your assignment?***

  Examples:
  - ❑ Jim achieved 100% of an assigned special project.
  - ❑ Katherine complied with 100% of audit standards.
  - ❑ Larry accomplished 100% of his assignments.
  - ❑ Melvin complied with 100% of the contract.

  Note: The minimum job requirement is 100%. You are hired to do your entire job–*all of it*. Anything less would not be meeting minimum job standards.

Power Resume Builder | **Accomplishments Peanut Butter Principle**

Purpose: Demonstrates ***how well*** you have done your job with the intent of promising similar future success.

Formula: The Hill & Associates Peanut Butter Principle.

Question: Have you ever made a peanut butter sandwich?

1. How long did it take you the first time (before)?
2. How long would it take you now (after)?
3. What is the **difference**?
4. What is your **increase in productivity?**

		Time
1.	Ask: What was it **before**?	10 minutes
2.	Ask: What was it **after**?	2 minutes
3.	Ask: What was the **difference**?	8 minutes
4.	Quantify in a %(**Increase in** profitability/productivity/sales/ clients/cost savings, etc.	400% (8 divided by 2 x 100%)
5.	Statement: 400% increase in productivity through developing a system for making peanut butter sandwiches.	

Express Power Quick Tips

Don't:

1. Use *subjective* words, e.g., successful, terrific, wonderful, etc.
2. Write accomplishments like duties.
3. Write more than 2 lines of copy for each accomplishment.

Do:

1. Quantify your accomplishments using the "Hill & Associates Peanut Butter Principle."
2. Always have your percent or number as the first word in your sentence.
3. Quantify everything you do so you will become a natural at focusing on the *bottom line.*
4. Remember, the only reason companies are in business is to make a profit and the only reason they need employees is to increase the bottom line. That's business.
5. Create at least 15 accomplishments so you have a resource of goodies from which to draw significant bits of trivia to sell you.
6. Once you arrive at your perfect job, continue to apply the Peanut Butter Principle to everything you do. This fosters job security!

Power Resume Builder

Accomplishments: How to Figure the Percents

Use the following thought process to develop your percentages for accomplishments. Use samples on page 76.

SALES:

1. What was the sales volume for this position *before* I started? $3 million
2. What was the sales volume *after* my first year? $5 million
3. What was the difference? $2 million
4. What was the increase in a percent? 2 divided by 3 = 66% increase in sales

Accomplishment: 66% increase in sales through (*what you did*).

1. What was the number of clients *before* I created the marketing campaign? 140
2. What was the number of clients *after*? 230
3. What was the difference? 90
4. What was the increase in a percent? 90 divided by 140 = 64% increase in client base

Accomplishment: 64% increase in client base through (*what you did*)

COST SAVINGS:

1. What was the cost of monthly supplies *before* I researched vendors? $345
2. What was the cost of monthly supplies *after*? $315
3. What was the difference? $30
4. What was percent cost savings? 30 divided by 345 = 8.6% cost savings

Accomplishment: 8.6% cost savings through (*what you did*).

PRODUCTIVITY:

1. How long did it take *before* I computerized forms? 15 minutes
2. How long did it take *after*? 5 minutes
3. What was the difference? 10 minutes
4. What was the percent increase in productivity? 10 divided by 5 = 200% increase

Accomplishment: 200% increase in productivity through (what you did).

Exhibit 6-3: How to Figure Percents

Power Resume Builder

Accomplishments Steps 1 - 4

What was it?	$	Manpower	Projects	Clients	Volume	Time
What was it... **Before**						10
What was it... **After**						2
What was the... **Difference**						8
Quantify (%) the difference.						400%

1. What did you do that was **significant**?

- **A SYSTEM FOR MAKING PBS** (peanut butter sandwiches)

2.How didyou do it?

- **THROUGH ACTION**
- **developing**
- creating
- initiating
- designing
- *streamlining*
- *refining*

POLITICALLY CORRECT
(DO NOT use words
such as reduce or decrease)

3. What did it **increase**?

BOTTOM LINE

- **productivity**
- profitability
- sales
- revenues
- cash flow
- clients
- cost savings
- ANYTHING that makes them $$$$

4. How much?

- **STATEMENT**
  (400% increase in ...)

- 100% accomplishment of ________________through____________________
- 100% compliance with ________________through____________________
- Recognized/Awarded/Ranked #___ for "_________" for/through ____________

ASK BEFORE WRITING ACCOMPLISHMENTS:

1. Think about what you want to say.
2. Ask: So what? Who cares? What's the benefit?
3. Is what I am presenting FACT and OBJECTIVE (a winner)?
   Or FICTION and SUBJECTIVE (a loser)?

Exhibit 6-4, Steps 1-4

Sample Accomplishments: Increase in Profitability

- ❑ __% increase in profitability through designing and patenting a product distribution system.
- ❑ __% increase in profitability through developing marketing strategies to create name recognition.
- ❑ __% increase in profitability through researching and adding new products to service clients.
- ❑ __% increase in profitability through developing targeted strategies to increase volume sales in customer base.
- ❑ __% increase in profitability through negotiating exclusivity on quality products to capture market.
- ❑ __% increase in profitability through developing innovative client-oriented proposal.
- ❑ __% increase in profitability through establishing guaranteed formula for return-on - investment.
- ❑ __% increase in profitability through strategizing rate increases while maintaining total client base.
- ❑ __% average return-on-investment through strategically moving product.
- ❑ __% increase in profitability or productivity through developing an in-house servicing system.
- ❑ __% increase in profitability through expansion of client base.
- ❑ __% increase in collection activity for bad debt through development of positive client relations.
- ❑ __% increase in profitability through establishing standardized forms, inventory and signage.
- ❑ __% increase in profitability through providing positive monitoring of employee productivity, benefits and compensation program.
- ❑ __% increase in return-on-investment through controlling inventory turn.
- ❑ __% increase in return-on-investment and profit through controlling days outstanding receivables and bad debt loss.
- ❑ __% increase in profits through reduction of inventory shrinkage.

Sample Accomplishments: Increase in Sales/Revenues

- ❑ __% increase in sales through designing a client-centered sales program.
- ❑ __% increase in sales through creating specific follow-up program to ensure benefit from special event promotion.
- ❑ __% increase in sales through designing activities to increase sales volumes and margins.
- ❑ __% increase in sales through designing creative marketing strategies.
- ❑ __% increase in sales through developing strategic marketing program promoting add-on sales.

Sample Accomplishments: Increase in Productivity

- ❑ __% employee retention during acquisition process through developing employee-centered communications system.
- ❑ __% increase in community exposure through developing special event promotional activity.
- ❑ __% increase in productivity of auction event through developing specific programming procedures.
- ❑ __% increase in productivity through creating a scheduling and monitoring system to ensure compliance with established standards.
- ❑ __% increase in productivity through promoting and monitoring safety program in compliance with OSHA standards.
- ❑ __% increase in productivity through developing client network resulting in greater return with less manpower.
- ❑ __% increase in productivity through developing an effective management/staff communications program.
- ❑ __% increase in productivity and profitability through implementing time management process and job training.
- ❑ __% increase in productivity through developing rotation system for materials and efficient order pulling process.
- ❑ __% increase in productivity through standardizing policies and procedures to establish corporate culture.
- ❑ __% increase in productivity through establishing a procedure for problem resolution.
- ❑ __% increase in productivity through streamlining procedure for contract preparation.

Sample Accomplishments: Increase in Clients

- ❑ __% increase in client base through targeting market.
- ❑ __% increase in client retention through developing and implementing customer relations program.
- ❑ __% increase in client base through the creation of innovative promotional programs.
- ❑ __% increase in listings through developing innovative marketing strategies.
- ❑ __% customer retention resulting in achieving sales goals during acquisition through designing a "customer-oriented" education program.
- ❑ __% increase in client base through developing client referral system.
- ❑ __% increase in client base through developing targeted client and customer product movement through successful advertising campaign.

Sample Accomplishments: Cost Savings

- ❑ __% increase in cost savings through negotiating fleet purchases.
- ❑ __% cost savings through minimizing shrinkage while maximizing sales.
- ❑ __% cost savings through recycling product resources and establishing a FIFO system.
- ❑ __% cost savings through minimizing warehousing through implementation of JIT system.
- ❑ __% cost savings in manpower through streamlining full-time staff, expanding manpower resources through job sharing and temporary employees, while maintaining quality production.

Sample Accomplishments: Recognition/Awards/Commendations.

- ❏ Ranked "#1 in United States" for Highest Profit Division in total net earnings and ROI for three consecutive years.
- ❏ Named "Salesman of the Year" in 1999 and consistently awarded "Salesman of the Month" on a recurring basis.
- ❏ Ranked #1 in rate integrity and received the "Leadership Award."
- ❏ Ranked "All Time High" salesperson over 30-day period and received $1,000 bonus.
- ❏ Awarded "Spirit of Life," company's highest award, for 0 accidents.
- ❏ Awarded "Top Listing Agent in Dollar Volume and Amount of Listings" - 1998
- ❏ Awarded "Million Dollar Producer" for 1998 & 1999.

Sample Accomplishments: Compliance/Achievement

- ❏ 100% achievement of all assigned goals and objectives through developing a specific plan of action.
- ❏ 100% compliance with all contract specifications established by clients through establishing a specific follow-up and accountability system.
- ❏ 100% compliance with audit standards for three consecutive years.
- ❏ 100% compliance with OSHA, JCAHO, HAZMAT and other governing entities for the years 19XX through 2XXX through developing a focused training program.
- ❏ 100% accomplishment of assignment to create and implement a preventive maintenance program.
- ❏ 100% accomplishment of all assigned goals and objectives on time and within budget through designing a specific plan of action.
- ❏ 100% achievement of business goals during transition through precision planning.

Power Resume Builder

Accomplishments
My Starter List

4. How much?	3.What did it increase?	2. How did you do it?	1. What did you do that was significant?
200% increase	in profitability	through developing	a system for making PBS

Exhibit 6-6
My "Starter" List

Power Resume Builder | **Accomplishments From A - Z**

This section provides a more indepth look at accomplishments and offers some frequently requested information that includes:

- Strategies for selling *how well you can do your job* for a company through presentation of your *quantitative* achievements.
- The magical Hill & Associates "Peanut Butter Principle" that makes quantifying a piece of cake.
- Ways to put your work experience into quantifiable accomplishments using the Power Resume Builder Accomplishment Samples.

It's easy, fun and eye-opening.

Understand the basics! The only reason a company is in business is to make money. The only reason a company hires employees is for what they can do to support the company making money. If a company doesn't make money, neither does the employee and they are both out of business. The importance of this chapter is critical to your resume development. You must understand the power you have in presenting your value to a potential employer. This is achieved by quantifying what you have accomplished in previous jobs.

Most resumes are obituaries that say " This is what I did," not "This is how well I did it!" The obituary resume provides a history of what was, and runs the risk of generating the response, "Who cares? Next resume, please!" Employers want to see in quantitative terms what you did to increase productivity, profitability, cost savings—anything that would have a positive effect on the bottom line. Employees must be able to understand the bottom line.

"But I can't quantify my achievements!" How often this cry is heard. But hold on—we are going to make it quick and easy!

Lesson #1: Learn the Hill & Associates Peanut Butter Principle. This principle should be everyone's lifelong buddy. It opens doors, provides rewards, and achieves promotions. It targets business basics...a positive bottom line.

What is the Hill & Associates Peanut Butter Principle?

It's simple. Remember back to when you were a kid. You're in the kitchen and your mom is teaching you how to make a peanut butter sandwich. You are probably about 3 to 5 years old, depending on how brave your mom was. She shows you how, and monitors your progress. You have a knife, what seems to you to be a gigantic jar of peanut butter, two slices of bread and maybe some jelly.

______1. How long do you think it took you to make *your first* peanut butter sandwich?
______2. How long would it take you to make a peanut butter sandwich *today*?
______3. What is the *difference* ?
______4. What is your *increase in productivity*?

Let's do a sample.

Exhibit 6-7 Accomplishments A-Z

10 1.	Let's say it took 10 minutes to make a peanut butter sandwich when you were a kid.
- 2 2.	Today it takes you 2 minutes.
8 3.	What is the difference? 8 minutes. (10 original time - 2 minutes now = 8 minutes)
400%4.	Your increase in productivity is about how many more peanut butter sandwiches you can make now than in the *original* time. It now takes 2 minutes to make each sandwich, so we divide the difference, 8, by 2, which equals 4. Multiply by 100%. The answer is that you can make 4 more sandwiches now than you could in the original 10 minutes; therefore, you would have a 400% increase in productivity.

(NOTE: If the production of peanut butter sandwiches was important to a potential employer, presenting a resume that stated, "“400% increase in productivity through developing a system for making peanut butter sandwiches "would be pretty impressive!)

What is the formula for implementing the Peanut Butter Principle?

The kick-off for the formula is to *create an achievement* that will:

- Sell how well you have done your job.
- Demonstrate your potential future success to the company interviewing you.

Remember: If you don't tell them how great you are, they will never know.

1. ***What did you do that was significant?***

Identify 10 significant contributions you have made to a company.
"Ten," you say. "I can't even think of one!" Just brainstorm. Don't worry about having a finished statement. Simply make a list of ideas to give you a starting point.

- ➔ Write your ideas on Exhibit 6-6, Column 1 (Page 79).
- You may want to copy Exhibit 6-6 for additional entries.
- Once your resume is completed, continue to note your accomplishments in a log as items for future positions.

What other notable things have you done?

Once you start thinking and giving yourself credit—you probably will be impressed with yourself. You are by no means limited to 10 accomplishments. As you identify others, continue to add them to your list. Make this a lifelong habit. This is the foundation for selling yourself.

2. ***How did you do it?***

- *Expand your 10 statements by asking yourself, "How did I do it?"*
- Here are some ideas: You can match anything from the *action* column with the *what* column. This will get you started.

Exhibit 6-7 Accomplishments A - Z

Action		What	
❑	developing	❑	program
❑	creating	❑	special projects
❑	establishing	❑	policies and procedures
❑	standardizing	❑	systems
❑	reconciling	❑	records
❑	refining	❑	processes
❑	targeting	❑	manpower
❑	innovating	❑	clients
❑	strategizing	❑	marketing
❑	forecasting	❑	market share

Example: "Developing" (Action list) "clients" (What list) formulates the accomplishment, "developing clients"

• ➔ Add the words you selected to "My starter list," Exhibit 6-6, Column 2.

3. ***What did it increase?***

- Expand your 10 statements by asking yourself, "What did I increase? What was the benefit to the company?"

- Here are some ideas:

  ❑ productivity
  ❑ profitability
  ❑ cost savings
  ❑ cash flow
  ❑ sales
  ❑ customer satisfaction
  ❑ revenues
  ❑ profit margin
  ❑ return on investment
  ❑ customer satisfaction

• ➔ Add to Exhibit 6-6, Column 3.

4. ***How much?***

- Expand your 10 statements by asking yourself, "How much did I increase/improve things?"
  So often clients say, "I don't do anything that can be quantified!" We say *everything* you do can be made into an accomplishment.

- Here are some ideas:
  - Refer to the exhibits:
    - 6-1 Accomplishments: Ideas to Get You Thinking
    - 6-2 Peanut Butter Principle Formula for Quantification
    - 6-3 Accomplishments: How to Figure Percents
    - 6-4 Quantification Steps 1-4
    - 6-5 Accomplishments Samples
    - 6-6 "My Starter List" for Building Accomplishments
    - 6-7 Accomplishments: A - Z
  - ➔ Add your new informtion to "My Starter List," Exhibit 6-6, column 4.

Remember:

- When using numbers or percents on your accomplishments, put them at the *front* of the sentence. This provides a structured format, so simply by scanning, the reader's attention will zoom in on the numbers.

- Employers will be impressed and relate what you have done for another company to what you can do for them—and your name will be placed on the interview list.

- *Do not put a percent on an accomplishment that you cannot easily explain.* You do not need internal reports as proof, but you must be able to explain how you arrived at your numbers.

- It is important to have other accomplishments ready to use in addition to the ones on your resume. One of my clients reported, "The interviewer was so impressed with my resume that he asked me what other accomplishments I had. To be honest, I really hadn't given it any thought and I felt like a fool."

The Story of Alex, an Engineer

Alex: You expect me to use accomplishments in my resume?!

Counselor: Yes, they will get you a lot of attention and will result in some good dialogue about your skills and bottom line commitment to the company.

Alex: But I am an engineer! Sometimes we never know whether we have had an impact on the bottom line or not. We don't even know if our part of a project gets used.

Counselor: Alex, that may be true. But are you in control of the parts of the projects they assign to you?

Alex: Of course.

Counselor: Over the years have you developed streamlined processes in planning and implementing your projects?

Alex: Sure.

The counselor led Alex through the Peanut Butter Principle formula. Alex computed an activity in which he was involved and was amazed.

Alex: 1400% percent increase in ...! No one would believe this! If I put this on my resume they would think I was crazy!

Counselor: Is what you computed the truth?

Alex: Well, of course it is!

Counselor: Alex, how long have you been out of work?

Alex: Eight months.

Counselor: Well, evidently something you are doing isn't working. Why not give this a try? Hey, what can you lose?

Alex: I don't want to miss an opportunity for a job. These 8 months have been tough.

Counselor: I know you are anxious to get a job. Let's see what we can do to maximize your results. Alex, why don't you send out two resumes: one with the percents and one without and see which one works best for you?

Two weeks later, Alex called.

Alex: I didn't think I would ever be having this conversation with you. You won't believe what happened! I sent my resume out, got a phone call four days later, have been on three interviews and got a job offer with a major company making more money than I made at my last job! This is pretty incredible!

Counselor: Terrific! Which resume got the interview, Alex?

Alex: The one with the percents! I couldn't believe it!

Counselor: Did they ask you about the 1400% increase in...?

Alex: Yes, and they marveled that I could explain it in terms of the bottom line. They said I would be great as an interface between engineering and management since I had the business sense they were looking for!

Just as Alex has found success with the use of the Peanut Butter Principle, so have thousands of others. It doesn't matter what the profession is or the part of the world someone lives in—it works.

Other Accomplishments That Will Sell You:

- **Ranked/Awarded/Recognized** for something. (Exhibit 6-5)

  Stop and think about a time you have been recognized for outstanding performance, employee of the month, supreme team leader, No.1 sales person, excellence in customer service and hundreds of other forms of recognition. Give yourself credit. This is important.

- **Compliance** with something. (Exhibit 6-5)

  Is compliance important to a company? Most certainly. Procedures result in streamlining processes, having fair practice standards and ultimately increasing productivity and profitability. Think about contract specifications, audits, deadlines, budgets, standards, policies and procedures, and other items with which you must comply.

- **Achievement/Accomplishment** of something. (Exhibit 6-5)

  Every job requires that we do *all of it*! The funny thing is when resume reviewers see 100% achievement/accomplishment on a resume, they are impressed. Hey, that is the minimum standard! If you do all of your job, complete 100% of a special project/activity, you have the right to use that as an accomplishment.

- **So now you are an expert!**

  Having an inventory of potential accomplishments is invaluable. You should always have a data bank of accomplishments ready to use. As you begin to target specific jobs, the accomplishments that relate to the needs of the company should be chosen to reflect the successes you have already had. This increases your opportunity for an interview. Now let's complete your accomplishments statement.

  1. Target a specific job that interests you.
  2. Select the 5 most significant things you have done from your list of 10 by placing a check next to it.
  3. Prioritize them in order of importance.
  4. ➔ Transfer them to the Resume Builder Form 4.

- **Finale! This is a "winning approach."**

  Everything is targeted toward FACT—not fiction, objectivity or subjectivity—so only the truth is presented. The objective of the resume is to get the interview. Clients tell us they have more fun using this concept. The results of this approach is that potential employers are impressed and the job seeker quickly gets an interview—and often, a job offer!

Step 7

Work Experience

Translate It So It Sells

Your work history tells a story about the companies for which you have worked, your progression, skills sets, and how well you have done your job. It is important that this information is presented in such a way that whatever the reader is looking for jumps out. Unfortunately, most resumes try to cram 10 pounds of information into a 1 pound package. The more concise the resume is, the better. Of equal importance is the selection of words you use. Some resumes are full of *stuff* that really doesn't sell the best part of what a job seeker can do.

Review the "focused" tools for completing your work history:

- Work Experience—The Old Way (Exhibit 7-1)
- Work Experience—The Power Approach (Exhibit 7-2)
- Keys to Targeting Your Work History (Exhibit 7-3)
- Sample Work History Focus Points (Exhibit 7-4)

•→ Follow the step-by-step process to complete your work history and transfer the information as directed on Power Resume Builder Form 5.

In Step 7, you will learn the easy way to develop your work history by ensuring it is targeted for the job you want, no periods of time are unaccounted for, and you positively position the information to catch the attention of the reviewer. Remember, your work history is more than an *obituary*, a dull and boring recount of everything you used to do. It must come alive by selling *what I can do for you!* In Step 8, we will next look at some powerful tools that will assist you in promoting your credentials—plus:

Express Power Quick Tips:

- Company, City and State, page 92.
- Job Title, Duties and Accomplishments, page 93.
- Period of Employment, page 94.

WORK EXPERIENCE

UPS, Little Ferry, New Jersey
1998 - Present

COURIER: OPERATED DIFFERENT VEHICLES, PICKING UP AND DELIVERING PACKAGES TO CUSTOMERS. WAS MEASURED BY A STOP PER HOUR RATIO INVOLVING A SPECIFIC DEADLINE FOR EACH INDIVIDUAL STOP. INVOLVED CONTINUOUS CUSTOMER INTERACTION. HANDLED LARGE SUMS OF CASH ON A DAILY BASIS.

1998

CARGO HANDLER: WORKED ON SEVERAL DIFFERENT TYPES OF AIRCRAFT, OPERATING A WIDE VARIETY OF MACHINERY, TRANSPORTING CONTAINERIZED FREIGHT. WAS PROMOTED TO COURIER POSITION.

World Gym Fitness Center, Little Ferry, New Jersey
1997

ACCOUNT EXECUTIVE: RESPONSIBLE FOR BRINGING IN NEW ACCOUNTS AND RENEWING PRESENT ACCOUNTS. PHONED GUESTS IN AN ATTEMPT TO REVISIT AND PURCHASE MEMBERSHIPS. ESTABLISHED CORPORATE ACCOUNTS. ENSURING CUSTOMER SATISFACTION.

Johnston Corporation, Maryville, New Jersey
1996

LOSS PREVENTION OFFICER: OBSERVED CUSTOMERS FOR SUSPICIOUS BEHAVIOR. APPREHENDED SHOPLIFTERS. CONTACTED LOCAL AUTHORITIES AFTER COMPLETING REQUIRED PAPERWORK.

Able Brothers, Inc., Halston, New Jersey
1995

DATA ENTRY: RECORDED DIFFERENT MEASUREMENT DATA INTO COMPUTER FOR INDUSTRIAL PLANT.

Telecon Telecenters, Hampershire, New Jersey
1995

TELEMARKETING: TELEPHONE SALES. CALLED POTENTIAL BUYERS FROM LIST.

Exhibit 7-1 Work History — The Old Way

EXPERIENCE WHILE WORKING WAY THROUGH SCHOOL

- UPS
Little Ferry, NJ

  Courier/Part-Time — Jul 1998 - Present
Territory: NE New Jersey.
Customer Service, Customer Relations, Problem Solving, Territory Management, Cash Handling, Scheduling, Product Management, Sales & Marketing.
115% Goal Achievement.

  Cargo Handler — Jun 1997 - Jul 1998
Customer Service, Problem Solving.

- World Gym Fitness Center
Little Ferry, NJ

  Account Executive — Jun 1996 - Jun 1997
Sales Volume: $1M Annually.
Corporate Sales.
Clients: Banks, Businesses, Retail Operations, Technical Facilities.
160%Quota Achievement.

- Johnston Corporation
Maryville, NJ

  Loss Prevention Officer — Aug 1995 - May 1996
Customer Relations, Safety, Security, Surveillance, Liaison with Law Enforcement.

- Able Brothers Inc.
Halston, NJ

  Data Entry Clerk — May 1995 - Aug 1995
Statistical Data Entry & Reports.

- Telecon Telecenters
Hampershire, NJ

  Telephone Sales — Feb 1995 - May 1995
Clients: Financial/Commercial Companies.

- Other experience includes working in various positions in sales and customer service.

Power
Resume

Exhibit 7-2 Work History The Power Approach

Keys to Targeting Your Work History

- Divide your paper into 3 columns and follow steps 1-3.

Step #1

- Company
  City, ST

Name of **Company** for which you worked.

City and state. Use 2 letter abbreviation for state. Do not include address, zip or phone.

Step #2

Job Title
Managed/Performed...
Clients:
Products:
Companies:
Industries:
Gross Margin:
Net Profit:
Sales:
Staff:
Territory:
Special Projects:
Projects:
__% Goal Achievement
100% Audit/Project/Contract Compliance
Accomplishment

The **job title** you held. Make it bold.

What you did in this job as it relates to the job you ***want.***

1. Use key words to represent major areas of responsibility, e.g., Managed Purchasing, Distribution, Shipping & Receiving.
2. Begin each word with a capital (except words such as to, and, by, the, through).
3. Use "&" in lieu of "and."
4. Use heading titles (Client Service) or maximize experience through listing significant names, products, industries, etc.
5. If possible, include a percentage accomplishment in no more than 3 words.

Step #3

Jan 1996 - Jun 1999

Period of Employment. Do not make this a mystery List month (3 letters) and the full year (1996).

Example

- White Company
  City, ST

Regional Sales Manager
Annual Sales: $12M
Staff: 24; Territory: U.S.
Managed Sales & Marketing Program.
Gross Margin: 24%; Net Profit: 18%.
Products: Medical, Technical, Aeronautics.
Special Projects: New Product Promotion, Media Packages & Precision Campaign.
190% Goal Achievement.

Jan 1990 - Jun 1999

Maintain the integrity of the 3 columns.

Place a period at the end of each thought.

Exhibit 7-3

SALES & MARKETING
Annual Sales Volume: $_____
Territory: _____
Key Accounts: _____
Products: _____
Clients: _____
Staff: _____
Duties: _______
Achievements: _________

OPERATIONS MANAGEMENT
Annual Sales Volume: $_____
Annual Budget: $_____
Locations/Branches: _____
Key Accounts: _____
Products: _____
Staff: _____
Duties: _______
Achievements: _________

BANKING
Portfolio Volume: $_____
Locations/Branches: _____
Products: _____
Staff: _____
Duties: _______
Achievements: _________

HUMAN RESOURCES
Annual Budget: $_____
# of Employees: _____
Training Programs: _____
Staff: _____
Duties: _______
Achievements: _________

INFORMATION SYSTEMS
Projects: _____
Clients: _____
Programs: _____
Languages: _____
Achievements: _________

RESTAURANT MANAGEMENT
Annual Sales Volume: $_____
Seats: _____
Dining Rooms/Clubs/Banquets
Theme: _____
Special Events: _____
Staff: _____
Duties: _______
Achievements: _________

PURCHASING
Annual Volume: $_____
Products: _____
Key Accounts: _____
Special Projects: _____
Vendors: _____
Staff: _____
Duties: _______
Achievements: _________

HOSPITALITY
Annual Sales Volume: $_____
Hotel Rooms: _____
Theme: _____
Special Events: _____
Clients: _____
Staff: _____
Duties: _______
Achievements: _________

HEALTHCARE
Annual Budget: $_____
Staff: _____
Facilities: ______
Beds: _____
Duties: _______
Achievements: _________

Exhibit 7-4

Here are some important details to keep in mind as you follow Steps 1-3 to target your work history.

Step 1: Company, City, and State of Employment.

- Compare the resumes in Exhibits 7-1 and 7-2.

Express Power Quick Tips: Company, City and State of Employment

Don't:

1. Put company, city and state in bold type.
2. Write out the name of the state; abbreviate.
3. Use the full name of the company out if it can eliminate you. (Example: Bartenders School of America, Inc. Instead, use letters: BSA, Inc.)
4. List more than 7 companies unless you are a consultant.
5. List your own name as a company for which you have worked. Generally, employers are threatened by entrepreneurs.
6. Include the complete address and phone number of companies you've worked for.

Do:

1. Abbreviate all states using postal service two-letter method (Florida=FL, Mississippi=MS).
2. Modify name of company, if it is to your benefit to do so.
3. Keep it simple, as shown in Exhibits 7-2 and 7-3.
4. Always use regular type, with upper and lower case letters.
5. ➔ Fill in your work history in terms of *company, city, and state* on the Power Resume Builder Form 5.

Step 2. Job Title, Duties and Accomplishments. Compare:

Work History—The Old Way

COURIER. Operated different vehicles, picking up and delivering packages to customers. Was measured via a stop per hour ratio involving a specific deadline for each individual stop. Involved continuous customer interaction. Handled large sums of cash on a daily basis.

Work History—The Power Approach

Courier - Part-Time
Territory: NE New Jersey.
Customer Service, Customer Relations, Problem Solving, Territory Management, Cash Handling, Scheduling, Product Management, Sales & Marketing.
115% Goal Achievement.

Which work history best sells Carlos for a position as a pharmaceutical representative? The *Power Resume*! The *"before"* resume is an obituary! It simply lists what Carlos did, not what he can do. It also doesn't tell how *well* he did it. The Power Resume demonstrates what Carlos can do, and *how well*—115% Goal Achievement! Look at all the transferable skills that would apply to pharmaceutical sales: customer service, customer relations, problem solving, territory management, cash handling, scheduling, product management, sales and marketing. It all fits!

Express Power Quick Tips: Job Titles, Duties, and Accomplishments

Don't

1. Write complete sentences.
2. Take words verbatim from a job description.

Do:

1. Use key words to represent major areas of responsibility, e.g., Sales & Marketing, Customer Service, etc.
2. Begin each word with a *capital,* except words such as to, by, the, through. People are more inclined to read headlines than sentences.
3. Use "*&*" instead of "*and.*"
4. Use *heading titles* to maximize experience through listing significant names, products and industries. See Exhibit 7-4 Sample Work History Focus Points, for examples.
5. Include, if possible, a percentage accomplishment in no more than 3 words.

6. ➔ Fill in your work history in terms of *job title, duties and accomplishments* on the Power Resume Builder Form 5.

Step 3. Period of Employment.

It is critical to include complete information on dates of employment. Leaving months out, as on Carlos's *"before"* resume, would cause the reviewer to wonder: "What is this applicant trying to hide?" Technically, you could work one day in 1999, and list that as a year on your resume—which is what creates suspicion. It is better to be specific—you avoid any mystery or questioning.

If you look at Carlos's old resume, he had two jobs in 1998; one, 1997; one in1996; and two in 1995—six jobs in three years! (Meet Mr. Job Hopper!) This could be an automatic eliminator—"Hire Carlos, and he will move on in no time. Forget him. We would just be looking for a replacement soon."

In the Power Resume Approach, by adding the heading "EXPERIENCE WHILE WORKING WAY THROUGH SCHOOL," Carlos' numerous jobs become a selling point. The employer notes, "Wow, this guy worked all through school!" Also, by adding the months on the resume, it demonstrates that Carlos worked his way straight through school—there are no periods of unemployment. The resume, in combination with a cover letter, would tell an employer that Carlos is seeking a full-time permanent position as a *recent college graduate*. (Note: Carlos used that approach, and is now working as a pharmaceutical representative—and he loves it!)

Express Power Quick Tips: Period of Employment

Don't:

1. Leave out the month in your job chronology.
2. Leave unexplained periods of time.

Do:

1. Include Month/Year to Month/Year (Jan 1996 - Jun 1998).
2. Use 3 letters to indicate month: Jan, Feb, Mar, Apr, etc.
3. Write out the complete year (1994, 2001).
4. ➔ Fill in your work history in terms of *dates of employment* on the Power Resume Builder Form 5.

Step 8

Education

Share the Qualifications that Make You the Best Candidate

In this chapter you will learn:

- The different ways of presenting educational/continuing education credentials.
- What to do if you don't have a degree.
- When to use all your credentials.
- Which ones to use/not use and when. (Review "Keys to Listing Your Education," Exhibit 8, and "Education: A Case Study.")

Both the lack of a college or university education or too much education can be an eliminator. Learn what will work for you and then proceed with confidence. Through using the Power Resume Strategies, many clients have overcome not having the *desired* educational credentials and won the interview. What we have proven over and over again is "it is not always the best-credentialed candidate who wins." Personality, enthusiasm and the ability to convince a company that you are the person to do the job gives you the competitive edge.

Express Power Quick Tips: Education

Don't:

1. Overwhelm them with every educational program you have ever attended, beginning with high school.
2. Use anything that can be used against you.
3. Include your AS/AA, high school, vocational/trade school credentials, etc. if you have a bachelor's degree, unless it is critical to meeting the job requirements for which you are applying.
4. Include the fact that you are not a high school graduate, if that fact is applicable.

Do:

1. Represent your educational background as it *supports* the job for which you are applying.
2. Use your GPA if you are a *recent graduate* and it is 3.3 or higher.
3. Include significant events, scholarships, and awards *if you are a recent graduate.*
4. Include dates of graduation *only if you are a recent graduate.*
5. Include continuing education courses that support the focus of your resume.
6. ➔ Go to Power Resume Builder Form 6 and fill in your educational background following the rules presented.

Power Resume Builder
Use the education that supports the job!

Education

If you have...	Formula	Example
BS/BA/AS/AA - **One Degree**	**Degree in Field-GPA-Honors** School, City, State	**BS in Biology- GPA 3.9 Cum Laude** Stetson University, Deland, Florida
Multiple Degrees	Most Important/Highest **Degree in Field-GPA-Honors** School, City, State Second Most Important **Degree in Field-GPA-Honors** School, City, State	**MS in Biology- GPA 4.0 Cum Laude** Miami University, Miami, Florida **BS in Biology- GPA 3.9 Cum Laude** Stetson University, Deland, Florida
Some College - **No Degree**	**School,** City, State Major: Your intended major.	**Miami University**, Miami, Florida Major: Biology
Vocational/Trade School - Certificate/ Diploma - Only use if you do not have higher degrees/education that support your job interest.	**School**, City, State **Diploma/Certificate:** Profession	**Lindsey Vo-Tec**, Lindsey, VT **Diploma: Engineering Technology**
High School Diploma - Only use if you do not have any college coursework.	**School**, City State (List Significant Honors, Awards, Scholarships, etc. only if you are a recent HS graduate.)	**Lake High School,** Lake, Florida • National Honor Society - 4 years • Valedictorian • Future Business Leaders • Awarded 4 year Scholarship:Sports
High School No Graduation - Do not list your HS so as not to bring attention. Enroll in a GED program.	**Continuing Education** Focus on the *courses* you have taken since high school that support the job for which you are applying.	**Continuing Education** • Microsoft Office • Customer Service • Certificate: Accounting
Continuing Education	**Continuing Education** List courses that will support the job for which you are applying and the school/ institution providing the course. Also include required Continuing Education Courses and Credits.	Continuing Education • TQM, Crosby & Associates • Crises Management, Duke Univ. • Leadership I, Hill & Associates

Keys to Listing Your Education
Exhibit 8-1

Story of Bill:

Bill: You know, I really messed up in high school. I hated school and was a master at getting out of class. I never graduated. I dropped out when I was 16. I thought, 'Why go to school if I can make big bucks an hour in the automotive industry?' I finally did get my GED, and worked my way up in the industry—but now I am stuck. I think it is because I never went to college. I send out my resume and don't get responses. One time a friend even set up an interview for me, and then I learned the truth. The first question the interviewer asked was, "Tell me about your educational background." I blurted out, "I know I don't have much education,but..." Well, it was as though the interview and my life ended at the same time, in a split second. Before I knew what was happening, the interviewer was shaking my hand and wishing me well.

Coach: Tell me a little bit about what you want.

Bill: Well, I am not 16 any more and have worked my way up in the industry. I have 23 years in already. I don't want to do *hands-on* any more. I am the best when it comes to knowing parts and automotive systems, and I would really like to get a corporate job in a Parts Department, with a major tool maker. It's just that *education* thing.

Coach: Let's take a look at how you presented the education you have on your resume.

"The Old Way" Education

Education: High School Equivalency, Morton Vocational School

Coach: Well, Bill, after reviewing your resume, I see that your educational background is pretty sparse.

Bill: I know, but I am the best—better than any of these young engineering guys. I can do circles around them.

Coach: While you have been working your way up within the industry, have you had any continuing education courses?

Bill: Yes. I have been to the best schools in the automotive field.

Coach: Do these courses result in certification?

Bill: You bet. I have the best credentials in the field.

Coach: Bill, would you consider signing up with Western University for some college courses? This would demonstrate your interest in continuing your education and better help us to position you.

Bill: I will do anything. However, the demands of my job require so much overtime, it probably would take me forever to get a degree. I really don't think I need one any way. I have the experience.

Coach: Sometimes you need the ticket to get through the door. Just begin and see where it takes you.

After coaching, Bill did sign up with the university and declared a major. We also picked his brain about the continuing education courses he had taken over the years, and selected five of the most impressive to include on his resume. See what you think of Bill's "after" resume.

"The Power Approach" Resume: Education

- **Western University**, Maurytown, Nevada
  Major: Business & Engineering
- Automotive Engineering Course, General Motors: Certified Automotive Engineer
- Chrysler Supervisory Management: TQM and Quality Controls
- Leadership America: Automotive Industry's Best: Graduated #1 in class
- President's Roundtable on Process Management: Innovative, Cost- Saving Prototype Development
- Automotive Master Product Manufacturing and Management

Which approach to education do you think worked best for Bill? You're right—the Power Approach resume! It worked so well, Bill was hired as regional manager for a major engineering tool manufacturer in Ilkhart, Indiana. When Bill called to share the good news, he was so excited. "Once I had the Western University and continuing education information on my resume, no one asked me about my educational background anymore. They were more interested in my technical skills and knowledge—and that was *my* thing! It was easy to beat out the competition once interviewers began to hear what I could do for them!"

Understanding how to position yourself on your resume is everything.

In this chapter you have learned how to make your educational background work for you. It is all in the presentation. Remember, only tell what will sell you to the potential company. We are always amazed when a new client tells us, "I really don't have any educational credentials..." and then we find the truth. They do have some real treasures that will enable us to position them for success. Now that we have discussed education, let's explore some other headings used in resumes.

Step 9

Other Headings

• Professional Affiliations • Memberships • Certifications • Licensure • Publications • References

The headings you use on a resume can have a major impact on whether you are called for an interview. Choose your headings wisely. Review the tools that will promote you in your job search.

- Power Tips! Membership/Affiliations (Page100).
- Power Tips! Certification/Licensure (Page 101).
- Power Tips! Publications/Articles (Page 101).
- Power Tips! Project Lists (Page 102).
- Power Tips! References (Page 102).

Express Power Quick Tips: Headings

Don't:

1. Include anything that can be used against you: religion, politics, activist organizations, interests, personal information, etc.
2. Tell too much—stick to *business*.

Do:

1. Use the Seven Key Resume Headings
   - Objective/Qualified for
   - Professional/Executive Profile
   - Areas of Expertise/Skills/Knowledge
   - Professional Background/Experience
   - Accomplishments (Not labeled as a heading)
   - Experience/Experience While Working Way Through School/Work History
   - Education
2. Review Exhibit 3-2, page 25, Sample Headings
3. Do review Exhibit 3-3, page 26, Sample Resume Layout
4. → Do complete Power Resume Builder Forms 7A, 7B, 7C.

In this chapter you have completed the final part of your resume. Now just fine tune it, put it in your computer and you are on your way to success! In the next chapter you will learn about the different ways of presenting and using a variety of resumes: functional, chronological, performance based, one-page, two-page, internet resumes and scannable resumes.

Keys to Using the Optional Headings

- **Affiliations/Memberships**

The Lament of Several Clients. "I just don't know why I am not getting the response to my resume. With my background, credentials and recognition, I would expect to get a lot of attention." In reviewing the clients' resumes, here are some examples of what we found:

MEMBERSHIPS/AFFILIATIONS:
- National Organization of Women, Vice-President, Regional Chapter
- Black Women's Caucus, Past President, Southeastern United States
- Gay and Lesbian League, Member
- The Patriots, Treasurer
- The American Nazi Party, Member
- The Christian Coalition, Member
- The Republican Party, Area Chairman
- The Democratic Party, Campaign Chairman
- The Holy Pentecostal Church, Southern Division, Elder

Before including any organization on your resume, be sure there is no way it can be offensive to ANYONE. Politics, religion, activist organizations and sensitive groups may result in a red flag with an automatic, "Naw...don't think I'll even bother interviewing this one. There could be a risk. Why take the chance?" Keep these tips in mind as you develop your membership heading.

Power Tips! Memberships/Affiliations

1. Be smart. Only tell what sells you!
2. Ask: Can it be used against me in any way?
3. Does it relate directly to my profession and the job for which I am applying?
4. Have I included all the professional memberships that are pluses (or mandatory) in my field?
5. ➔ *Complete the Affiliation/Memberships* section on Power Resume Builder Form 7A.

- **Certification/Licensure**.

Story of Bud: "I can't believe I didn't get that job because of Little League."

Bud was quite proud that he was a certified referee for the Little League, but you just never know what turns a potential resume reviewer on or off. Little did Bud know that the hiring authority hated sports and had a previous employee who had put a community sports roster on the *company computer*, done mailings on the *company's* account, talked on the phone, and counseled team members on *company* time—which resulted in the hiring manager stating bluntly, "That's the last time I will ever have someone like that on staff!"

Once again, keep the resume focused strictly on business—and for all other affiliations, when in doubt, leave it out. Once you get the interview, *if* you find the interviewer loves Little League, share your experience. Otherwise, hush!

Certification and Licensure is fairly straightforward.

Power Tips! Certification/Licensure

1. Use those credentials that are required by your profession on your resume.
2. Do not use a license or certification that does not relate to your work.
3. ➔ *Complete the Certification/Licensure* section on Power Resume Builder Form 7A.

- **Publications/Articles**

All companies love to be in the press, magazine articles, on television—anything that provides publicity to enhance the company's image. If you are published, don't miss an opportunity to make it known. If you have a few articles that relate to your industry, all the titles may fit on your resume. If you have numerous articles, you may wish to create a Publications section.

Power Tips! Publications/Articles

1. Include all articles on your resume that relate to your industry.
2. Create a Publications section if you are a prolific writer.
3. ➔ *Complete the Publications/Articles* section on Power Resume Builder Form 7A.

- **Projects**

Project lists are great for many professions–project managers, engineering, creative artists, theater and many others. Having a project list provides an interviewer with a quick overview of the magnitude of the projects you have been involved in, a description and the results. This can be a great sales tool.

Power Tips! Project Lists

1. *Journal all your projects*. Over time you will even impress yourself!
2. *Include related projects* on your resume.
3. ➔ *Complete the Projects* section on Exhibit Power Form 7B.

- **References**

Of course, references are important to your job search process. However, NEVER write "References provided upon request." Believe me, companies know you will provide references and to write this is just a waste of space. Your references are treasures.

Power Tips! References

1. **Ask permission to use someone as your reference**. There is nothing worse than to call a reference and have them say, "Yeah, I fired the guy...sure didn't think he would use me as a reference." References do not have to be previous employers. Pick people who love you and will sell you positively. They should all be professionals—even your *personal references*.
2. **Keep in touch with your references**. There is nothing worse than to call a reference and have them say, "Hey, how is Cal? Haven't seen him in 15 years! What's he doing now, anyway?" This will *not* get you hired.
3. **Educate your references.** Provide them with a copy of your resume and cover letter. This will enable them to better sell you when they are contacted.
4. **Keep your references up-to-date**. When a company asks if they can contact your references, call your references and educate them as to what the job is all about. One client was so excited because she just knew she was going to get her dream job. Her experience was diverse, with expertise in both training and public relations. She was being considered for a *public relations* job. She did not educate her references. They gave her a wonderful *training* reference. She did not get the job. Get smart! Your references are not mind readers.
5. **Thank them**. Send thank you notes when you know your references have provided a good recommendation. If you do, they will continue to take the time to do a good reference for you. Thank you notes are a wonderful way to build and maintain relationships.
6. ➔ **Complete the Reference section** on Power Resume Builder Form C.

Part III

The Toolbox

Tricks of the Trade

The Toolbox provides some creative resources you can use as references for developing and refining your resume. Review these and enjoy!

Appendix 1 Action Verbs - Just in case you need help!
Appendix 2 15 Resume Tips - How to Groom Your Resume
Appendix 3 7 Ways to Present Your Power Resume

1. Combination Chronological and Functional Resume (Preferred format—Sample: Cameron Clarkson)
2. Chronological Resume (Sample: Joseph Darlin)
3. Multiple Functions Resume (Sample: Randolph Martin)
   Functional - One-page Resume (Sample: Alice Parker)
4. Performance Resume (Sample: Henry Lawson)
5. One Page Resume
6. Scannable Resume
7. Internet/Electronic Resume

Appendix 4 Resume Samples

Appendix 1

Action Words

Just in case you need help!

Abbreviating
Accepting
Accrediting
Accommodating
Accomplishing
Achieving
Acknowledging
Acquainting
Acquiring
Acting
Activating
Adapting
Addressing
Adhering
Adjusting
Administering
Advertising
Advising
Aiding
Aiming
Alerting
Allocating
Amending
Analyzing
Answering
Anticipating
Appealing
Applying
Appointing
Approving
Arbitrating
Arranging
Arriving
Assembling
Assessing
Assisting
Associating
Auditing
Authorizing
Avoiding
Balancing
Bidding
Blending
Buying
Briefing
Broadening
Budgeting
Building
Calculating
Calibrating
Calling
Calming
Carrying
Cataloguing
Causing
Centralizing
Chairing
Changing
Checking
Choosing
Chronicling
Circulating
Circumventing
Clarifying
Classifying
Cleaning
Clearing
Collaborating
Commencing
Communicating
Confirming
Compiling
Completing
Composing
Computing
Conceiving
Conceptualizing
Condensing
Conducting
Configuring
Consolidating
Constructing
Contracting
Controlling
Converting
Conveying
Coordinating
Correcting
Corresponding
Counseling
Creating
Critiquing
Cultivating
Deciding
Defining
Delegating
Delineating
Delivering
Demonstrating
Describing
Designating
Designing
Detailing
Determining
Developing
Devising
Diffusing
Directing
Discovering
Discussing
Dispatching
Displaying
Disseminating
Distributing
Dividing
Documenting
Donating
Doubling
Drafting
Driving
Duplicating
Editing
Educating
Effecting
Eliciting
Eliminating
Enforcing
Engaging
Enhancing
Enlarging
Enlisting
Enrolling
Ensuring
Entering
Equipping
Establishing
Extending
Evaluating
Examining
Executing
Exhibiting
Expanding
Expediting
Explaining
Expressing
Fabricating
Facilitating
Familiarizing
Fashioning
Feeding
Fielding
Filing
Finalizing
Financing
Focusing
Following
Forecasting
Forming
Formulating
Forwarding
Founding
Fulfilling
Functioning
Garnering
Gathering
Generating
Governing
Greeting
Grouping
Guaranteeing
Handling
Harvesting
Heading
Heightening
Helping
Hiring

Holding
Hosting
Hurrying
Identifying
Illustrating
Implementing
Importing
Improving
Incepting
Incorporating
Increasing
Indexing
Influencing
Informing
Initiating
Innovating
Installing
Instituting
Instructing
Insuring
Integrating
Interpreting
Interviewing
Introducing
Inventing
Investigating
Keeping
Launching
Leading
Learning
Lecturing
Liaising
Locating
Maintaining
Managing
Manipulating
Marketing
Marking
Measuring
Mediating
Minimizing
Moderating
Modernizing
Modifying
Molding
Monitoring
Motivating
Moving
Multiplying
Negotiating
Notifying
Observing
Obtaining
Omitting
Operating
Ordering
Organizing
Originating
Outlining
Overhauling
Overseeing
Packaging
Packing
Pairing
Patrolling
Perceiving
Performing
Persuading
Pioneering
Placing
Planning
Preparing
Presenting
Presiding
Preventing
Printing
Prioritizing
Processing
Procuring
Producing
Profiling
Programming
Promoting
Proofreading
Proposing
Providing
Publicizing
Publishing
Purchasing
Quantifying
Questioning
Querying
Reaching
Receiving
Recognizing
Recommending
Recording
Recruiting
Reducing
Refining
Registering
Relating
Releasing
Remaining
Remodeling
Reorganizing
Replying
Reporting
Representing
Requesting
Retooling
Researching
Resolving
Responding
Restoring
Restructuring
Retrieving
Revamping
Reviewing
Revising
Rotating
Routing
Scanning
Scheduling
Screening
Selecting
Separating
Sequencing
Serving
Setting
Settling
Shipping
Simplifying
Selling
Solving
Sorting
Sourcing
Speaking
Spearheading
Specifying
Staffing
Standardizing
Starting
Streamlining
Strengthening
Structuring
Studying
Submitting
Suggesting
Supervising
Supplying
Supporting
Surveying
Synthesizing
Teaching
Tending
Thanking
Totaling
Tracking
Training
Transferring
Translating
Transmitting
Transporting
Troubleshooting
Typing
Updating
Upgrading
Using
Utilizing
Validating
Verifying
Visiting
Visualizing
Voicing
Writing

Appendix 2

15 Resume Tips

How to Groom Your Resume

1. Pages	• No more than two pages (15 years or 2 pages).
2. Margins	• Remember, white space sells.
3. Letterhead	• Should be same as on resume for all correspondence. • Font should be different from body of text.
4. Second Page	• Should be standardized for all correspondence. • Should use same font as for letterhead. • Name should be printed on the bottom right of second page. • 18-point text is recommended.
5. Paper	• Colored paper (*light* blue, pink, peach) or white, if mandated. • Test paper to make sure it faxes and copies clearly. • Expensive paper is not necessary. • Size: 8 1/2" x 11"
6. Type	• Preferred: laser printed. • Other printers with good black ribbon. • Do not use dot matrix. It cannot be scanned.
7. Type style	• Use an easy-to-read font: Times, Helvetica, Arial, Palatino. • Don't mix a lot of different fonts and point sizes.
8. Format	• Be consistent with your use of indentations, underlining, bolding, etc. (Internet resumes have special requirements.)
9. Spacing	• Double-space between new subjects/jobs. • Single space within sections.
10. Bullets	• Line up. Use round, square, diamond shaped. • Indent 5 spaces from left margin (Standard: 1/2-inch tab). • Tab over from indent before beginning text.
11. Reproductions	• Use quality copy machines. Prefer original laser prints. • Reproducing resumes in large quantities is not recommended as each resume should be tailored as much as possible to meet the specific matching job requirements.
12. Proofing	• Proofing is critical! Spell Check, and don't depend on yourself!
13. Objective	• Indicate specific job for which applying if known. • If applying to a company where you are not sure if there is a position available, list no more than three job titles.
14. Job Duties	• Follow the formula. (*Verb, verb,* and *verb* the overall activities of the *dept./project /unit/program/organization* which includes: *verbing* ____; *verbing* ____; and *verbing* ____.)
15. Accomplishments	• Follow the formula. (___% increase in profitability/productivity through________)

Appendix 3 — 7 Ways to Present Your Power Resume

Appendix 3-1 — **Combination Chronological and Functional**
(The Preferred Format. Sample: Cameron Clarkson)
This is the best way to present yourself in a job search. This resume focuses on what you have that the company wants, and it also eliminates the "eliminators."

Appendix 3-2 — **Chronological** (Sample: Joseph Darlin)
You should have a chronological work history in your file as a basis from which to pull information for other resumes.

Appendix 3-3 — **Multiple Functions** (Sample: Randolph Martin)
Use a multiple function resume if you have experience in areas that the company is targeting. Limit your use of this resume as it can present you as being *overqualified*.

Appendix 3-3 — **Functional One-Page** (Sample: Alice Parker)
This version can be used by someone with limited experience or multiple jobs of similar positions.

Appendix 3-4 — **Performance** (Sample: Henry Lawson)
Many sales-oriented companies will request a one-page performance/achievement resume which focuses on how well the employee performed.

Appendix 3-5 — **One-Page Resume**
The one-page resume is used mostly for those who have limited experience, recently graduated, or worked in one company for the majority of their career.

Appendix 3-6 — **Scannable**
A scannable resume is configured so it may be scanned by state-of-the art resume readers that match key words. If you know a company is scanning resumes, send 2: one pretty resume and one scannable.

Appendix 3-7 — **Internet/Electronic**
This version should be used when posting resumes on the internet and when e-mailing to a company. The format must be ASCII (text only).

Power Resume Builder
Combination: Functional & Chronological

Job Attack Power Preferred Resume

Benefits
- Focuses on Job
- Minimizes eliminators
- Matches your skills with those of the company

Name

Street • City, State Zip • (XXX) xxx-xxxx • Email abc@xyz.net

Qualified for:

Job I want → • Exact Job Title •

Who I am → **PROFESSIONAL PROFILE**

- Your whole life in one sentence focused on your next job.
- 5 statements of who you are as a person
- Self-starter...
- Analytical planner...
- Team player, etc...

What I can do for you → **AREAS OF EXPERTISE** (Approximately 24 - 33 bulleted skills)

• Budgeting	• Finance	• Taxes
•	•	•
•	•	•
•	•	•

My work experience in a nutshell → **PROFESSIONAL BACKGROUND**

FUNCTIONAL AREA YOU ARE FOCUSING ON

Plan, organize and manage the overall activities of____, which include: evaluating _______; providing _______; and ensuring compliance with _____________.

Accomplishments →

- (List 5 major accomplishments using the Peanut Butter Principle.)
- 100% compliance with...
- 250% increase in productivity...
- 150% increase in revenues/sales/profitability...
- Awarded/Ranked/Recognized for...

Work History → **EXPERIENCE**

- Company City, ST — **Job Title** Key Word Duties. Accomplishment. — Mon 19XX - Mon 19XX

Credentials → **EDUCATION**

- Degree in ____, School, City, State

AFFILIATIONS/MEMBERSHIPS/LICENSURE/CERTIFICATION

- Name of Group/Certification, Organization/Licensing Body

Appendix 3 -1
Preferred Resume: Combination Chronological and Functional

CAMERON CLARKSON

10 A Street, Any Town, Florida 32746 • (555) 339-1907 • Fax: 323-9799 • Pager 555-1212• EMail Jld124a@aol.com

Qualified for:

• Director of Human Resources, Training & Development •

PROFESSIONAL PROFILE

- Dynamic professional employing more than 10 years of progressive accomplishments in staff training, special projects coordination, media services and communications.
- A loyal and dedicated self-starter exhibiting strong organizational skills and attention to detail.
- Results-oriented team leader demonstrating skills in organization and planning.
- Diverse achiever able to follow strict budgets, evaluate personnel and achieve all goals and requirements on time and within budget.
- Analytical planner, able to comprehend complex and unrelated information and translate them into workable terms.
- Motivated team player, eager to learn, meet challenges, and assimilate new concepts quickly.

AREAS OF EXPERTISE

- Seminars
- Budgeting
- Curriculum
- Recruitment
- Planning
- Organization
- Interviewing
- Budgeting
- Scheduling
- Program Development
- Staff Development
- Cross-Cultural Communications
- Employee Relations
- Counseling
- Special Projects
- Multi-Task Management
- Inventory Control
- Testing
- PC/Mac
- Graphic Design
- Writer/Editor
- Safety/OSHA
- Problem Solving
- Special Events
- Client Relations
- Publications
- Evaluations

PROFESSIONAL BACKGROUND

RECRUITMENT, TRAINING AND DEVELOPMENT

Planned and directed overall continuing education programs for organizations ranging from health care facilities (75 hospitals) to professional organizations (4,000+ employees representing 69 nationalities) which included: assessing needs, developing programs and resources for educational seminars and coordinating continuing education activities.

- 18% increase in program offerings specifically targeted to meet organizational needs.
- 24% increase in program participation resulting in 32% increase in profitability.
- 20% increased application activity in first year resulting in 32% increase in placement.
- Ranked #1 recruiter for East Coast Division for four years.
- 400% of quota achieved through target marketing.

EXPERIENCE

- The Best Company
  City, ST

  Director, Staff Training & Special Projects — Mar 1996 - Present
  Staff 8; Budget $3.5 Million.
  Staff 23; Employees 3500.
  Training, Safety, Recruitment, Employee Relations, Curriculum Development, Special Projects.
  100% Compliance with Goals & Objectives.

  Supervisor, Media Services — Jan 1993 - Mar 1996
  Staff 8; Budget $650,000.
  Audio-Visual Library; Media Presentation Development; State-of-the-Art Media Production.
  1st Place in National Media Awards.

- Joint Venture: Automatic Telephone Project
  City, ST

  General Assistant to the Director — May 1991 - Dec 1992
  Liaison between Dutch & Swedish Company; Developed Operational Systems and Support Functions.
  International Project: $17 Billion to Install Telecommunications Systems in Saudi Arabia.

- Major Company
  City, ST

  Supervisor, Employment Processing & Records — Jan 1987 - May 1991
  New Hires, Employee Evaluations & Counseling; Payroll; Promotions and Special Projects.

Provide a BRIEF overview of specific functions and accomplishments. Include such items as: budget, quota accomplishment, functional areas for which you are responsible, territory or any other notable item.

EDUCATION

- **M.S. in Management** - GPA 3.9
  International University, Town, Florida
  Emphasis: Finance

- **B.S. in Education** - GPA 3.8
  Commonwealth University - City, Virginia
  Minor: Business & Economics

Note: This resume provides total focus on WHAT THE COMPANY WANTS and WHAT YOU WANT TO DO. Leave out superfluous experience that does not directly support the job for which you are applying.

CAMERON CLARKSON

Power Resume Builder | **Chronological Resume**

Benefits
- Good for companies who demand a chronological resume.
- Everyone should have one for your own purposes.

Name

Street • City, State Zip • (XXX) xxx-xxxx • Email abc@xyz.net

Job I want ➔

Qualified for:

• Exact Job Title •

Who I am ➔

PROFESSIONAL PROFILE

- Your whole life in one sentence focused on your next job.
- 5 statements of who you are as a person
- Self-starter...
- Analytical planner...
- Team player, etc.....

What I can do for you ➔

AREAS OF EXPERTISE (Approximately 24 - 33 bulleted skills)

• Budgeting	• Finance	• Taxes
•	•	•
•	•	•
•	•	•

Work History ➔

PROFESSIONAL BACKGROUND

NAME OF COMPANY (Most Recent)
City, State

Month 19XX - Month 19XX

Plan, organize and manage the overall activities of____which include: evaluating _______; providing _______; and ensuring compliance with _____________.

Accomplishments ➔

- (List 5 major accomplishments using the Peanut Butter Principle.)
- 100% compliance with...
- 250% increase in productivity...
- 150% increase in revenues/sales/profitability...
- Awarded/Ranked/Recognized for...

(Repeat this format for each company for which you have worked to cover the last 15 years or 7 companies or 2 pages. Do not exceed 2 pages.)

Credentials ➔

EDUCATION

- Degree in ____, School, City, State

AFFILIATIONS/MEMBERSHIPS/LICENSURE/CERTIFICATION

- Name of Group/Certification, Organization/Licensing Body

JOSEPH DARLIN

10 A Street, Any Town, Florida 32746 • (407) 339-1907 • Fax: 323-9799 • Pager 555-1212• EMail Jld124a@aol.com

Qualified for:

- **SPECIAL PROJECTS MANAGEMENT**

Exact Job Title

PROFESSIONAL PROFILE

The 1st line only - entire work life in one sentence as it supports job for which you are applying.

Who **YOU are**: personally, professionally, and socially - the generic you.

- Dynamic professional employing more than 10 years of progressive accomplishments in staff training, special projects coordination, media services and communications.
- A loyal and dedicated self-starter exhibiting strong organizational skills and attention to detail. Results-oriented team leader demonstrating skills in organization and planning.
- Diverse achiever able to retain strict budgets, evaluate personnel and achieve all goals and requirements on time and within budget.
- Analytical planner, able to comprehend complex and unrelated information and digest them into workable terms.
- Motivated team player, eager to learn, meet challenges and assimilate new concepts quickly.

AREAS OF EXPERTISE

- Seminars
- Budgeting
- Curriculum
- Program Development
- Staff Development
- Cross-Cultural Communications
- PC/Mac
- Graphic Design
- Writer/Editor

Everything you can do for them - You can have up to 33 skills.

PROFESSIONAL BACKGROUND

THE BEST COMPANY
Houston, Texas

Most Recent Company

March 1994 - Present

DIRECTOR, STAFF TRAINING AND SPECIAL PROJECTS - Planned, controlled and directed the overall activities of the Staff Training and Special Projects Department which included: supervising and training staff; preparing and allocating budget for all training programs; and ensuring compliance with corporate directives in directing management projects.

- 95% student success rate in first year through the development of a new training program for 900 foreign students.
- 212% increase in training program participation resulting in 22% increase in employee retention.
- 32% increase in productivity through new program development.

Accomplishments - How well you did your job.

January 1992 - March 1994

SUPERVISOR, MEDIA SERVICES - Planned, organized and managed the overall activities of the Media Services Department which included: supervising the media library and graphics/media production services; coordinating continuing education and community education programs; and ensuring quality products were provided and approved by appropriate government agencies and company levels.

- 12% increase in productivity through creation of in-house video and materials library.
- 300% expansion of programs and services through reorganization of system with the addition of only one more staff person.
- 250% increase in profitability through promotion to increase sales.

Chronological Resume - 2-page

JOINT VENTURE: AUTOMATIC TELEPHONE PROJECT
Any City, Any Country

May 1985 - December 1991

GENERAL ASSISTANT TO THE DIRECTOR - Planned, organized, and coordinated the overall activities of the Operations Department which included: recruiting support staff and supervising office services, housekeeping, clerical functions, dietary and other support services, coordinating documentation of contracts with the government; and directing public relations/social activities for the organization.

- 20% increase in productivity and project profitability through designing layout for $1 million office building and getting project on-line ahead of schedule.
- 38% increase in productivity through implementation of new organization communications system.
- Recognized for "Outstanding Performance" for establishing support systems for $17 billion project to monitor productivity and budget.

MAJOR COMPANY
Little City, Big State

January 1981 - May 1985

SUPERVISOR, EMPLOYMENT PROCESSING AND RECORDS - Supervised and coordinated the overall activities of the Employment Processing and Records Department which included: directing recruitment, performance evaluations and termination activities; benefits management, employee relations and other personnel functions.

- 28% increase in productivity through design and implementation of new hire on-line training program.
- 60% increase in recontracting activity efficiency through standardizing process.
- 22% increase in on-the-job training due to implementing liaison programs with community academic institutions and other facilities.
- 50% increased enrollment in Education Programs resulting in 32% increase in productivity and 20% reduction in turnover.

Other experience includes public relations, sales and training.

EDUCATION

- **M.S. in Management** - GPA 3.9
  International University, Town, Florida
  Emphasis: Finance

- **B.S. in Education** - GPA 3.8
  Commonwealth University - City, Virginia
  Minor: Business & Economics

JOSEPH DARLIN

Benefits
- Focuses on what the company wants.
- Eliminates confusion due to diverse backgrounds.
- Highlights positives.

Name

Street • City, State Zip • (XXX) xxx-xxxx • Email abc@xyz.net

Job I want →

Qualified for:

• Exact Job Title •

Who I am →

PROFESSIONAL PROFILE

- Your whole life in one sentence focused on your next job.
- 5 statements of who you are as a person...
- Self-starter...
- Analytical planner...
- Team player, etc...

What I can do for you →

AREAS OF EXPERTISE (Approximately 24 - 33 bulleted skills)

• Budgeting	• Finance	• Taxes
•	•	•
•	•	•
•	•	•

My work experience represented through functional areas →

PROFESSIONAL BACKGROUND

FUNCTIONAL AREA ON WHICH YOU ARE FOCUSING

Plan, organize and manage the overall activities of____which include: evaluating _______; providing _______; and ensuring compliance with _____________.

Accomplishments →

- (List 5 major accomplishments using the Peanut Butter Principle.)
- 100% compliance with...
- 250% increase in productivity...
- 150% increase in revenues/sales/profitability...
- Awarded/Ranked/Recognized for...

(Repeat this format for all your functional areas of expertise.
Do not exceed 2 pages.)

Credentials →

EDUCATION

- Degree in ____, School, City, State

AFFILIATIONS/MEMBERSHIPS/LICENSURE/CERTIFICATION

- Name of Group/Certification, Organization/Licensing Body

Appendix 3 -3
Functional: Sample Layout

RANDOLPH MARTIN

10 A Street, Any Town, Florida 32746 • (407) 339-1907 • Fax: 323-9799 • Pager 555-1212• EMail Jld124a@aol.com

Qualified for:

• **Vice President, Corporate Development Programs** •

PROFESSIONAL PROFILE

- Dynamic professional employing more than 10 years of progressive accomplishments in staff training, special projects coordination, media services and communications.
- A loyal and dedicated self-starter exhibiting strong organizational skills and attention to detail.
- Results-oriented team leader demonstrating skills in organization and planning.
- Diverse achiever able to retain strict budgets, evaluate personnel and achieve all goals and requirements on time and within budget.
- Analytical planner, able to comprehend complex and unrelated information and digest it into workable terms.
- Motivated team player, eager to learn, meet challenges, and assimilate new concepts.

AREAS OF EXPERTISE

- Seminars
- Budgeting
- Curriculum
- Program Development
- Staff Development
- Cross-Cultural Communications
- PC/Mac
- Graphic Design
- Writer/Editor

PROFESSIONAL BACKGROUND

Functional area that SUPPORTS the job for which you are applying. You may only wish to include one functional area in your resume to indicate total focus on what the company wants so as not to appear overqualified.

RECRUITMENT

Planned, controlled and directed overall recruitment programs which included: providing career counseling and recruitment for business professions; organizing Career Days and Career Fairs in shopping centers, hotels , home shows, etc.; presenting career seminars for counselors; and organizing professional and voluntary organizations in supportive activities.

Clients: AT&T, AAA, Westinghouse, AMA and others.

Here's a great place for name dropping! Headings to use: Clients, Facilities, Industries, Organizations or Companies.

- 20% increased application activity in first year; 32% increase in placement.
- Ranked #1 recruiter for East Coast Division for four years.
- 400% of quota achieved through target marketing.

TRAINING AND DEVELOPMENT

Planned and directed overall continuing education programs for organizations ranging from health care facilities (75 hospitals) to professional organizations (4,000+ employees representing 69 nationalities) which included: assessing needs, developing programs and resources for educational seminars, and coordinating continuing education activities.

- 18% increase in program offerings specifically targeted to meet organizational needs.
- 24% increase in program participation resulting in 32% increase in profitability.

PUBLIC RELATIONS

Planned, developed and managed the overall public relations activities for organizations, hospitals and companies which included: coordinating news media releases; designing, writing and producing videos, pamphlets, presentations, reports and guides; and providing desktop publishing (Macintosh) consulting services.

- Received 1st place award for creativity in 1991 Florida Public Relations Convention.

ADMINISTRATION

Established and directed basic office systems, procedures, programs, units and departments for various organizations.

- 100% achievement of special project to reorganize division and develop new systems in 80% of time allocated.

POPULATIONS WORKED WITH

- Professionals - representing professional organizations and working with physicians, administrators, etc.
- **Minority groups** - Community Action Program
- **Educational institutions** - junior high to college level students.
- **Cultures** - people representing **69** different nationalities. Areas included: Florida and various overseas multi-cultural settings.

Be creative! If there is a particular skill/philosophy/ or experience the company is looking for, include it in your resume!

PERSONAL PHILOSOPHY FOR GETTING THE JOB DONE

- **Participatory management:** people are the key and team building is essential.
- **Results oriented**: achieve the goals of the organization.

EXPERIENCE

- The Best Company, City, State — **Director, Staff Training & Special Projects** — Mar 1994 - Present
  Supervisor, Media Services — Jan 1992 - Mar 1994
- Joint Venture: Automatic Telephone Project, City, State — **General Assistant to the Director** — May 1986 - Dec 1991
- Major Company, City, State — **Supervisor, Employment Processing & Records** — Jan 1981 - May 1986

It's always important to include where you have worked and account for all time.

EDUCATION

- **M.S. in Management** - GPA 3.9
  International University, Town, Florida
  Emphasis: Finance
- **B.S. in Education** - GPA 3.8
  Commonwealth University - City, Virginia
  Minor: Business & Economics

ALICE E. PARKER

10 A Street, Any Town, Florida 32746 • (407) 339-1907 • Fax: 323-9799 • Pager 555-1212• EMail Jld124a@aol.com

Qualified for:

• **Manager, Education, and Training** •

PROFESSIONAL PROFILE

- Dynamic professional with more than 10 years of progressive accomplishments in staff training, special projects coordination, media services and communications.
- A loyal and dedicated self-starter exhibiting strong organizational skills and attention to detail.
- Results-oriented team leader demonstrating skills in organization and planning.
- Diverse achiever able to follow strict budgets, evaluate personnel and achieve all goals and requirements on time and within budget.
- Motivated team player, eager to learn, meet challenges and assimilate new concepts quickly.

AREAS OF EXPERTISE

- Seminars
- Budgeting
- Curriculum
- Recruitment
- Planning
- Program Development
- Staff Development
- Diversity Training
- Employee Relations
- Counseling
- PC/Mac
- Graphic Design
- Writer/Editor
- Safety/OSHA
- Problem Solving

PROFESSIONAL BACKGROUND

TRAINING AND DEVELOPMENT

Planned, designed, and directed overall continuing education programs for organizations ranging from health care facilities (75 hospitals) to professional organizations (4,000+ employees representing 69 nationalities) which included: assessing needs, developing programs and resources for educational seminars, and coordinating continuing education activities.

- 18% increase in program offerings specifically targeted to meet organizational needs.
- 24% increase in program participation resulting in 32% increase in profitability.
- 20% increased application activity in first year resulting in 32% increase in placement.
- 250% increase in productivity through standardizing scheduling and course planning.

EXPERIENCE

• The Best Company	**Director, Staff Training**	Mar 1996 - Present
	Supervisor, Media Services	Jan 1994 - Mar 1996
• Automatic Project	**Coordinator, Education**	May 1991 - Dec 1993
• Major Company	**Supervisor, Employment**	Jan 1987 - May 1991

EDUCATION

- **M.S. in Management** - GPA 3.9, International University, Town, Florida
- **B.S. in Education** - GPA 3.8, Commonwealth University - City, Virginia

Functional Resume - 1-page

Power Resume Builder

Performance Based Resume

Benefits
- Focuses on accomplishments and presents them in quantitative terms.
- Good for Sales.

Name

Street • City, State Zip • (XXX) xxx-xxxx • Email abc@xyz.net

Qualified for:

Job I want ➔

• Exact Job Title •

Who I am ➔

PROFESSIONAL PROFILE

- Your whole life in one sentence focused on your next job.
- 5 statements of who you are as a person
- Self-starter...
- Analytical planner...
- Team player, etc...

What I can do for you ➔

AREAS OF EXPERTISE (Approximately 24 - 33 bulleted skills)

• Budgeting	• Finance	• Taxes
•	•	•
•	•	•
•	•	•

Accomplish-ments ➔

ACCOMPLISHMENTS

- (List 10 major accomplishments using the Peanut Butter Principle.)
- 100% compliance with...
- 250% increase in productivity...
- 150% increase in revenues/sales/profitability...
- Awarded/Ranked/Recognized for...
- __% cost savings...
- —%increase in sales...
- 100% achievement of...
- Recognized for "Outstanding..."
- Ranked #1 in U.S. for...

Work History ➔

EXPERIENCE

- Company, City, ST — **Job Title**, Key Word Duties. Accomplishment. — Mon 19xx - Mon 19xx

Credentials ➔

EDUCATION

- Degree in ____, School, City, State

AFFILIATIONS/MEMBERSHIPS/LICENSURE/CERTIFICATION

- Name of Group/Certification, Organization/Licensing Body

Appendix 3 -4
Performance: Sample Layout

HENRY R. LAWSON

10 A Street, Any Town, Florida 32746 • (407) 339-1907 • Fax: 323-9799 • Pager 555-1212• EMail Jld124a@aol.com

Qualified for:

• **Regional Sales Manager** •

PROFESSIONAL PROFILE

- Results-oriented professional employing more than 15 years of progressive accomplishments in territory development, marketing, and sales management.
- Catalytic problem solving leader who thinks logically and values creativity and innovation.
- Diplomatic communicator, able to motivate diverse populations toward achieving goals.
- Analytical planner, demonstrating the ability to interpret task directions and provide solutions in a timely manner.
- Goal-directed self-starter, exercising strong organizational skills and attention to detail.

AREAS OF EXPERTISE

- Customer Service
- Customer Relations
- New Business
- Presentations
- Marketing Strategies
- Product Marketing
- Wholesale Distribution
- Sales
- Cost Reduction
- Advertising Strategies
- Inventory Control
- International Marketing
- Budgeting
- Spanish
- Planning & Organization
- Target Marketing
- Travel
- Operations Management
- Territory Development
- P&L
- Manufacturing

ACCOMPLISHMENTS

- 40 - 120% increase in revenues annually through launching a pharmaceutical product line to new territory. (Pharmaceuticals, Inc.)
- 300% increase in consumer product line sales through developing innovative advertising initiatives and product acquisition. (Pharmaceuticals, Inc.)
- 20% increase in revenues annually over a 5 year period for Frito-Lay through launching new products and maximizing market share in established sales territory.
- 15% increase in annual profitability for Frito-Lay over a 6 year period through aggressive pricing strategies.

EXPERIENCE

- Pharmaceuticals, Inc. — **General Manager** — Dec 1994 - Present
  New Product Development
  Director of Marketing — Apr 1989 - Nov 1994
- Frito-Lay — **General Manager** — Jan 1984 - Mar 1989
  Developed Sales Force, Built & Opened New Plant, 20% Average Annual Growth

EDUCATION

- **Bachelor in Business Administration**, University of Miami, Miami, Florida

Resume Builder
Entry Level/New Graduates/One Field

One-Page Resume

Benefits
- Good for those with limited experience or new graduates.

Name

Street • City, State Zip • (XXX) xxx-xxxx • Email abc@xyz.net

Qualified for:

Job I want → • **Exact Job Title** •

Who I am →

PROFESSIONAL PROFILE

- Your whole life in one sentence focused on your next job.
- 5 statements of who you are as a person
- Self-starter...
- Analytical planner...
- Team player, etc...

What I can do for you →

AREAS OF EXPERTISE (Approximately 24 - 33 bulleted skills)

• Budgeting	• Finance	• Taxes
•	•	•
•	•	•
•	•	•

PROFESSIONAL BACKGROUND

My work experience in a nutshell →

FUNCTIONAL AREA YOU ARE FOCUSING ON

Plan, organize and manage the overall activities of____which include: evaluating _______; providing _______; and ensuring compliance with _____________.

Accomplishments →

- (List 5 major accomplishments using the Peanut Butter Principle.)
- 100% compliance with....
- 250% increase in productivity...
- 150% increase in revenues/sales/profitability...
- Awarded/Ranked/Recognized for...

Work history →

EXPERIENCE

• Company City, ST	**Job Title**	Mon 19XX - Mon 19XX
• Company City, ST	**Job Title**	Mon 19XX - Mon 19XX
• Company City, ST	**Job Title**	Mon 19XX - Mon 19XX

Credentials →

EDUCATION

- Degree in ____, School, City, State

Appendix 3-5
One-Page: Sample Layout

Tips:
Do not use:
- Underlining
- Italics
- Colored paper
- Fancy type faces
- Dot matrix print

Name

Street • City, State Zip • (XXX) xxx-xxxx • Email abc@xyz.net

Qualified for:

Job I want ➔ • **Exact Job Title** •

PROFESSIONAL PROFILE

Who I am ➔
- Your whole life in one sentence focused on your next job.
- 5 statements of who you are as a person...
- Self-starter...
- Analytical planner...
- Team player, etc....

AREAS OF EXPERTISE (Approximately 24 - 33 bulleted skills)

What I can do for you ➔

• Budgeting	• Finance	• Taxes
•	•	•
•	•	•
•	•	•

PROFESSIONAL BACKGROUND

FUNCTIONAL AREA YOU ARE FOCUSING ON

My work experience in a nutshell ➔

Plan, organize and manage the overall activities of____which include: evaluating _______; providing _______; and ensuring compliance with _____________.

Accomplish-ments ➔
- (List 5 major accomplishments following the Peanut Butter Principle.)
- 100% compliance with...
- 250% increase in productivity...
- 150% increase in revenues/sales/profitability...
- Awarded/Ranked/Recognized for...

EXPERIENCE

Work history ➔
- Company City, ST | **Job Title** Key Word Duties. Accomplishment. | Mon/19XX-Mon/19XX

EDUCATION

Credentials ➔
- Degree in ____, School, City, State

AFFILIATIONS/MEMBERSHIPS/LICENSURE/CERTIFICATION
- Name of Group/Certification, Organization/Licensing Body

Appendix 3 -6
Scannable Resume: Sample Layout

Power Resume Builder

Internet/Electronic Resume

Tips:
Do not use:
- Underlining
- Italics
- Formatting
- Fancy type faces
- Bolding

Do:
- Left align
- Use text/ASCII
- 10/12 pt. font

NAME
Street
City, State Zip
(XXX) xxx-xxxx
Email: abc@xyz.net

Job I want ➔

OBJECTIVE: Exact Job Title

Who I am ➔

PROFESSIONAL PROFILE

Your whole life in one sentence focused on your next job.
5 statements of who you are as a person
Self-starter...
Analytical planner...
Team player, etc...

What I can do for you ➔

AREAS OF EXPERTISE (Approximately 24 - 33 key words/skill areas)

Budgeting, Finance, Taxes, Reports, Customer Relations, Presentations, Planning & Organizing, Cost Controls, Financial Analysis, etc.

PROFESSIONAL BACKGROUND

My work experience in a nutshell ➔

FUNCTIONAL AREA YOU ARE FOCUSING ON

Plan, organize and manage the overall activities of____which include: evaluating _______; providing _______; and ensuring compliance with _____________.

Accomplishments ➔

(List 5 major accomplishments using the Peanut Butter Principle.)
100% compliance with....
250% increase in productivity...
150% increase in revenues/sales/profitability...
Awarded/Ranked/Recognized for...

Work history ➔

EXPERIENCE

Job Title - Company - City, ST - Mo 19XX - Mo 19XX
Key Word Duties.
Accomplishment.

Credentials ➔

EDUCATION

Degree in ____, School, City, State

AFFILIATIONS/MEMBERSHIPS/LICENSURE/CERTIFICATION

Name of Group/Certification, Organization/Licensing Body

Appendix 3 -7
Internet/Electronic Resume: Sample Layout

Sample Resumes

STEPHANIE MERVIN

345 Old Forest Road • Longwood, Florida 32779 • (407) 788-2987

Qualified For:

• Accounting Manager •

PROFESSIONAL PROFILE

- Results-oriented professional employing more than 15 years of progressive accomplishments in financial software training and overall financial operations management.
- Diplomatic leader, able to empower others to achieve common goals.
- Effective communicator, dedicated to excellence in service and relationships.
- Analytical planner, able to take complex and unrelated information and organize into workable terms.
- Diverse achiever, able to interpret task directions and provide solutions in a timely manner.
- Motivated self-starter, exhibiting high ethics, competence and confidence underscored by a personal commitment to outstanding professional performance.

AREAS OF EXPERTISE

- Customer Service
- Data Communications
- Reconciliations
- Accounts Payables
- General Ledger
- Auditing
- Information Technology
- Risk Management
- Financial Operations
- Team Building
- Multi-Task Management
- Accounts Receivables
- Budgeting
- Financial Reporting
- Problem Solving
- Presentations
- Training
- Financial Analysis
- Interpersonal Relations
- Purchasing
- Financial Planning
- Computer Proficient
- Cash Control
- Billing

PROFESSIONAL BACKGROUND

FINANCIAL OPERATIONS

Plan, organize and manage the overall financial activities for various companies which include: evaluating customer needs; developing creative strategies and solutions; and monitoring process in compliance with established standards and corporate objectives.

- 350% increase in productivity through reorganizing and streamlining policies and procedures.
- 165% cost savings through streamlining manpower requirements while boosting morale.
- 500% increase in client base through developing a "client-centered" marketing approach while ensuring quality service.
- 100% accomplishment of assigned projects on time and within budget through developing "results-oriented" plan of action identifying time lines.
- Recognized for "Dedication & Hard Work" for commitment to project completion on-time and within budget.

EDUCATION

- **Bachelors Degree in Business Administration**, Emphasis: Accounting
  Roger Williams College, Providence, Rhode Island

EXPERIENCE

- InfoSource Inc.
  Orlando, FL
  Financial Training Specialist — Dec1990 - Present
  Software: (Financial - Ledger, Budget, AR, Cash Receipts)
  Accounts: 300 - National & International;
  Training; Presentations; Client Relations;
  Troubleshooting; Liaison; Customer Service.

- EBS
  Orlando, FL
  GM & Bookkeeper — Jul 1988 - Dec 1990
  Offices Managed: 56; Staff: 4;
  Total Operations; Bookkeeping; Contract Negotiations;
  Liaison; Accounting Management; Training;
  Staff Development; Client Relations.

- Carlton Corporation
  Orlando, FL
  Controller — Feb 1986 - Jun 1988
  Staff: 25;
  Auditing; Financial Planning/Budgeting; Cash
  Control; Procurements; Financial Administration;
  General Operations.

- Smith Properties, Inc.
  Orlando, FL
  Controller/Office Administrator — Feb 1982 - Dec 1985
  Staff: 8; Offices: Pensacola & Orlando;
  Accounting; Policies & Procedures; Expenses;
  Budgets; Investments; Closing Records.

NORQUIST W. MONAHAN

Deer Run Path • Heathrow, Florida 32708 • Office (407) 332-0928 • Home (407) 332-0495

Qualified for:

• Chief Executive Officer •

PROFESSIONAL PROFILE

- Results-oriented professional employing more than 15 years of progressive accomplishments in domestic and international operations.
- Motivated self-starter, exhibiting high ethics, competence and confidence underscored by a personal commitment to outstanding professional performance.
- Proven leader, eager to learn, meet new challenges and assimilate new concepts and ideas quickly.
- Diplomatic leader able to empower others to achieve common goals.
- Effective communicator dedicated to excellence in service and relationships.
- Loyal and goal-directed achiever demonstrating integrity in achieving all goals and objectives.

AREAS OF EXPERTISE

- Turnaround Specialist/ Restructuring
- Operations
- Manufacturing
- Master Planning
- Feasibility Studies
- Banking Relations
- P&L
- Financial Reporting
- Accounts Receivable
- Negotiations
- Sales Promotions
- International Business
- Cost Containment
- Capital Plans
- Quality Controls
- Financial Analysis
- Forecasting
- Accounting
- Problem Solving
- Computerized Operations
- Planning & Organization
- Marketing Strategies
- Global Purchasing
- Productivity Improvement
- New Product Development
- Corporate Tax Returns
- Budgeting
- Auditing
- Accounts Payable
- Multi-Task Management

PROFESSIONAL BACKGROUND

FINANCIAL MANAGEMENT AND OPERATIONS

Plan, organize and manage the overall accounting and financial activities for CompuCo International Trading Companies and Worldwide Operations which include: evaluating annual fiscal requirements (manpower, resources & equipment); developing budgets, financial controls and marketing strategies; and ensuring compliance with established standards and corporate objectives.

- $4.2 million increase in profitability in 1995 for product manufacturing company which previously had a loss of $6.5 million through turnaround process.
- 30% annual cost savings through developing and implementing a global purchasing strategy for resins.
- 18% cost savings in annual manufacturing costs through sharing of best-practices among 25 plants.
- 97% increase in profitability, 40% increase in sales and 30% cost savings in manpower requirements through developing "results-oriented", measurable marketing strategies. (CompuCo Trading Companies)
- Recognized for "Excellent Customer Service/Relations" through developing positive banking and community relationships.
- 100% compliance with IRS Tax Reporting requirements resulting in no audits or penalties.
- 100% accomplishment of assigned projects on time and within budget through developing "results-oriented" plan of action identifying time lines.

EXPERIENCE

- CompuCo Trading Companies & Worldwide Operations
  Orlando, FL

Vice President & CFO Jul 1991 - Present
$798MM Sales; $140MM Profit
40% Sales Increase; 97% Profit Increase
Total Operations Management
Restructuring
Scope of International Operations Expanded.
Satellite Production Company:
$18MM Sales; $4.2MM Profit
Total Restructuring & Strategies Shift

Vice President, Financial Planning Mar 1986 - Jul 1991
U.S. Division
New Direct Delivery Methods Introduced.
Innovative Marketing Methods for Isolated Consumers and Geographic Markets.
Payment by Credit Card Introduced.
10% Cost Savings

- CompuCo- Canada
  Toronto, Ontario

Controller - Vice President Jul 1983 - Feb 1986
Profit 28% Increase; 70% ROI Increase
Line of Credit Established for Distributors.
Demographic/Market Analysis: Increased Market Share.
Head Office Relocation; Restructuring.

Controller Aug 1982 - Jul 1983
Computerized Distributor Operations.
$1.4MM Automotive Cost Savings.
$1MM Annual Savings: Printing Department Reorganization.

Director Finance & Planning Nov 1981 - Aug 1982
Financial Operations Automated.

Chief Accountant Jan 1981 - Oct 1981

EDUCATION

- **Professional Management Development**, Harvard University, Boston, Massachusetts
- **BA in Political Science & English,** Carleton University, Ottawa, Ontario, Canada
- **Certificate in Manufacturing Management**, Saint Lawrence College, Cornwall, Ontario, Canada
- **Certified Public Accountant** (CPA): Florida
- **Certified Management Accountant** (CMA)

NORQUIST W. MONAHAN

Carmen Alvarez

2904 North Bay Road • San Antonio, Texas 43987 • (507) 451-1798

Qualified in:

• **Financial Services** •

PROFESSIONAL PROFILE

- Proficient professional with more than 15 years of progressive accomplishments in financial services.
- Dependable team player, always gets the job done.
- Disciplined self-starter, with the unique ability to comprehend complex, unrelated information and digest it into workable terms.
- Eager to learn, meet new challenges and assimilate new concepts and ideas quickly.
- Level-headed communicator, respectful of others and able to work with all types of people.
- Motivated self-starter, exhibiting high ethics, competence and confidence underscored by a personal commitment to outstanding professional performance.

AREAS OF EXPERTISE

- Budgeting
- Planning & Organization
- Financial Analysis
- Strategic Planning
- MS Excel
- Financial Controls
- Multi-Task Management
- Forecasting
- Training
- Presentations
- Interpersonal Skills
- Client Liaison
- Collections
- Problem Solving
- Tracking Systems
- Troubleshooting
- Lotus 1-2-3
- Capital Expenditures
- Direct Margin Planning
- Bilingual: Spanish

PROFESSIONAL BACKGROUND

FINANCIAL SERVICES ADMINISTRATION & SUPPORT

Plan, organize and manage the assigned financial services activities for various companies which included: evaluating financial service requirements (manpower, resources and equipment); developing financial plans, monitoring and reports; and ensuring compliance with corporate goals and objectives.

Companies: J. Walter Thompson, Coca-Cola and Others.

- 300% increase in productivity for financial reporting through automating information processing while maintaining quality control.
- 100% compliance with corporate standards in managing expenditures and project costs through establishing results-oriented monitoring practices.
- Recognized for "Excellence in Budget Preparation and Monitoring" resulting in minimal variances.
- 250% increase in productivity through standardizing workflow process.
- 100% accomplishment of assigned projects on time and within budget through developing a targeted timeline, plan of action.

EDUCATION

- **Bachelor in Business Administration**, Pace University, The Lubin School of Business Administration, New York City, New York
  Major: Marketing & Accounting

EXPERIENCE:

•	BMES Orlando, FL	**Coordinator** Spanish, Program Planning, Special Events, Numbers in Business, Financial Analysis	Jul 1996 - Present
•	Harcourt Brace & Company	Short-Term Project Educational Product Evaluations; Historical Analysis	Jun 1995 - Jun 1996
•	J. Walter Thompson Company New York, NY	**Financial Services Supervisor** Financial Reporting/Analysis, P&L, Budgeting, Project Billings, New Business Activity Reporting, Approvals: Expenditures	Jul 1989 - Oct 1992
		Financial Services Administrator Equipment Leases/Expenditures; Direct Margin Planning; Coordinated Capital Expense Budget; Financial Controls & Reporting	Oct 1986 - Jul 1989
		Senior Financial Account Controller Liaison: Account Exectives & Clients' Financial Staff; Estimating, Invoicing, Revenue Planning, Monitoring Accounts Receivables, Customer Service/Relations	Jun 1986 - Oct 1986
		Financial Account Controller Collections, Client Relations, Troubleshooting; Financial Tracking	Jul 1983 - May 1986
		Print Estimator Purchased/Costed Advertising Space in Media; Contracts; Discounting	Jan 1981 - Jul 1983

Randolph Evans

2984 Harcourt Drive, Heathrow, Florida 32729 • (407) 332-9876

Qualified for:

• **Chief Financial Officer** •

PROFESSIONAL PROFILE

- Dedicated professional employing more than 7 years of progressive accomplishments in financial management.
- Eager to learn, meet new challenges and assimilate new concepts and ideas quickly.
- Hard working and goal-oriented achiever with exceptional analytical, financial and organizational skills.
- Inspiring self-starter, able to organize resources to achieve goals.
- Resourceful problem solver who thrives on translating complex and unrelated information into understandable terms.
- Goal-directed team leader, demonstrating the ability to motivate diverse groups towards achieving a common goal.

AREAS OF EXPERTISE

- Accounting
- Reconciliations
- Account Analysis
- Monthly/Quarterly Reports
- LAN
- MS Office
- Oral Communications
- General Ledger
- Financial Analysis
- Inventory Control
- Inventory Audits
- Financial Statements
- Lotus 1-2-3
- PCHUB
- Written Communications
- AP/AR
- Budgeting
- Banking
- Planning & Organization
- Novell
- WordPerfect
- Property Management System

PROFESSIONAL BACKGROUND

FINANCIAL MANAGEMENT AND ACCOUNTING

Plan, organize and manage the overall financial activities for Walt Disney World Resort which include: identifying organizational requirements/goals; performing financial responsibilities and developing reports; and providing audits to ensure compliance with government and commercial regulations.

- 400% increase in productivity through automating ticket control, accountability and reconciliation process.
- 100% compliance with special project to open new resort at the Walt Disney World on time and within budget.
- Recognized for "Excellence in Accountability and Organizational Development" for creating an inventory reconciliation/control report resulting in cost savings.
- 100% compliance with government regulations for documentation and reporting.
- 100% accomplishment of assigned projects on time through developing a results-oriented plan of action.

EXPERIENCE

- Walt Disney World
  Walt Disney World Resort
  Buena Vista, FL

  Assistant CFO Feb 1993 - Present
  Staff: 10.
  Departments: MIS, AR/AP, Payroll, General Cashier, Auditors, Food & Beverage Controller.
  Financial Reports, Reconciliations (Bank & Inventory), General Ledger, Internal Controls.
  400% Goal Achievement.

  Contracting Directorate

  Contracting Specialist Jun 1990 - Nov 1993
  Staff: 6 in Services Department.
  Purchase Orders, Contracts (up to $1MM), Bids/Proposals, Negotiations,
  500% Productivity Increase.
  Contract Administration & Closing.
  Special Project: Opened new ventures on Walt Disney World Resort.

- Halprin Construction
  Washington, D. C.

  Accountant Jun 1989 - Jun 1990
  Accounting Functions, Forecasting, Financial Analysis & Reports, Negotiations, Contract Review.

- Worked various positions while in school ranging from retail operations to park ranger.

EDUCATION

- **MBA in Financial Affairs, George Washington University - GPA 3.9**
  Washington, D.C.

- **BS in Business Administration in Accounting - GPA 4.0**
  George Washington University, Washington, DC

- **Continuing Education:**
  - Novell IntranetWare Netware 4.11 Administration
  - Novell IntranetWare Netware 4.11 Advanced Administration
  - Novell IntranetWare Net Ware 4.11 Installation and Configuration
  - Financial Planning & Control Techniques
  - Internal Control Programming
  - Cost & Price Analysis

MARSTON E. NAUGHTON

4146 Sweetbriar Parkway • Richmond, Virginia 22601 • (540) 281-4955

Qualified For the Management of:

• **Trust & Estate Administration & Private Banking** •

PROFESSIONAL PROFILE

- Results-oriented professional with over 25 years of progressive accomplishments in managing trust and estate administration, taxes, budget control, new business and overall operations.
- Motivated self-starter, exhibiting high ethics, hard work, dedication, competence and confidence, underscored by a personal commitment to outstanding professional performance.
- Analytical planner, with exceptional financial, management and organizational skills.

AREAS OF EXPERTISE

- Financial Planning
- Trust Administration
- Sensitive Accounts
- Strategic Planning
- Policies & Procedures
- Estate Administration
- Investment Services
- Portfolio Management
- Budget Planning
- New Business
- Corporate Accounting
- Organizational Planning
- Operations Coordination
- Presentations
- Public Relations
- Taxes
- Client Relations
- Problem Solving

PROFESSIONAL BACKGROUND

ADMINISTRATION, INVESTMENTS & PRIVATE BANKING

Plan, organize and manage private banking and administrative activities for high net worth individuals which include: trust and estate administration, taxes, new business and general overall operations.

- $600 million in asset management has been developed for a new organization since February 1995 by providing developmental support. (First Union Private Capital Group)
- As Executive Vice President of Big Company, firm grew approximately 270%. Assets under management increased by $105 million, with an additional $32 million of investment advisory business from a local bank.
- 100% client retention in all positions by providing excellent customer service and attaining results through goal-directed management.
- 100% compliance with Regulations and banking principals.

EDUCATION

- **BS in Business Administration (Accounting Emphasis),** University of Richmond - Richmond, Virginia
- **Trust & Estate Law/Advanced Bank Management,** Canisius College, Buffalo, New York
- **Trust & Estate Administration Schools,** New York State Bankers Association

EXPERIENCE

•	First Union Private Capital Group Capital Management, NA Richmond, VA	**Senior Vice President Administration/Investments Private Banking**	Feb 1995 - Present
•	Bankers Trust Company of Virginia, NA Richmond, VA	**Vice President Administration/Investments Private Banking**	Jun 1990 - Feb 1995
•	First Union, NA Richmond, VA	**Vice President Administration/Investments Private Banking**	Feb 1987 - Jun 1990
•	Big Company, Inc. Buffalo, NY	**Executive Vice President**	Aug 1985 - Feb 1987
•	The National Bank New York, NY	**Vice President/Trust Officer**	Oct 1983 - Aug 1985
•	MM Banks, Inc. (Holding Company)	**Vice President Stateside Consultant on Estate & Trust Administration**	Oct 1974 - Oct 1983
•	MM Bank, NA Buffalo, NY	**Vice President**	Apr 1972 - Oct 1974

- **Teaching Experience:** New York State Bankers Association, Estate & Trust Taxation, Trust & Estate Administration Schools, Certified Life Underwriters, Trust & Estate Income Taxes

BANK COMMITTEES

- **Regional:**
  - Officers Trust Investment
  - Trust Committee on Real Estate & Mortgages
  - Closely-Held Business Committee
  - New Business Acceptance Committee
  - Administrative Officer for Discretionary Common Trust Funds
- **Statewide:**
  - Chairman Statewide Closely Held Business Committee
- **Other Committees:**
  - New York State Bankers Committee on Fiduciary Income & Estate Taxation

ROBERT W. LASSITER

627 Grand Lake Boulevard • Orlando, Florida 32836 • (407) 876-1886 • Email: Lassiter1@aol.com

Qualified for:

• Conference Services Management •

PROFESSIONAL PROFILE

- Motivated professional with more than 15 years of accomplishments in conference planning, group sales & marketing, banquet services and meeting/travel coordination.
- Dedicated to excellence in customer service and relationships.
- Effective achiever, able to meet all projects within budgetary constraints.
- Eager to learn, meet new challenges and apply new concepts and ideas quickly.
- Flexible team player, always willing to help out wherever and whenever needed.
- Hardworking, loyal and goal-oriented, with strong organizational skills and attention to detail.

AREAS OF EXPERTISE

- Conference Planning
- Catering/Banquet Services
- Customer Service
- Group Presentations
- Written Communications
- Contract Negotiations
- Operations
- Client Relations
- Special Events
- New Business
- Internet & Websites
- Meetings/Workshops
- Transportation & Lodging
- Sales & Marketing
- Trade Shows
- Creative Design
- Problem Solving
- Budgeting
- Microsoft Office Products
- Time Management
- Client/Business Liaison
- Destination Services
- Conventions
- AV Equipment Set-up
- Business Plan
- Travel
- Verbal Communications
- Community Service
- Public Relations
- Database Management
- Promotional Materials
- Office Administration
- Cost Estimation /Proposals

PROFESSIONAL BACKGROUND

CONFERENCE SERVICES

Plan, organize and manage the overall conference services activities which include: evaluating event requirements (resources, manpower & equipment); developing and implementing strategic plans of action; and supervising events to ensure conceptual development goals are achieved on-time and within budget.

- 32% cost savings achieved through negotiating corporate rates for frequent business travelers with area hotels and transportation companies.
- 46% increase above sales rate goals through utilizing quality and value selling techniques.
- 33% increase above predetermined event confirmation goals by developing time-lined incentives through targeted follow-up.
- 10% increase in revenues through up-selling group food and beverage products and events.
- Consistently awarded for "Above Average Performance and Exceeding Sales Goals".
- Awarded "Manager of The Month" as a result of "Dedication to Quality Customer Service".
- Recognized for "Outstanding Event Planning & Coordination" documented by customers, managers and executive committee members.

EXPERIENCE

- Armstrong International Inc..
  Stuart, FL & Orlando, FL
  Director of Corporate Services — Apr 1996 - Oct 1997
  Clients: Florida State University, Mobil, Honeywell & Anheuser Busch.
  Projects: Conference/Meeting Planning (Domestic/International), Incentive Travel Planning (Up to 1200 Travelers), & Business Travel Coordination.
  Liaison: Transportation, Hotels, Airlines.
  Duties: New Site Development & Startup, Internal Travel Guideline Development, Office Administration, Corporate Liaison, Special Events Planning/Coordination (Olympics).

  Westin Hotels & Resorts
  The Westin Regina Resort, Los Cabos
  National Group Sales Manager — Aug 1987 - Apr 1996
  Clients: AT&T, Seagrams, American Express & Maritz BGT.
  Duties: Hotel Pre-Opening, Sales & Marketing, Destination/Facility Promotion, FAM Trips/Travel Coordination.

  The Westin Kauai at Kauai Lagoons Events:
  Conference Services, Sales & Banquet Management
  Group Meetings, Conferences, Banquets, Catering & Special Events.
  Participants: 10 - 1400 (Corporate & Incentive)
  Key Projects: NFL Quarterback Challenge, PGA Grand Slam & Post-Hurricane Strategic Plans.
  Duties: Event Planning/Organization/Coordination, Contract Negotiations, Hotel Liaison, Office Administration, Public Relations/Image Building.

- Princess Cruises Hotels
  Garden Grove, CA
  Banquet Management — Aug 1986 - Aug 1987

- Meridien Hotels
  Newport Beach, CA
  Banquet Management — Jan 1985 - Jul 1986

- Hilton Hotels Corporation
  Kansas City, MO/Los Angeles, CA/Reno, NV
  Banquet Management — Jul 1982 - Jan 1985

- Holiday Inns of America
  Morgan City, LA
  Beverage Management — Oct 1980 - Jul 1982

EDUCATION

- Bachelors Degree Program, Hospitality Management Emphasis, University of Hawaii, Lihue, Kauai
- Certificate in Business Management, University of Michigan, Ann Arbor
- Certified Meeting Professional (CMP), Convention Liaison Council, Completion June 1998

PROFESSIONAL ORGANIZATIONS

- Meeting Professionals International, 1994 - 1998
- Rotary Club International, 1994 - 1998

ROBERT W. LASSITER

MARYBETH CRAMER

365 Burbon Street • Flemington, New Jersey 08822 • (908) 806-8765

Qualified for:

• **Corrections Officer** •

PROFESSIONAL PROFILE

- Motivated professional with more than 5 years of accomplishments in governmental corrections and instruction roles.
- Dependable, always gets the job done on-time.
- Eager to learn, meet new challenges and assimilate new concepts and ideas quickly.
- Hardworking and goal-oriented team player, employing strong organizational skills and attention to detail.
- Loyal and dedicated, demonstrating integrity in achieving goals and objectives.

AREAS OF EXPERTISE

- Federal/State Regulations
- Computer Proficient
- Corrections
- Planning & Organization
- Scheduling
- Auditing
- Public Relations
- Supervision
- Safety Regulations
- Problem Solving
- Labor Relations
- Juvenile/Adult Residents
- Communication Skills
- Training
- First Aid/CPR
- Coaching & Counseling
- Legal Documents
- Logs & Records
- Operations
- Recreational Programs
- Interviewing & Hiring
- Customer Relations
- Monitoring Equipment
- Reports
- Maximum Security
- Policies & Procedures

PROFESSIONAL BACKGROUND

GOVERNMENTAL CORRECTIONS & REHABILITATION

Plan, organize and perform corrections and rehabilitation activities which include: evaluating resident needs; developing and monitoring operational and rehabilitation procedures; and following process to ensure compliance with targeted objectives and governmental regulations.

- 340% increase in productivity through standardizing processing procedures.
- 100% accomplishment of projects on-time through developing a schedule and a plan of action.
- 100% compliance with internal policies & procedures and governmental regulations.
- Awarded for "Outstanding Service and Dedication" for consistently going above and beyond the call of duty.

EXPERIENCE

• County Youth Detention Center, Freehold, NJ	**Juvenile Detention Officer**	Mar 1993 - Present
• NJ Dept. of Labor & Industry, Trenton, NJ	**Principal Audit Account Clerk**	Jul 1988 - Mar 93
	Senior Audit Account Clerk	Sep 1986 - Jul 1988
	Audit Account Clerk	May 1984 - Sep 1986
• Robert Conroy, Attorney at Law, Trenton, NJ	**Assistant Legal Secretary**	Aug 1980 - May 1984

EDUCATION

- **Mercer County Community College,** Accounting & Social Sciences, West Windsor, NJ
- **Correction Officer Training Academy,** Juvenile Detention Officer Basic Training, Skillman, NJ

MELISSA ANN MAYOR

3955 Bay Road East • Kissimmee, Florida 32888 • (407) 246-8394

Qualified for:

- **Customer Service Representative**

PROFESSIONAL PROFILE

- Results-oriented professional employing more than 10 years of progressive accomplishments in insurance and customer service.
- Goal-oriented achiever, demonstrating strong organizational skills and attention to detail.
- Levelheaded service provider, dedicated to excellence in service and relationships.
- Creative problem solver, able to meet challenges and provide effective solutions in a timely manner.
- Enthusiastic self-starter, able to work independently or with groups to achieve common goals.
- Eager to learn, meet new challenges and assimilate new concepts and ideas quickly.

AREAS OF EXPERTISE

- Customer Service
- Insurance
- Customer Relations
- Liaison: Insurance Companies
- Property/Casualty Policies
- Sales
- Personal Lines
- Accounting
- Claims
- MS Windows
- Umbrella/Excess Insurance
- Interpersonal Relations
- AR/AP
- Problem Solving
- PC: IBM
- Specialized PC Programs
- Rating (ISO)

PROFESSIONAL BACKGROUND

CUSTOMER SERVICE

Planned, organized and managed assigned customer service activities for the John A Pierce Insurance Agency which included: assessing client concerns and needs; providing services and solutions; and following process from inception to completion to ensure compliance with client needs and appropriate Division of Insurance regulations.

- 80% increase in productivity through standardizing a problem resolution process in handling customer concerns.
- Recognized for "Excellence in Customer Service" documented by clients and management.
- 100% compliance with insurance regulation in policy development, problem solving and other services provided.

EXPERIENCE

- John A. Pierce Insurance Agency, Inc.
  Winchester, MA
  Customer Service Representative
  Oct 1987 - Mar 1998
  Relocated to Florida
  Customer Service, Billing, Accounting, AP/AR, Customer Relations, Liaison: Insurance Companies for Policy Changes
  Clients: Residential & Commercial.

EDUCATION

- **BS in Business Administration - May 1987,**
  Whittemore School of Business and Economics, University of New Hampshire, Durham, NH
- CIC: Certified Insurance Counselor

CHARLES A. SHELBY

5189 Watercrest Way • Palm Beach, Florida 32909 • (407) 768-3592

Qualified for:

• Journeyman Electrician •

PROFESSIONAL PROFILE

- Results-oriented professional employing more than 15 years of progressive accomplishments as a journeyman electrician, leader, foreman and supervisor.
- Dedicated to excellence in service and relationships.
- Motivated self-starter, able to get the job done on time and within budget.
- Levelheaded team leader, respectful of others and able to work with all types of people.
- Goal-directed team player, able to work independently and in a group setting.
- Flexible, willing to do whatever needs to be done to achieve targeted goals and objectives.

AREAS OF EXPERTISE

- Commercial
- Industrial
- Residential
- Maintenance
- Operations
- Quality Assurance
- New Construction
- Inspections
- Power Distribution Systems
- Troubleshooting
- Service Upgrades
- Rewiring
- Repairs/Wiring
- Lighting
- Installations
- Testing
- Security Systems & Monitoring
- Emergency Power Systems
- Remodeling/Renovations
- Training
- Scheduling
- NEC
- Counseling
- Safety/OSHA/HAZMAT
- Multi-Task Management
- Home Improvements

PROFESSIONAL BACKGROUND

JOURNEYMAN ELECTRICIAN

Plan, organize and manage the overall activities for assigned electrical projects for the Panama Canal which include: evaluating project requirements; providing overhauls, installation and maintenance; and ensuring quality service is provided in accordance with designated standards and organizational objectives.

- 500% increase in productivity through refining operations and troubleshooting non-routine problems, such as machine breakdowns, accidents and unusual operating situations.
- Awarded "Superior Achievement Award" repeatedly for exceeding targeted goals and objectives.
- 100% compliance with NEC/OSHA and organizational goals and objectives through establishing quality controls and time-lined project management.
- Recognized for achieving project goals prior to targeted date while maintaining quality electrical renovations, installations and maintenance services.

EDUCATION

- **Electrician Journeyman Apprenticeship,**
  Panama Canal Company/Canal Zone Government

EXPERIENCE

- Panama Canal Commission

Senior Control House Operator/ Lockmaster — Jan 1989 - Present
Manage & Maintain: Operation & Maintenance of Electrical Controls (Electrical Switching, Remote Control Operations, Power Distribution, Lighting, Flood Control & Fire Protection Systems).

Operations Foreman- Electrical — May 1988 - Jan 1989
Managed: Electricians, Machinists & Other Support Crew.

Control House Operator — Jan 1986 - May 1988
Operation & Maintenance of Electrical Controls (Electrical Switching, Remote Control Operations, Power Distribution, Lighting, Flood Control & Fire Protection Systems).

Electrician Leader — May 1982 - Jan 1986
Crew & Electrical Project Management.

Salvage Diver — Dec 1984 - Present
Lighting Systems Installations on Diving Hoses, Helmets & Barges.

CONTINUING EDUCATION

- **Salvage and Diving Training Course**, Salvage and Diving School
  Panama Canal Commission

- **Continuing Education**: Various Supervisory Management Programs, Leadership, Decision Making, Diving Emergencies and others

Amanda Spitzer

899 Lake Eva Parkway • Apopka, Florida 32712 • (407) 880-2246 • AS9000@aol.com

Qualified In:

• Electronics Manufacturing •

PROFESSIONAL PROFILE

- Dedicated professional employing more than 15 years of progressive accomplishments in systems development, electronics manufacturing and quality assurance.
- Analytical planner, able to take complex and unrelated information and organize it into workable terms.
- Disciplined self-starter with the unique ability to complete projects on-time and within budget.
- Diverse achiever, able to interpret task directions and provide solutions in a timely manner.
- Resourceful problem solver who thrives on pursuing unique methods to attain goals and objectives.

AREAS OF EXPERTISE

- IBM: PC
- Cost Reduction
- Problem Solving
- Manufacture Electronics
- Lotus 1-2-3
- UNIX
- Analysis
- Lotus Notes
- Computer Maintenance
- SPC
- Team Leader
- Policies & Procedures
- Staff Development
- Auditing
- MS Office
- Trouble Shooting
- Interfaces
- Oracle
- Liaison
- C-Shell/K-Shell
- Quality Assurance /TQM
- ISO-9000 Certification
- Operations Management
- WordPerfect
- DOS
- Test & Measurements
- Informix SQL
- Indy Workstations
- Inspections
- HTML Programming

PROFESSIONAL BACKGROUND

ELECTRONICS MANUFACTURING, SYSTEMS DEVELOPMENT & QA

Plan, organize and manage the overall quality assurance, electronics manufacturing and systems development activities for various companies which include: analyzing client/project needs; designing custom product/program/ solution; and delivering a quality product on time and within budget.

Companies: Time Warner; Acer America; MYLEX; Lockheed Martin; National Semiconductor; and Others

- 20% increase in quality products through developing and implementing ISO-9000 Certification procedures.
- 300% increase in cost savings and 15% increase in manufacturing yields through creating incoming inspection processes and procedures.
- Increase in demographic database accuracy through certification of interactive television applications ($700MM Project).
- Recognized for "Excellence in Trouble Shooting and Problem Solving" through spearheading a barcode tracking system resulting in product reliability.

EXPERIENCE

- Time Warner Cable, Maitland, FL — **Senior Certification Analyst** — Jul 1995 - Present
  Debug, Final Certification, Interactive Applications, Problem Solving, Reporting. Liasion, C-Shell/K-Shell Script Writing, Policies & Procedures, HTML Programming.

- MYLEX Corporation, Fremont, CA — **Quality Assurance Manager** — Feb 1994 - Jul 1995
  Certified ISO-9000 Lead Assessor/Auditor
  Staff: 9; Departments: 3;
  TQM, Policies & Procedures, QA Databases, Manufacturing/Test Data, Cost Reduction, Bar Code Tracking, Process Improvement, Inspection, Auditing, Vendor Liaison, Customer Service.

- Special Project, Sunnyvale, CA — **Career Development** — Nov 1992 - Jan 1994

- Acer America, San Jose, CA — **Senior Quality Engineer** — Jun 1984 - Oct 1992
  Quality Reports, Inspection Criteria, Policy & Procedures, Test Equipment Maintenance, SPC Databases, Vendor/ Supplier Liaison, Engineering, Field Service, Customer Service, Analysis.

- Custom MOS Arrays, Inc., Milpitas, CA — **Test Engineer** — Aug 1983 - Jun 1984
  Wrote Programs, Test Vectors, Program Simulation, Set-up & Calibration.

- Geo Reliability Services, Sunnyvale, CA — **Test Maintenance Manager** — Jan 1980 - Aug 1983
  Staff: 3 Engineering Technicians.
  Hiring, Training, Engineering Trouble Shooting, Repairing/Calibrating/Maintaining Computerized Testors/Component Handlers.

EDUCATION

- **Associates Degree in Electrical Engineering,** ITT Technical Institute, Ft. Wayne, Indiana
- **Certified, Computer Programmer,** Lasalle Extension University, Scranton, Pennsylvania
- **Certified ISO-9000 Lead Assessor,** Perry Johnson, San Jose, California

CONTINUING EDUCATION

- **Computer Courses:** UNIX, Oracle, Lotus Notes, Informix SQL
- **Quality Assurance Courses:** ISO-9000, Statistical Process Control

CARLA MILTON

458 Park Drive • Clermont, Florida 32779 • (407) 334-9987

Qualified:

• Quality Engineer •

PROFESSIONAL PROFILE

- Dynamic professional employing more than 15 years of progressive accomplishments in software and hardware quality engineering.
- Results-oriented self-starter, able to achieve all goals and objectives.
- Dependable and dedicated team player demonstrating effective communications skills with diverse populations.
- Enthusiastic team leader, able to plan, organize and complete projects on time and within budget.
- Analytical planner, able to take complex and unrelated information and organize them into workable terms.
- Eager to meet new challenges and assimilate new concepts and ideas quickly.

AREAS OF EXPERTISE

- Quality Assurance
- Audit Preparation
- Troubleshooting
- Mechanical/Electrical Engineering
- MS Office
- Basic
- Part Specifications
- Training
- Customer Relations
- Test Equipment
- Reports
- ADA
- Cobol
- Planning & Organization
- Staffing
- Vendor Liaison
- Policies & Procedures
- DOS
- Fortran
- Multi-Task Management

PROFESSIONAL BACKGROUND

QUALITY ASSURANCE ENGINEERING

Plan, organize and manage the overall assigned Quality Assurance Engineering projects which include: assessing project requirements and designing hardware and software systems; staffing and training to support project requirements; and following projects from inception to completion ensuring compliance with contract standards.

Companies: Lockheed-Martin, Smith Industries, Sperry Univac

- 300% increase in productivity through designing and developing software, hardware and audit systems. (Smith Industries)
- 100% accomplishment of assigned goals and objectives through strategically managing five research and development programs for advanced systems. (Lockheed-Martin)
- 100% compliance with contract specifications to design and integrate hardware and software for a multinational (France, Germany & Great Britain) program through establishing and managing international control procedures.
- 500% improvement in product performance through the development and implementation of a corrective action system for complex target and navigation system.
- 100% accomplishment of project goals for converting and developing a management information system for the U.S. Military Academy on time and within budget. (Sperry)

EXPERIENCE:

- Webster University, Orlando, Florida — **Graduate Student** — Sep 1994 - Oct 1996

- Smiths Industries, Clearwater, FL — **Senior Quality Engineer** — Sep 1991 - Aug 1994
  Established Systems & Audit Department: Designed Software Quality Assurance Program, Configuration Management, Trend Analysis System for Non-Conforming Hardware, Database for Component Control System, Cost of Quality Financial Report and Trainer for Certifying Employees in New Technology.

- Martin Marietta Aerospace, Orlando, FL — **Group Quality Engineer** — Dec 1981 - Sep 1991
  Managed Commercial & Government Projects Ranging from $10MM - $300MM. Contract Financial Requirements, Budgeting & Scheduling. Program Plans, Project Data & Proposal Inputs.

- Sperry Univac, Orlando, FL — **Scientific Programmer** — Feb 1978 - Dec 1981
  Designed, Coded, Tested, Documented Sub-System for Academic Management Information System for U.S. Military Academy.

EDUCATION

- **MA in Business**, Webster University, Orlando, Florida
  Emphasis: Financc

- **BA in Social Sciences,** University of Central Florida, Orlando, Florida

MICHAEL W. O'RILEY

198-C Vista Run • McLean, Virginia 20191 • (703) 850-4112 • oriley@aol.com

Qualified for:

- Software Engineer
- Systems Analyst

PROFESSIONAL PROFILE

- Results-oriented professional with more than 10 years of progressive accomplishments in computer and communications operating systems.
- Hard-working achiever, demonstrating strong organizational skills and attention to detail.
- Flexible, always willing to help out whenever needed.
- Level-headed team player, respectful of others and able to work with all types of people
- Energetic self-starter, able to get the job done on time and within budget.
- Motivated team leader, able to implement workable solutions within diverse situations.

AREAS OF EXPERTISE

- MS Windows NT Server
- MS Windows NT Workstation
- Outlook
- Lotus CC:Mail
- HP Open Mail
- MS Front Page
- Novell Netware
- WINS/DHCP/TCP/IP
- FTP/Telnet/SMTP
- Eicon WAN Services for NT
- MS Exchange
- MS Mail 3.2
- MS Windows 95
- Live Test Demonstration
- Design & Implementation
- Customer Interface
- Assessments & Analyses
- MS Access
- MS Remote Access Service
- MS Word
- Multi-platform Interoperability · MS
- MS Windows 3.11
- MS Lan Manager
- MS Internet Information Server
- Quality Control
- Installation & Configuration
- OSI/X.400

PROFESSIONAL BACKGROUND

COMPUTER/COMMUNICATIONS SYSTEMS MANAGEMENT

Plan, organize and manage the overall technical activities for computer/communications systems which include: evaluating customer/project requirements; developing installation, administration and maintenance programs; and monitoring to ensure compliance with targeted goals and objectives while maintaining quality.

- 45% increase above targeted deadlines through improvement of fast-cycle engineering change proposals.
- 50% increase in productivity through building reusable test plans, increasing hardware and software integration.
- 100% accomplishment of targeted goals and objectives on time and within budget, through developing a strategic plan of action.
- Awarded 10 Achievement Awards for combining technical research and creative promotion, resulting in increased productivity and cost savings.
- Awarded Microsoft Certified Product Specialist, achieved August 20, 1997, for MS Windows NT 4.0.
- Awarded Microsoft Certified Systems Engineer (MCSE) achieved September 19, 1997.

EXPERIENCE

- UNISYS Corporation
  McLean, VA

  Software Engineer,
  Federal Systems Division — Nov 1988 - Present
  Clients: Government (U.S. Coast Guard).
  Projects: Standard Workstation III Team ($187 M).
  Operations, Installations, Configurations, Maintenance, Troubleshooting, Technical Support, Planning, Preparation, Interoperability Research, Compliance Solutions, Live Test Demonstrations.

- Computer Sciences Corporation
  Reston, VA

  Associate Management Analyst,
  Network Control Center — Dec 1986 - Nov 1988
  Clients: U.S. Government.
  Projects: Data Base Management, Quality Control, Network Analysis, Provide Status Reports, System Design & Implementation, Programming, Daily Customer Interface, Inter-departmental Liaison.

- AT&T/Sparks Personnel
  Reston, VA

  Programmer/Data Entry — Jul 1986 - Dec 1986
  Technical Documentation, Hardware/Software Installation, Data Base Analysis.

EDUCATION

- Bachelors Program, Park College, Arlington, VA
  Major: Computer Science & Management/Computer Information Systems
- Microsoft Certified Product Specialist - Professional ID #11220
- Microsoft Certification Exams (All Successfully Completed)
- Networking Essentials - Aug 5, 1997
- Implementing & Supporting NT 4.0 Workstation - Aug 20, 1997
- Implementing & Supporting NT 4.0 Server - Aug 28, 1997
- Implementing & Supporting NT 4.0 Server in the Enterprise - Sep 12, 1997
- Internetworking with TCP/IP on Windows NT 4.0 - Sep 18, 1997
- Implementing and Supporting Exchange Server 5.0 - Sep 19, 1997

CONTINUING EDUCATION CONFERENCES

- Microsoft Exchange Developers Conference, 1996
- Microsoft Exchange Deployment Conference, 1996
- Microsoft Access/Visual Basic Developers Conference, 1996

MICHAEL W. O'RILEY

TIMOTHY RALSTON

989 South Lake Way • Orlando, Florida 32821 • (407) 445-1254

Qualified in Engineering:

- Waste Water Treatment • Water Resources Engineering • Hydrology • Geohydrology

PROFESSIONAL PROFILE

- Goal-oriented professional employing more than 9 years of progressive accomplishments in research and engineering.
- Analytical planner, able to take complex and unrelated information and organize them into workable terms.
- Creative and open-minded; offers outstanding growth potential in any capacity.
- Eager to learn, meet new challenges, assimilate new concepts and ideas quickly.
- Diverse achiever able to interpret task directions and provide solutions in a timely manner.
- Resourceful and creative team player, with the ability to pursue unique methods for attaining goals and objectives.

AREAS OF EXPERTISE

- Hydrology
- Processing Modflow
- Matlab
- Dos
- Seismic Surveying
- Geostatistics/Kriging
- Water Quality
- Supervision
- Geohydrology
- PC: IBM/Mac
- UNIX
- Spanish
- Sonic Well Logging
- Watershed Runoff
- Problem Solving
- Waste Water Treatment
- MS Office
- VAX
- Mathematical Analysis
- Field Engineering
- Statistical Analysis
- Interpersonal Relations
- RO Desalinization

PROFESSIONAL BACKGROUND

ENGINEERING

Plan, organize and manage the overall engineering activities which include: identifying and analyzing project needs; developing creative strategies and solutions; and ensuring established standards are met.

- 89% increase in test reliability through filtering and streamlining the data into a computerized program.
- 100% accomplishment of targeted goals and objectives.
- Recognized for "Hard work and Dedication" by management.
- Recognized for "Visionary Excellence" for thesis project solving the solution to particle movement within a fluid of unsteady and non-homogenous velocity.

EXPERIENCE

- EnviroTech Inc., Orlando, FL — **Systems Analyst**, Research & Development — Apr 1997 - Present
- Johns Hopkins University, Laurel, MD — **Systems Analyst** — Jun 1989 - Apr 1997

EDUCATION

- **Master of Engineering, in Civil and Environmental Engineering, University of California,** Berkeley, California
  Emphasis: Environmental Water Resources Engineering and Environmental Engineering
- **Master of Science in Electrical Engineering, Boston University,** Boston, Massachusetts
  Emphasis: Communication & Control Systems
- **Bachelor of Science in Systems Science & Engineering, Washington University,** St. Louis, Missouri

Morris E. Entemons

870 Drake Road • Melbourne, Florida 33399 • (407) 887-5544

Job Objective:

- Production/Graphic Artist
- Computer Drafting/Design

PROFESSIONAL PROFILE

- Enthusiastic recent graduate with over 2 years of progressive experience in desktop publishing.
- Results-oriented innovator, exhibiting focused planning and attention to detail.
- Flexible team player, always willing to help out wherever needed.
- Resourceful and creative self-starter who pursues unique methods to attaining goals and objectives.
- Dependable achiever, always gets the job done.
- Dedicated to excellence in service and relationships.

AREAS OF EXPERTISE

• Customer Service	• Macromedia Freehand	• AutoCad
• MS Excel	• Problem Solving	• Video Editor
• Print Production	• PageMaker	• QuarkXPress
• Creative Designs	• MS Word	• ClarisWorks
• Planning & Organization	• Quicken	• FormZ
• Adobe Illustrator	• Adobe Photoshop	• MacroMedia Director
• KPT Bryce	• ElectricImage	• Desktop Publishing
• Fractal Design Painter	• Electronic PrePress	• Adobe Premiere

PROFESSIONAL BACKGROUND

DESKTOP PUBLISHING & COMPUTER GRAPHIC DESIGN

Plan, organize and manage the assigned design activities for various companies which included: evaluating customer/ project needs; developing creative design strategies; and following project from inception to completion to ensure customer satisfaction.

- 500% increase in productivity through developing a results-oriented procedure for locating graphics files.
- 100% compliance with targeted goals and objectives through developing a strategic plan of action.
- 120% increase in client base through developing a "customer-centered" computer training approach.

EXPERIENCE

• Halloran & Associates	Graphics Designer	Feb 1997 - Present
• Kal Graphic Studios Inc.	**Desktop Publisher**	Sep 1996 - Jan 1997

EXPERIENCE WHILE WORKING IN SCHOOL

• GraphLine	**Internship**	Mar 1996 - Apr 1996
• Kinko's	**Desktop Publisher**	Jul 1995 - Oct 1995
• Pizza Hut	**Customer Service**	Feb 1993 - Apr 1993

EDUCATION

- **Associate of Fine Arts in Computer Graphics**, International Fine Arts College, Miami, Florida
  Emphasis: Animation, Desktop Publishing, Multi Media
- **Associate of Applied Science in Drafting & Design Technology,** Clark State Community College
  Certificate: Computer Aided Design & Emphasis on Drafting, Technical Illustration
- **Mechanical Engineering**, University of Dayton, Dayton, Ohio

Brent D. Parze

249 Pinto Lane • Orlando, Florida 32801 • (407) 877-6031 • bdp@aol.com

Qualified For:

- **Technical Support**
- **Database Administration**
- **Software Support**

PROFESSIONAL PROFILE

- Dedicated professional employing more than 3 years of progressive accomplishments in database systems and customer service/support.
- Resourceful problem-solver who thrives on translating complex and unrelated information into workable solutions.
- Creative and open-minded, offering outstanding growth potential in any capacity.
- Eager to learn, meet new challenges and assimilate new concepts and ideas quickly.
- Flexible, always willing to help out wherever needed.
- Results-oriented achiever, able to accomplish all goals and objectives.

AREAS OF EXPERTISE

- Database Management
- Analysis
- Windows NT
- Database Tuning
- Liaison
- Technical Support
- Planning & Organization
- Oral Communication
- Problem Solving
- Workstations
- Written Communication
- Replicated Environments
- Interpersonal Relations
- Installation/Maintenance
- Training & Education
- Customer Service
- Oracle Database
- UNIX
- Backup/Recovery
- Troubleshooting
- Conflict Resolution
- Research
- SQL/SQL* Plus
- Security/Access

PROFESSIONAL BACKGROUND

COMPUTER DATABASE ADMINISTRATION

Plan, organize and manage the overall computer database administration activities which include: evaluating client/project requirements; developing creative solutions and support strategies; and following client/project from inception to completion to ensure quality service.

- 100% increase above targeted goals through researching client needs and developing creative support strategies for Technical Assistance Requests.
- 77% increase above targeted productivity levels through actively monitoring call volume and utilizing a client-centered work ethic.
- Recognized for "Dedication and Commitment to Outstanding Customer Support" documented by managers and clients.
- Awarded "Oracle's Peer Recognition Award for Outstanding Work Ethic".

EXPERIENCE

• Oracle Corp. - Orlando,	**Associate Technical Analyst**	Jun 1996 - Present
• BancTec Service Corp.	**Technical Assistant**	Dec 1995 - Jun 1996
• University of Florida	**CIS Consultant**	Jan 1994 - Aug 1995

EDUCATION

- **Bachelor of Science in Materials Science and Engineering,** University of Florida, Gainesville, FL

CONTINUING EDUCATION

- Introduction to Oracle: SQL and PL/SQL
- Administering Oracle7 Database I
- Windows NT Administration
- Advanced SQL & SQL* Plus
- Database Backup & Recovery
- Windows NT Core Technologies

RANDY RUTHERFORD

444 Halston Road • Hempstead, NY 11550 • (516) 489-5534

Career Objective:

• Graphic Designer • Mac Operator • Production Artist

PROFESSIONAL PROFILE

- Motivated professional with more than 4 years of accomplishments in all facets of graphic design.
- Creative and resourceful in meeting goals and objectives.
- Flexible, always willing to help out wherever needed.
- Loyal and dedicated team player, with strong organizational skills and attention to detail.
- Deadline-oriented, able to plan, organize and complete projects on-time.

AREAS OF EXPERTISE

- Advertising Strategies
- Presentations
- Word Perfect
- Illustrator
- ClarisWorks
- Advertisements
- Fine Arts
- Client Relations
- Layout
- Photography
- Graphics
- Editing
- Pagemaker
- Photoshop
- Scanning
- Color/Photo Copiers
- Paste Up
- Newsletters
- Brochures
- Agency Liaison
- Macintosh Proficient
- Training
- QuarkXPress
- Internet/WWW
- Pre-Press
- Research
- Comps
- Publications
- Package Design
- Commercial Art

PROFESSIONAL BACKGROUND

GRAPHIC DESIGN

Plan, organize and manage the overall graphic design activities which include: evaluating client/project needs; developing innovative designs and support strategies; and monitoring projects to ensure compliance with targeted objectives and deadlines.

- 100% accomplishment of assigned projects on-time through effectively planning, organizing and prioritizing events.
- Recognized for "Outstanding Talent, Creative Design, Reliability and Hard Work" documented by managers and clients.
- Increased revenues for various companies through researching trends and developing creative advertising strategies.

EXPERIENCE

- The Ad Team - N. Miami, FL — **Mac/Production Artist** — Sep 1996 - Jan 1998
- Innovation - Franklin Square, NY — **Advertising Coordinator** — Oct 1995 - Aug 1996
- Telegraphics International - N. Miami, FL — **Computer Graphics Intern** — Mar 1995
- Miami Jewish Tribune - Miami, FL — **Production Artist** — Sep 1993 - Feb 1994
- Other Freelance Experience includes Crispin & Porter Advertising, Tropical Tribune Magazine, Coconut Grover Newspaper, New Millennium Associates, Richner Publications & Vanguard Graphics.

EDUCATION

- **Associates Degree in Computer Graphics & Commercial Art (Dual Degree),** International Fine Arts College - Miami, Florida
- Continuing Education:
  - **QuarkXPress Certificate,** The Center for Desktop Publishing, Garden City, NY
  - **Advertising Art Certificate,** Nassau Community College, Garden City, NY

DAVID W. GREGORY, JR.

137 East Unis Street • Milwaukee, Wisconsin 53207 • (414) 744-1038

Qualified for:

• **Group Vice President** •

PROFESSIONAL PROFILE

- Performance-driven professional employing more than 7 years of progressive accomplishments in healthcare operations management and project administration.
- Diplomatic leader, employing strong communication skills to motivate diverse populations.
- Effective achiever, able to meet all goals while staying within budgetary constraints.
- Motivated self-starter, exhibiting high ethics, competence and confidence, underscored by a personal commitment to outstanding professional performance.
- Poised innovator with strong people skills and leadership ability.
- Respected team builder, able to empower others toward common goals.

AREAS OF EXPERTISE

- PPS Knowledgeable
- Team Building
- Quality Assurance/CQI
- Corporate Compliance
- Survey Readiness
- Presentations/Seminars
- Staff Development
- Sub-Acute/Post-Acute
- Computer Literate
- HCFA & State Regulations
- Patient Services
- Planning & Organization
- Systems Development
- Cost Control
- Marketing/Advertising
- Business Plans
- Problem Solving
- Community Liaison
- Creative Strategies
- RUGS/Case Mix Management
- Budgeting/Financial Controls
- Customer Service
- Project Management
- Policies & Procedures
- Negotiations
- Operations
- Public/Patient Relations
- Medicare/Managed Care/ Medicaid

PROFESSIONAL BACKGROUND

HEALTHCARE ADMINISTRATION/OPERATIONS

Plan, organize and manage the overall healthcare administration/operations activities for various facilities which include: identifying facility/resident needs; trouble shooting programs and developing operational strategies; and monitoring activities to ensure targeted goals and objectives are accomplished and are in compliance with federal/state/local regulations.

- 350% increase in profitability in one year through researching and enhancing ancillary services resulting in increased patients/residents while maintaining quality care.
- 50% cost savings through eliminating outside employment agency and actively recruiting for in-house staff.
- 25% increase in cost containment through researching and developing a computerized cost control process.
- 200% increase in revenues through strategic trouble shooting of internal improvements (ancillary programs and cost controls) also resulting in improved public relations.
- Awarded Superior Rating for Quality Healthcare for 100% compliance with regulations.
- Recognized for "Outstanding Leadership and Business Development" for implementing employee-centered training programs resulting in increased census and increased employee retention.
- Awarded for creating "City Sidewalks", a simulated outdoor environment indoors, assisting patients with rehabilitation to re-enter society.

EXPERIENCE

- Adventist Health Care Centers, Orlando, FL — **Administrator, Florida Living Center** — Jul 1997 - Present
  Budget: $14.5MM Annually;
  Employees: 250; Beds: 224;
  Patients: Subacute, Long-Term & Assisted Living;
  Therapy Programs: PT/OT, Speech, Respirator, Cardiac Rehab, CVA Rehab, Pain Management, Wound Care; Rehab Discharges per Month: 90%.
  Total Facility Operations (Therapy, Nursing, Admission, Social Services, Dietary & Environmental Services): Budgeting (P&L), Forecasting, Superior Program, Staff Development, Marketing, Public Relations, Community Liaison, Labor/Supply/Productivity Tracking.

  Covington, KY — **Administrator, SJHCC** — Jun 1996 - Jun 1997
  Budget: $22MM Annually;
  Employees: 450; Beds: 390 (64 Medicare);
  Patients: Long-Term & Subacute;
  Therapy Programs: Basic;
  Rehab Discharges per Month: 15%;

- GranCare Inc., Christopher East, Milwaukee, WI — **Executive Director** — May 1994 - May 1996
  Budget: $20MM Annually;
  Employees: 250; Beds: 308 (62 Medicare);
  Patients: Long-Term & Subacute;
  Therapy Programs: Advanced;
  Rehab Discharges per Month: 20%.

  Executive Director — Apr 1993 - Apr 1994
  Renaissance Health & Rehab - Milwaukee, WI
  Budget: $14MM Annually;
  Employees: 180; Beds: 174;
  Patients: Long-Term;
  Therapy Programs: Basic.

  Lancaster Healthcare Center, Lancaster, CA — **Associate Administrator** — Sep 1992 - Mar 1993
  Employees: 110; Beds: 99 (23 Subacute);
  Patients: Long-Term & Subacute;
  Therapy Programs: Advanced.

  Administrator in Training — Sep 1991 - Sep 1992

EDUCATION

- **Bachelor of Business Administration in Business Management**
  Southwestern Adventist University, Keene, Texas
- **Licensed Nursing Home Administrator,** Wisconsin, California, Kentucky and Florida
- **Continuing Education:** CEU Courses in Advanced Medicare/Managed Care, Clinical, CQI and Other Health-Related Seminars

PROFESSIONAL AFFILIATIONS

- American College of Healthcare Administrators (ACHCA)
- Alzheimer's Association
- Committee on Aging

DAVID W. GREGORY, JR.

KELLY BRANSON

165 Mason Boulevard • Palm Beach, FL 33418 • (561) 753-1234

Career Objective:

• Health Services Administration •

PROFESSIONAL PROFILE

- Hardworking recent graduate with more than 2 years of accomplishments in health services.
- Dependable and dedicated individual, employing strong communication skills with diverse groups.
- Loyal team player, demonstrating integrity in achieving goals and objectives.
- Conscientious and goal-oriented, with solid organizational skills and attention to detail.
- Motivated self-starter, able to plan, organize and complete projects on-time.

SKILL AREAS

- Health Services
- Patient Care
- Home Health Care
- Medical Manager
- Problem Solving
- Lotus 1-2-3
- Team Building
- Medical Charts
- Insurances
- Laws & Regulations
- Patient Relations
- Medical Records
- Medicare
- MS Office
- Hospital Referrals
- Special Projects
- Scheduling
- Confidentiality
- Finance
- Business Operations
- First Aid/CPR
- Medical Products
- Email/Internet
- Word Perfect
- Supervision
- Consult-A-Nurse
- X-rays & Labs
- Physician/Clinic/ Pharmacy Liaison

PROFESSIONAL BACKGROUND

HEALTH SERVICES

Plan, organize and complete the assigned health service duties which include: evaluating center/patient needs; coordinating support strategies; and monitoring process to ensure compliance with targeted goals and health standards.

- 45% increase in productivity through maximizing manpower abilities while maintaining quality patient care.
- 100% compliance with patient confidentiality, OSHA/Safety and other health standards.
- 100% accomplishment of targeted clinic goals on-time (while undergoing construction and reorganization) through "stepping up" and increasing personal responsibility.
- Recognized for "Outstanding Dedication and Motivation" for "Demonstrating a conscientious work ethic" as documented by managers, physicians and center directors.

EXPERIENCE

- Student Health Center
  University of Central Florida
  Orlando, FL
  Medical Records Night Supervisor Aug 1997 - Present
  Medical Records Assistant & Immunizations Clerk Oct 1995 - Present

EDUCATION

- **Bachelor Science Degree in Health Service Administration (Computer Science Minor),** University of Central Florida - Orlando, Florida - May 1998
  - American College of Health Care Executives, VP of Communication
  - Volunteer: American Heart Association & Second Harvest Food Bank

JASON WILSON

515 Cedar Place • Allentown, Idaho 87504 • (987) 333-3333

Job Objective:

- Security
- Sales

PROFILE

- Dynamic student with over 4 years of progressive experience in providing excellent customer service and sales.
- Eager to learn, meet new challenges and do whatever needs to be done.
- Dedicated to excellence in customer service.
- Enthusiastic, positive attitude and dependable.

SKILLS

- Customer Service
- Sales
- Medical Skills
- Security Officer
- Territory Management
- Problem Solving
- First Aid/CPR
- Leadership
- Reports
- PC:IBM/MAC
- Customer Relations
- Team Player
- Liaison: Police

EXPERIENCE

• GLSS	**Security Officer/Sales**	Jun 1998 - Present
• Allentown Springs Mall	**Security Officer**	Aug 1998 - Sep 1998
• Sears	**Sales Associate**	Sep 1996 - Dec 1996
• Burlington Coats	**Sales Associate**	Jul 1996 - Oct 1996
• Retirement Home	**Server,** Dining Hall	Jan 1996 - Jul 1996
• AllentownDry Cleaners	**Clerk**	Sep 1994 - Oct 1995
• Lawn Service	**Self-Employed**	Jun 1991 - Aug 1994

ACCOMPLISHMENTS

- Most Distinguished Fire Explorer - Idaho1996-97
- Selected to go to Olympics - Kayak Water Rescue Team, Ocoee, Tennessee - Summer 1996 - as part of Medical Rescue Team
- Placed First in Sales - Specialty Exercise Equipment & Sporting Goods.

EDUCATION

- **Allentown High School Student**
  - WrestlingTeam
- **Allentown Fire Department** - President, Fire Rescue Explorers
  - FA/CPR
  - Water Rescue
  - Extensive Anatomy/Physiology Knowledge & Skills
- **Naval ROTC**
  - Navigations & Naval Sciences
- **Civil Air Patrol** - Leadership - Search & Rescue

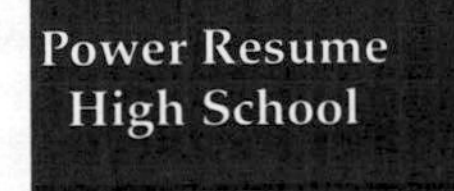

ROBERT BRAY

3226 Mango Boulevard • Orlando, Florida 32822 • (407) 345-2694 • RBBray@aol.com

Qualified for:

• **Hotel Manager** •

PROFESSIONAL PROFILE

- Motivated professional with 5 years of progressive accomplishments in the hospitality industry.
- Creative promoter, able to work independently or in a group setting.
- Disciplined self-starter, with the unique ability to comprehend complex, unrelated information and digest it into workable terms.
- Loyal and dedicated team player, demonstrating integrity in achieving all goals and objectives.
- Personable communicator, exhibiting the ability to make clients happy.

AREAS OF EXPERTISE

- Hospitality
- Front Office Operations
- Customer Service
- Quality Assurance
- Training & Support
- Reports/Statistics
- Oral Communications
- Lotus Smart Suite
- Staff Development
- Food & Beverage
- Tourism/Attractions
- Multi-Task Management
- Travel
- Computer Systems
- Special Events
- Written Communications
- Inventory Control
- Problem Solving
- Guest Relations
- Referral Programs
- Planning & Organization
- Scheduling
- Project Coordination
- Computer Systems
- MS Office
- Technical Training
- Operations Management

PROFESSIONAL BACKGROUND

HOSPITALITY MANAGEMENT

Plan, organize and manage assigned hospitality services which include: evaluating operational requirements (manpower, equipment and resources); providing training, supervision and solutions; and ensuring quality services are provided in compliance with corporate goals and objectives.

- Awarded by management and staff for "Excellence in Training, Mentoring & Team Building".
- 98% occupancy level achieved by developing a "client-focused" marketing and service approach.
- 150% increase in front desk productivity through streamlining process while enhancing quality through "hands-on" supervision and workflow analysis.
- Recognized for "Outstanding Performance" for balanced cash handling and customer service.

EXPERIENCE

- **The Orlando Hilton Hotel** — **Front Desk/Towers Manager** — Mar 1997 - Present
  Rooms: 580. Supervised: 25.
- **Walt Disney World Resort** — **Hospitality/Guest Services** — Feb 1993 - Mar 1997
  - Disney All-Star Resorts — **Front Desk Supervisor** — (3/94 - 3/97)
    Rooms: 790. Supervised: 12.
  - Caribbean Beach Resort — **Food & Beverage Host** — (3/93 - 3/94)

EDUCATION

- **Bachelors Degree in Restaurant, Hotel and Institutional Management** - December 1993
  Texas Tech University, Lubbock, Texas
- **Disney Internship Program**

Rachel M. Rothchild

6771 Wilson Boulevard • Gainesville, Florida 32607 • (352) 380-9869 • RRothchild@ncr.net

Qualified for:

• **Human Resources Manager** •

PROFESSIONAL PROFILE

- Results-oriented professional with more than 15 years of progressive accomplishments in human resources, employee relations, organizational development and training.
- Energetic self-starter, possessing strong personal and business ethics and a "whatever it takes" attitude.
- Focused motivator, with strong interpersonal and leadership skills.
- Team player able to plan, organize and complete projects on time and within budget.
- Dependable team leader, demonstrating effective communications skills with diverse groups.
- Resourceful project manager, able to see the "big picture" and provide cost-effective solutions to achieve short and long-term objectives.

AREAS OF EXPERTISE

- HR Management
- Performance Systems
- Job Descriptions
- Employee Relations
- Strategic Planning
- Assessments & Analysis
- Operational Liaison
- Change Management
- Employement Law
- HR Systems
- Training
- Policies & Procedures
- Employee Assistance
- Staff Development
- Team Building
- Succession Planning
- Group Facilitation
- Project Management
- HR Compliance
- Organizational Development
- Employment Services
- Multi-Task Management
- Recruiting & Hiring
- Coaching & Counseling
- SOP Writing
- Curriculum Development
- Benefits & Compensation

PROFESSIONAL BACKGROUND

HUMAN RESOURCE MANAGEMENT

Plan, organize and manage human resources, organization development and training responsibilities/projects by integrating business goals with human resources solutions.

Industries: Health Care, Financial Services, Transportation, Energy, Public Utilities, Educational Institutions, Retail, Engineering, Construction, Professional Organizations and others.

- 37% increase in productivity through developing innovative "results-oriented" team building and training processes, resulting in the highest level of technical competency and quality. (Chevron)
- $1.4 million cost savings by improving work processes during privitization. (Texas Public Utility)
- 89% increase in staff retention through targeting qualified candidates and using performance models and systems for career matching/planning. (Florida Hospital System)
- Recognized for "Professional Excellence" by national human resource and training organizations. (SHRM & ASTD)
- 35% increase in productivity by developing an integrated system of strategic planning, performance management, coaching/counseling and evaluation. (First Union Bank)
- Awarded "Woman of the Year" by the 10,000 member professional society. (Dallas Chamber)

EXPERIENCE

- Eagle Group, Dallas, TX — **HR Management Consultant** — Jan 1994 - Present
  Employees: 200. Staff: 35 Consultants.
  Clients: Chevron, Shell, Caltex,
  Texas Commerce Bank, MW Kellogg,
  Orlando Healthcare, Coulter Electronics,
  Texas A&M, HCM Transit Authority,
  JC Penney's Department Store & Others.
  Managed: All Aspects of HR Consulting
  (Training, Performance Improvement Measures,
  Organizational Development & HR Management).
  • 85% increase in employee retention.
  • $250K average cost savings per client.

- Bechtel Engineering, Dallas, TX — **Training & Organizational Development Manager** — Mar 1987 - Jan 1994
  Employees: 3,500. Staff: 8.
  Training Programs: Train-the-Trainer,
  Change Management, Consultative Sales,
  Customer Service, TQM, Process Improvements,
  Executive/Leadership Development & Team Building.
  Managed: Rebuilding of Training Function
  Within Matrix Organization, Training &
  Leadership Program Development,
  Staff Development & Direction.
  • 140% increase in departmental revenues.
  • Promoted from HR Administrator.

- SE Banking Corporation, Miami, FL — **Corporate Training & Organizational Development** — Feb 1973 - Mar 1987
  Employees: 7,500. Staff: 10.
  Facilities: 75 Banks & 13 Other Companies.
  Managed: Overall Corporate Training &
  Organization Development Functions,
  Operations Liaision Projects, Sucession Planning,
  Curriculum Development, National Presentations
  & Change Management Systems.
  • 98% increase in training retention and quality.
  • 25% cost savings achieved annually.

EDUCATION

- **Bachelors Degree in Education, Major in English**
  University of Tulsa - Tulsa, Oklahoma

- **Continuing Education & Professional Development:**
  - Leadership Development
  - Total Quality Management
  - Simulated Education
  - Train-the-Trainer
  - Change Management
  - Management Training
  - Sales & Customer Service
  - Psychological Assessments

MEMBERSHIPS

- American Society for Training and Development
- Society for Human Resource Management

RACHEL M. ROTHCHILD

MARGARET A. GREEN

4696 Pershing Drive West • Orlando, Florida 32839 • (407) 888-8126

Qualified for:

- **Insurance Adjuster**
- **Insurance Claims**

PROFESSIONAL PROFILE

- Ambitious professional with more than 3 years of experience in the insurance industry.
- Dedicated problem solver, who thinks logically, values creativity and cares about people.
- Hardworking and goal-oriented, employing strong organizational skills and attention to detail.
- Eager to learn, meet new challenges and assimilate new concepts and ideas quickly.
- Effective listener and communicator, able to create a good rapport with clients and associates.

AREAS OF SKILL & KNOWLEDGE

- Insurance Claims
- Liability Claims
- Legal Documentation
- Coverages
- Customer Service
- Conflict Resolution
- Multi-Faceted Tasks
- Time Management
- Policies & Procedures
- First Reports
- Auto Claims
- Payout & Denial
- Liaison
- Quality Assurance
- Team Player
- Client Relations
- Travel
- All Lines 620 License
- Home Owners/Catastrophe
- Case Management
- Research
- Problem Solving
- Verifications
- Training
- Planning & Organization
- Scheduling

PROFESSIONAL BACKGROUND

INSURANCE

Plan, organize and complete the overall insurance activities which include: determining insured/insurer needs; researching claims and providing support services and solutions; and monitoring and documenting process to comply with industry standards.

- Awarded for "Outstanding Productivity and Accuracy" in processing insurance claims.
- 60% increase in efficiency by researching problems and offering creative solutions.
- Recognized and promoted for "being a creative problem-solver and hardworking team leader".

EXPERIENCE WHILE IN SCHOOL

- Travelers Insurance Company, Orlando, FL — **Customer Service Representative** — Sep 1995 - Present
  Lines: Personal, Commercial & Specialty. (Auto, Homeowners, Liability, Workers Comp, Disability & Property).
- Ryan Reporting , Orlando, FL — **Court Reporter** — Sep 1993 - Aug 1995
- Hyatt Regency, Orlando, FL — **Customer Service** — Jul 1992 - Aug 1993

EDUCATION

- **Adjustor's License, All Lines,** State of Florida #576355058 - January 1998
- **Bachelors Degree Program,** Florida Metropolitan University, Orlando, Florida
- **AA in Court Reporting,** Orlando College, Orlando, Florida
- **Continuing Education:** Jewelry Claim Training & Customer Service Courses

MALCOLM R. RAND, MS, CVE

2984 Harcourt Drive, Heathrow, Florida 32729 • (407) 332-9876

Qualified for:

- **Insurance Consultant**
- **Case Management**

PROFESSIONAL PROFILE

- Creative professional employing more than 15 years of progressive accomplishments in case management and education in a psychiatric and medical format.
- Dependable and dedicated team player, employing strong communication skills with diverse populations.
- Levelheaded and mature advisor, respectful of others and able to work with all types of people.
- Diverse achiever, able to interpret task directions and provide solutions in a timely manner.
- Resourceful and creative in pursuing unique methods to attain goals and objectives.

AREAS OF EXPERTISE

- Case Management
- Staff Development
- Training
- Medical Claims
- Education
- Counseling
- Risk Management
- Academic Education
- Team Leader
- Problem Solving
- Computer Proficient
- Evaluation & Assessment
- Psychiatric Medications
- Seminars/Presentations
- Rehabilitation Services
- Program Development
- Creative Strategies
- Research
- Psychiatric Diagnosis
- Cost Control
- Insurance Liaison
- Severity Analysis (Medical/Psychiatric)

PROFESSIONAL BACKGROUND

CASE MANAGEMENT

Plan, organize and manage the overall case management activities which include: assessing client needs; researching and developing support services and solutions; and monitoring process from inception to completion to ensure compliance with targeted goals and objectives.

- $1 Million annual cost savings achieved through researching and evaluating the severity of psychiatric/medical claims.
- 100% compliance with insurance policy provisions, insured confidentiality protection and medical guidelines.
- 70% increase in insured return to work status through actively liaisoning with medical providers.
- Recognized for "Hard Work and Innovative Program Development" for creating guidelines and direction, resulting in increased accuracy of pertinent medical information for claims resolution.
- Recognized by Yale University's Research Team and neuropsychologists for developing policy and procedure guidelines of medical/psychiatric conditions, using criteria to validate diagnosis, in effort to rate the severity and monitor the length of disability.
- Awarded for training nurses, physicians, and insurance personnel on the methodology of gathering medical information for assessment/claims handling purposes.

EDUCATION

- **MS in Counseling Psychology,** University of Central Florida, Orlando, Florida
- **BA in Psychology & Sociology,** University of Emporia, Emporia, Kansas
- **Continuing Education Seminars:** Psychiatric Medicine, Borderline Personality Disorder, Rehabilitation & Vocational Evaluation Techniques

EXPERIENCE

- Patient Care Systems, Chicago, IL — **Manager** — Jan 1996 - Present
  Staff: 15;
  Liaison: Physicians, Insurance & Attorneys;
  Duties: Program Development, Training, Staffing, Employee Evaluation & Counseling

- CNA Insurance Companies, Chicago, IL — **Case Manager Consultant** — Jan 1990 - Dec 1995
  Caseload: High Indemnity Claims ($10K Monthly);
  Claims: Psychiatric & Medical (Esoteric);
  Liaison: Physician, Psychiatrist & Psychologist;
  Duties: Program & Training Module Development, Rehabilitation Services Coordination, Claims & Appeal Resolution Team, Cost Control, Reporting, Research, Diagnosis & Treatment Review.

- HealthPlansCo, Orlando, FL — **Case Manager** — Jan 1985 - Dec 1989
  Caseload: 50; Claims: Workers Compensation;
  Liaison: Physician, Insured, Attorneys & Potential Employers;
  Duties: Vocational Rehabilitation (Limitation Assessment & Medical/Psychiatric Evaluations), Job Skills Training, Psychiatric Disability Training Seminars.

- NATLSCO, Orlando, FL — **Case Manager** — Jan 1983 - Dec 1984
  Same As Above.

- Mars Mental Health Center, Orlando, FL — **Therapist** — Mar 1980 - Jan 1983
  Caseload: 30, Ages: 14-65 (Mental Disorders);
  Liaison: Patient, Family, Department of Corrections, School Systems & Psychiatrist;
  Duties: Intake Evaluations, Treatment Plans, Group Therapy Facilitator.

RESEARCH EXPERIENCE

- University of Illinois, Champaign, IL — **Child Development Research**

CERTIFICATIONS

- **Certified Vocational Evaluator**
- **NCS MMPI 2 Certified** - Psychological Testing - A Qualification
- **NCS Millon Clinical Multiaxial Inventory III Certified** - Psychological Testing

MARLIN J. SANDFORD

298 Country Club Lane • Heathrow, Florida 32752 • (407) 324-6698

Objective:

• DIRECTOR OF INSURANCE SALES •

PROFESSIONAL PROFILE

- Goal-directed professional employing more than 15 years of progressive accomplishments in the insurance industry.
- Self-directed, confident initiator with the ability to motivate others to achieve/exceed common goals.
- Highly energetic and ambitious; able to accomplish tasks on time and within budget.
- Goal-oriented team leader, employing strong organizational and leadership skills.
- Proactive manager, able to assimilate new concepts and ideas quickly and create "results-oriented" projects.

AREAS OF EXPERTISE

- Market Penetration
- Budgeting
- Recruiting
- Sales
- Restructuring
- Multi-Task Management
- Sales Management
- Key Accounts
- Training
- Planning & Organization
- Territory Development
- Direct Marketing
- Advertising
- Intangible Products
- Strategic Planning
- Presentations
- Team Building
- Field Management
- Regulatory/Compliance
- Customer Relations
- Product Marketing

PROFESSIONAL BACKGROUND

MANAGEMENT

Plan, organize and manage the overall operations, marketing and sales activities for various companies which include: assessing and evaluating corporate goals and objectives; developing plans and strategies; and monitoring progress to ensure compliance with corporate objectives.

Clients: 20+ Trade Associations (Home Builders, General Contractors, Municipalities, United Businesses, Automobile Franchise Dealers, Petroleum Marketers and others)

- 1600% increase in revenues annually over a six year period through developing new territories (7 states) and team players to promote product and services.
- 650% increase in new premium volume for out of state affiliate through creating a wholesale distribution network.
- Ranked "Top Salesman" for $9 million in sales for new fund through strategically identifying market and creating innovative "results-oriented" presentations.
- Ranked #1 for achieving $3 million in direct sales in first four months of the year through establishing a new trust account for an existing association.
- 100% accomplishment of Special Assignment which resulted in increasing Corporate Image through developing a "goal-directed" advertising campaign involving seminars, marketing materials and media presentations in trade publications.
- Recognized for "Excellence in Marketing" for conducting marketing survey which resulted in revamping product line and increasing profitability.

EXPERIENCE:

- AAG, Longwood, FL — **Director of Sales** — Oct 1998 - Present
  Developing & Directing Florida & Tennessee Sales & Marketing Activities.
- Associated Commerce Insurance Corporation, Boca Raton, FL — **Vice President, Marketing** — May 1996 - Sep 1998
  $10MM Increase in New Premium Volume, Converted Self Insured Fund to Stock Insurance Company, Advertising Achieved Record Breaking Months in Sales 7 of 9 months in 1996
- Gulf Management Group, Inc., Pompano Beach, FL — **Marketing Manager** — Sep 1994- May 1996
  $10MM Increase in New Premium Volume
  Sales Staff: Hiring, Training & Management.
- Master Risk Consultants, Orlando, FL
  - **Executive Assistant to the President** — Mar 1992 - Sep 1994
    $25 MM Acquisition of New Trust
    $15 MM Increase in Existing Trusts
  - **Executive Assistant to the President - Out of State** — Mar 1990 - Mar 1992
    650% Increase in Existing Trust
    $2 MM New Trust
  - **Sr. Vice President** — Jan 1988- Mar 1990
    Clients: 20+ Trade Associations
    $500 MM Premium Volume, 7 States
    $50 MM Increase in Existing Trusts Out-Of-State
  - **Vice President** — Jan 1986 - Jan 1988
    $9 MM New Trust - Out-Of-State
    $20 MM New Trust - Out-Of-State
  - **Assistant Vice President** — Jan 1984 - Jan 1986
    $4MM New Trust - Florida
    110% Increase in Existing Trust
    $3 MM Direct Sales New Trust
    $8 MM New Trust - Out-Of-State
- Federated Insurance Co., Orlando, FL — **Direct Marketing Representative** — Jan 1982 - Dec 1984
  98% Client Retention,
  120+% Achievement of Sales Goals

EDUCATION

- **MS in Management**, American College, Bryn Mawr, Pennsylvania
- **MS in Financial Services,** American College, Bryn Mawr, Pennsylvania
- **BS in Honors Mathematics,** University of Manitoba, Winnipeg, Manitoba, Canada
- **Continuing Education**:
  - Philip Crosby International Quality Education System
  - Advanced Management Leadership Program, American College

LICENSES

- Series 6, 22, 63 Certification
- 2-18, 2-20, Insurance

DESIGNATIONS

- LUTCF, RHU, CLU, ChFC

MARLAN J. SANFORD

MICHAEL F. GROVES

4222 Walnut Grove • Lake Mary, Florida 32771 • Home: (407) 669-8666 • Office: (407) 332-4948

Qualified for:

• Investigator •

PROFESSIONAL PROFILE

- Dynamic professional employing more than 15 years of progressive accomplishments in safety and security.
- Motivated self-starter, demonstrating integrity and total dedication to getting the job done.
- Results-oriented team player, with strong organizational skills and attention to detail.
- Goal-directed team leader focusing on quality service and completing projects on time and within budget.
- Proven motivator, able to work independently or with diverse groups to achieve a common goal.
- Resourceful innovator, ready to meet challenges and provide results-oriented solutions.

AREAS OF EXPERTISE

- Policies & Procedures
- Problem Solving
- Operations Management
- Legal Consulting
- Supervision
- Investigative Training
- OSHA
- Presentations
- Employee Theft
- Security Clearance
- Multi-Task Management
- Safety Procedures
- Security Design
- Surveillance
- Planning & Organization
- PC: IBM
- MS Office
- Loss Prevention
- Insurance Investigations
- Client Relations
- Contract Negotiations
- Research & Development
- Liaison: Law Enforcement
- Customer Relations
- Safety & Security Seminars

PROFESSIONAL BACKGROUND

SECURITY AND INVESTIGATIVE MANAGEMENT

Plan, organize and manage the overall security operations and special investigative projects for various companies which include: assessing project requirements and concerns; developing "results-oriented" plan of action; and following process from inception to completion to ensure compliance with targeted goals and objectives.

Clients: CBS, Travelers, Aetna, Anheiser-Busch, Geico, Walt Disney World, Albertsons, State Farm, Greyhound International, major law firms and many others.

- Selected to develop and create "Special Investigative Unit: Insurance Fraud Manual" by selected insurance companies: Manual was adopted an industry standard. Result: Cost Savings through minimizing potential fraudulent cases. (Aetna, Travelers, Geico, American States and others)
- 250% increase in investigative productivity through standardizing creative approaches to achieving targeted objective.
- 50% increase in client base through developing "client-centered" solutions, resulting in client retentionand new client referrals.
- 100% accomplishment of assigned projects on time and within budget through developing "results- oriented" plan of action identifying time lines.

EXPERIENCE:

- MGI Services
  Longwood, FL

  Security Manager Nov 1995 - Present
  Territory: International.
  Staff: 20 Investigators.
  Clients: Major Fortune 500 Companies, e.g., CBS, Traveler's, Aetna, Anheiser-Busch, GEICO, Walt Disney World, Albertsons, State Farm, Greyhound.
  Industries: Major Law Firms, Insurance, Hospitality, Food & Beverage, Local & Federal Governments.
  Corporate Consulting: Risk Management, Seminars, Policies & Procedures, Research & Development.
  100% Goal Achievement on All Projects.
  Ranked Top 3% of Traveler's Investigators.

  Assistant Manager/Investigator Apr 1992 - Oct 1995
  Client: Florida Bar
  Investigated Issues Involving Attorneys & Unauthorized Practice of Law.
  Other Special Investigative Projects.
  100% Goal Achievement on All Projects.

  Investigator Aug 1987 - Mar 1992
  Supported Above Activities.
  100% Accomplishment of All Projects.

- Old South Investigations
  Winter Park, FL

  Investigator Jun 1984 - Aug 1987
  Work Comp Surveillance, Property & Casualty, Undercover Investigations.
  100% Accomplishment of All Projects.

- Equitable Insurance Co.
  New York City, NY

  Investigator Jan 1983 - May 1984
  Fraudulent Position Claims Investigations.

- Hillbrook Detention Center
  Syracuse, NY

  Counselor Jan 1982 - Jan 1983
  Juvenile Delinquent Counseling for State of New York.

EDUCATION:

- **AS in Criminal Justice**, Onondaga Community College, Syracuse, New York
- **Continuing Education:**
  - Certified Investigative Specialist
  - Certified Loss Prevention Specialist
  - Certified Arson Investigations
  - Certified Insurance Surveillance Specialist

SAM LENDER

987 Old Oak Road • Florence, Kentucky, 41042 • (606) 240-8394

Qualified as:

• Maintenance Foreman •

PROFESSIONAL PROFILE

- Results-oriented professional with over 15 years of progressive accomplishments in managing maintenance and pipeline projects.
- A loyal and dedicated professional committed to high ethical standards and attention to detail.
- Results-oriented team player able to manage and motivate staff to meet goals and objectives.
- Proactive achiever able to negotiate proposals and manage multiple projects in a competitive environment.
- Confident leader with innovative problem solving approaches.

AREAS OF EXPERTISE

- Project Management
- Proposal Preparation
- Bid Soliciting
- Team Building
- Training
- Inventory Control
- Tank Inspections
- Loss Prevention
- Quality Control
- Planning & Forecasting
- Construction Administration
- Purchasing
- Scheduling
- Construction Management
- OSHA/HAZMAT
- Quality Assurance
- Budgeting
- Cost Estimates
- Contracts
- Petroleum Pipelines
- DOT Regulations
- Welding
- Tube-a-Scope Log Readings

PROFESSIONAL BACKGROUND

SUN OIL COMPANY
Territory: Clarksville Tennessee to Lima, Ohio; 5 pumping stations, 1 metering terminal
Burlington, Kentucky
January 1980 - April 1997

MAINTENANCE FOREMAN - Planned, organized and managed maintenance projects in a territory covering Clarksville, Tennessee to Lima, Ohio, which included: forecasting and budgeting $1.7M; planning for labor and capital requirements; and coordinating contract development from bid process to final contract acceptance.

- 100% compliance with all project requirements through creating a plan of action to ensure assignments were completed on time and within budget.
- 400% increase in productivity through providing a results-oriented training program for new employees.
- 100% compliance with DOT rules and regulations through developing a checks and balance system.
- 200% increase in cost savings through coordinating bid process for materials and supplies and negotiating contracts.
- Recognized for "Outstanding Performance" in interfacing with all levels of workers and management, 2500 property owners and city and county officials to accomplish project goals.
- 300% increase in productivity through standardizing work schedules.

Sun Oil Company continued

- 200% increase in cost savings through developing a system for purchasing pipe and ensuring materials required were available.
- Recognized for "Outstanding Performance" in responding to leak in Grason County, Kentucky, pipeline in 1992; coordinated on-site cleanup efforts and repairs.
- Selected for Project Manager for 6 relocations due to "results-oriented performance".
- Received numerous "Safety Awards" for implementing successful "Vehicle Accident Prevention Programs".
- 100% increase in productivity through tracking quarterly, monthly and yearly progress to ensure compliance with construction project goals.

EDUCATION

- **University of Texas at Austin:** Tank Certification Preparation Course
- **Letournour College:** Welding Inspectors Seminar
- **Texas A&M:** Fire Fighting Training
- **Sun Oil Company**:
    - Creative Competitive Advantage - A Field Supervisor Workshop
    - Management Skills for Seasoned Managers
    - Management Skills for New Managers

CERTIFICATIONS

- **American Welding Society**: Certified Welding Inspector and Member

Erickson Eastman

6456 Sweetwater Drive • Longwood, Florida 32729 • (407) 332-9854

Qualified for:

• Management Trainee •

PROFESSIONAL PROFILE

- Dedicated recent graduate with 2 years of accomplishments in customer service and business.
- Creative and open-minded, deadline-oriented.
- Eager to learn, meet new challenges and assimilate new concepts and ideas quickly.
- Hardworking and goal-oriented achiever, employing strong organizational skills and attention to detail.
- Team player, able to plan, organize and complete projects on-time and within budget.

AREAS OF EXPERTISE

- Customer Service
- Sales & Marketing
- Time Management
- Presentations
- Forecasting
- Equity & Capital Markets
- Debt & Money Markets
- Inventory Control
- Business Operations
- PC: IBM/Mac
- Microsoft Word
- Microsoft Excel
- Microsoft Windows
- Problem Solving
- Reports
- Financial Analysis
- Public Relations
- Creative Solutions
- Oral/Written Communications
- Internet & Email
- Macro/Micro Economics
- Special Projects

PROFESSIONAL BACKGROUND

BUSINESS OPERATIONS

Plan, organize and complete the assigned business operations which include: determining customer/project/business needs; developing creative support strategies; and monitoring projects to comply with targeted goals and deadlines.

- 200% increase in productivity through completing tasks accurately and thoroughly the first time.
- 100% accomplishment of business project goals by analyzing business needs and implementing creative financial and operational strategies.
- Recognized by customers and managers for being "Friendly, Efficient and Professional".

EXPERIENCE WHILE IN SCHOOL (SUMMERS)

• Masters Tech Inc. - Lakeville, NY	Receptionist	May 1996 - Aug 1997
• General Corp - Rochester, NY	Customer Service	June 1995 - Jan 1996
• Harwell Center - Rochester, NY	Customer Service	May 1995 - June 1995

EDUCATION

- **Bachelors Degree in Business Administration** - GPA 3.54 - May 1998
  University of Florida Gainesville, Florida
  Minor in Economics (Concentration in Finance),
  - President's List & Dean's List
  - Golden Key National Honor Society

LARS S. NAYLOR

444 Wyethe Avenue • Orlando, Florida 32803 • (407) 888-9821• Fax (407) 888-9821• Lsnaylor@bellsouth.com

Qualified for Materials Management:

• General Manager •

PROFESSIONAL PROFILE

- Goal-oriented professional employing more than 15 years of progressive accomplishments in management and organizational development.
- Analytical planner, able to take complex and unrelated information and organize them into workable terms.
- Diplomatic leader, able to motivate diverse groups towards achieving a common goal.
- Disciplined self-starter, exhibiting the ability to achieve targeted goals on time and within budget.
- Motivated achiever, able to implement workable solutions to diverse situations.
- Catalytic problem solving team leader who thinks logically, values creativity and develops innovative solutions to marketing and logistics operations.

AREAS OF EXPERTISE

- Purchasing
- Procedures/Practices
- Goal Setting
- Vendor Relations
- Database Solutions
- Business Plan Development
- Customer Service
- Sales Management
- Contracts Management
- Workflow Analysis
- JIT
- Multi-Task Management
- Scheduling
- PC: IBM/Windows
- Market Analysis
- Troubleshooting
- Regulatory Guidelines
- Inventory Management
- QA
- Budgeting
- Cost Savings
- MS Office
- ISO9000
- Facility Management
- Transportation

PROFESSIONAL BACKGROUND

MATERIALS MANAGEMENT

Plan, organize and manage the overall management activities for various companies which include: assessing material requirements (manpower, equipment, resources); providing and monitoring services and inventory control; and ensuring compliance with corporate goals, objectives and regulatory standards.

Industries/Clients: Government, International, Textiles, Medical, Electrical Distribution

- 15% cost savings through streamlining purchasing process, minimizing distribution costs and ensuring product availability.
- 50% cost savings through reevaluating transportation system and switching from road to rail resulting in JIT availability.
- Recognized for "Excellence in Performance" for 100% compliance on materials management and budgetary objectives.
- 20% increase in productivity through developing an integrated database in support of sales, manufacturing, distribution and inventory management.

EXPERIENCE

•	NII Services Orlando, FL	**General Manager/Consultant** International Contracted Services Products: Textiles, Medical Hardware. Territory: Far East, Mid East. Product Development, Contracts, Negotiations, Transportation, Customs, Distribution Systems, Imports/Exports, Turnarounds.	Sep 1997 - Present
•	U.S. Army Charlotte, NC	**Manager,Materials Management** Budget: $18MM; Staff: 7 Contracts & Purchasing, Regulatory Guidance, Procedures & Practices Development, Workflow Analysis, Data Base Inventory Systems Development. 100% Audit Compliance; 25% Cost Savings.	Nov 1995 - Sep 1997
	Ft. Meade, MD	**Director, Materials Management** Budget: $14MM; Staff: 6/135; Inventory: $240MM. Inventory Management, Audits, Quality Assurance, Purchasing Activities Coordination, Standards Compliance. 100% Audit Compliance; 35% Cost Savings.	Nov 1992 - Nov 1995
	Tallahassee, FL	**Materials & Standards Auditor**	Jul 1987 - Nov 1992
	Saudi Arabia	**Purchasing Manager**	Jan 1986- Jun 1987
	Olathe, KS	**Internal Auditor, Materials & Standards**	Jan 1983 - Jul 1986
	Tampa, FL	**Warehouse Manager**	Jan 1982 - Jan 1983

EDUCATION

- **MBA in Technology Management**
  University of Central Florida, Orlando, Florida
- **BS in Business Management**
  BS in Political Science
  Northern Kentucky State University, Highland Heights, Kentucky
- **AA in Economics, Behavioral Statistical Analysis**
  University of Kentucky, Lexington, Kentucky

PROFESSIONAL DESIGNATIONS/AFFILIATIONS

- National Association of Purchasing Managers
- APICS
- CPM

LARS S. NAYLOR

JEFFREY CONTI

216 Windy Way • Fairfax, Virginia 22643 • (540) 667-0614 • Voice Mail (540) 667-3957 • JeffConti@aol.com

Objective:

- **Emergency Medical Technician**
- **Firefighter**

PROFESSIONAL PROFILE

- Goal-directed professional employing more than 6 years of experience in volunteer firefighting and emergency medical services.
- Results-oriented team player demonstrating strong organizational skills and attention to detail.
- Dedicated to excellence in service and relationships while working with people at all levels.
- Motivated self-starter able to implement workable solutions to challenging situations.
- Flexible team player, eager to learn, meet new challenges and assimilate new concepts and ideas quickly.

AREAS OF EXPERTISE

- BLS
- Emergency Transport
- EMS
- KEMS Software System
- Arson Detection
- Radiological Monitoring
- Oral Communications
- Tactical Operations
- CPR with AED
- Community Relations
- Patient Transport
- Conflict Resolution
- Problem Solving
- Firefighting
- Liaison: Patient & Healthcare Facilities
- Hazardous Materials
- Computer Literate
- Vehicle Operations
- Written Communications

PROFESSIONAL BACKGROUND

FIREFIGHTING & EMERGENCY MEDICAL SERVICES

Plan, organize and manage assigned emergency medical services and firefighting activities for various organizations which include: assessing transport/mission requirements; developing strategic plans of action; and ensuring compliance with targeted goals/objectives and state/local regulations.

- 100% accomplishment of targeted goals and objectives through developing a results-oriented plan of action.
- Awarded "Firefighter of the Year - 1995" by Fairfax Fire Company.

EDUCATION

- **BA Degree in History,** Fairfax University, Fairfax, Virginia - August 1998
- **Delaware State Fire School,** Dover, Delaware
  - Basic Firefighting Skills
  - Hazardous Materials Response Skills
  - Ropes & Rigging
  - Wildfire Suppression Skills & Tools
  - Structural Firefighting Skills
  - Vehicle Rescue
  - Crew Leader
  - Arson Detection
- **Virginia State Fire Academy**, Alexandria, Virginia
  - Firefighter Safety and Survival
  - Hazardous Materials Operations
- **Continuing Training:**
  - Fairfax County Fire Training School: Forcible Entry
  - Radiological Emergency Response Training: Radiological Monitoring I & II
  - Triad Safety Consultants, Inc.: Firefighter's Building Construction

EXPERIENCE WHILE WORKING WAY THROUGH SCHOOL

• First West Chester Fire Company Fairfax, VA	**Volunteer Firefighter**	Sep 1992 - Present
• GF Ambulance Club of Fairfax County, Inc. Fairfax, VA	**Emergency Medical Technician** BLS Care to Pre-Hospital Patients, Ambulance Operation, Documentation as Required on KEMS Software.	Jan 1998 - Present
• QVC Corporation Fairfax, VA	**Hard Goods Packer** Packaging & Shipping.	Sep 1997 - Jan 1998
• Keystone Quality Transport Fairfax, VA	**Driver** Transporting Wheel Chair Patients - Hospital Discharges & Inter-Facility.	May 1997 - Sep 1997
• County Seat, Inc. Alexandria, VA	**Assistant Sales Manager** Merchandising, Customer Service, Sales Staff Supervision, Scheduling, Customer Relations.	Aug 1995 - May 1997

LICENSES & CERTIFICATES

- **Emergency Medical Technician,** Virginia Department of Health
- **Emergency Vehicles Operators Course,** Emergency Health Services Federation, Inc.
- **Practical Skills Instructor, EMT,** Good Fellowship Training Institute
- **Emergency Medical Technician**, Florida Department of Health & Rehabilitative Services

Richard Sanders, M.D.

9809 Errinson Path • Longwood, Florida, 32779 • (407) 333-6042

Qualified as

• ASSOCIATE MEDICAL DIRECTOR •

PROFESSIONAL PROFILE

- Dynamic professional employing more than 15 years of progressive accomplishments in medical management and patient care.
- Creative promoter, able to work independently and in a group setting; dedicated to excellence in service and relationships.
- Respected team builder, able to empower others to achieve common goals.
- Hard working goal-oriented se;f-starter employing strong organizational skills and attention to detail.
- Level headed person respectful of others and able to work with diverse populations.
- Creative and open-minded; offers outstanding growth potential in any capacity.
- Eager to learn, meet new challenges and assimilate new concepts and ideas quickly.

AREAS OF EXPERTISE

- Administrator
- Utilization Review & Management
- Physician/Medical Staff Discipline
- Patient Access to Care
- Speaking
- Inpatient/Outpatient Referral
- Coaching
- Strategic Planning
- Medical/Surgical
- Management
- Insurance Contracts
- Patient Advocate
- Customer Service
- Clinical Components
- Quality Assurance
- Community Involvement
- Hospital Admission Review
- Case Analysis
- Written Communications
- Business Plan
- OB/GYN
- Committee Chairperson
- Negotiations
- Physician Credentialing
- Problem Solving
- HMO/PPO/Medicare
- Education & Training
- Provider Liaison
- Data Analysis
- Cost Controls
- Team Leader
- Recruiting
- Physician/Staff Relations

PROFESSIONAL BACKGROUND

PHYSICIAN IN GROUP CLINICAL PRACTICE

Planned, organized and executed the overall administrative functions for the group practice which included: supervising and training staff; evaluating patients and planning treatments; and ensuring practice standards were met.

- 100% compliance with American College of Obstetricians and Gynecologists standards in group practice through developing a specific plan of action.
- 300% increase in profitability through streamlining patient processing while maintaining quality standards.
- 70% increase in profitability through reorganization of insurance billing.
- 50% increase in profitability through research development of satellite provider locations.
- 30% increase in profitability and market share through patient encounter data evaluation resulting in strategic contract negotiation with targeted insurance carriers.
- 8% decrease in cesarean section rate due to initiation of 100% cesarean review at Florida Hospital; resulting in decreased hospitalization costs and length of stay.
- Elected as Chairman, Department of OB/GYN, Florida Hospital.

EXPERIENCE

• Physicians Womens Group	Manager	Jul 1994- Present
• NuCare OB/GYN Specialists	Managing Partner/Physician	Nov 1990 - Jun 1994
• Maitland OB/GYN Group	Managing Partner/Physician	Jul 1982 - Nov 1990

EDUCATION

- **M.D. in Medicine**, New York University School of Medicine, New York, New York
  - North Shore University Hospital Medical Center
    - Intern, Internal Medicine Rotation, PGY-1,
    - Resident in OB/GYN,
    - Chief Resident in OB/GYN
  - Resident, GYN Pathology, Sloane Hospital for Women
  - Resident: Galloway Fellow, GYN Oncology, Sloan Kettering Memorial Hospital

- **B.A.. in Chemistry**, Franklin and Marshall College, Lancaster, Pennsylvania
  - Chemistry Honors
  - Cum Laude
  - Phi Beta Kappa

LICENSES AND BOARD CERTIFICATION

- Florida Medical License #40000
- New York Medical License #100000
- Certified American Board OB/GYN

PROFESSIONAL ASSOCIATIONS

- Diplomate, American College of OB/GYN
- Diplomate, National Board of Medical Examiners
- American Medical Association
- Florida OB/GYN Society
- Central Florida OB/GYN Society

HOSPITAL AFFILIATIONS

- Florida Hospital Medical Center
- Arnold Palmer Hospital for children and Women
- Winter Park Memorial Hospital

RICHARD SANDERS, M.D.

9809 Errinson Path • Longwood, Florida, 32779 • (407) 333-6042

HOSPITAL AND COMMUNITY SERVICE

- Board of Directors, Children's School for Special Children, Winter Park, Florida
- Speaker, Displaced Homemakers, Valencia Community College
- Member, Patient Care Monitoring Committee, Florida Hospital
- Member, Cancer Committee, Florida Hospital
- Member, Medical Records Committee, Florida Hospital
- Member, Ad Hoc Committee for Cost Containment, OB & Nursery, Florida Hospital
- Member, Ad Hoc Committee for Breast Feeding, Florida Hospital
- Member, Ad Hoc Committee for Perinatal Development, Florida Hospital
- Member, Central Florida Health Care Task Force (Medical Cost Containment), Florida Hospital
- Member, Florida Medical Association Annual Meeting Delegate
- Chairman, Department of OB/GYN , Florida Hospital
- Member, Operating Room Committee, Florida Hospital
- Member, Credentials Committee, Florida Hospital
- Member, ByLaws Committee, Florida Hospital
- Member, Diabetes Advisory and Quality Assurance Committee, Florida Hospital
- Member, Physician Nurse Liaison Committee, Perinatal and Neonatal Medicine, Florida Hospital
- Mini-Internship Preceptor, Orange County Medical Society
- Speaker/Lecturer to Allied Medical Groups within Florida Hospital and to Community Public Service Organizations.

CAMERON CROMWELL, RN, BSN, CCM

4381 Thalford Avenue • Lake Mary, Florida, 32712 • (407) 388-9877

Qualified RN, BSN:

• Quality Management Coordinator •

PROFESSIONAL PROFILE

- Proficient healthcare professional with 14 years of progressive accomplishments in a variety of clinical and non-clinical settings.
- Resourceful self-starter, with the outstanding ability to gather, comprehend and convey information.
- Hard working team player, demonstrating strong organizational skills and attention to detail.
- Dedicated to excellence in service and relationships.
- Eager to learn, meet new challenges and assimilate new concepts and ideas quickly.

AREAS OF EXPERTISE

• Quality Assurance	• Utilization Management	• Case Management
• Discharge Planning	• Cardiology	• Agency/Client Liaison
• Triage	• Office Management	• Infertility
• Medical/Surgical	• Education	• Gastroenterology
• Workers Compensation	• Public Relations	• Supervision
• Medical Records	• Medications	• Training
• RN: FL 1948576	• Cost Reduction	• Patient Advocate

PROFESSIONAL BACKGROUND

CASE MANAGEMENT/QUALITY ASSURANCE

Planned, organized and managed the overall utilization/case management activities which included: assessing and representing patient needs and services; recommending alternative levels of care and coordinating discharge planning; and ensuring compliance with NCQA standards.

Case Load: An average of 60 workers compensation patients served telephonically; interfacing with claims adjusters, medical providers and patients in a team environment to ensure medical management and return-to-work coordination.

- 100% achievement of all assigned goals and objectives through developing specific plan of action for servicing 5 healthcare facilities in Central Florida.
- 350% increase in productivity through establishing a network of resources and clinical support services for efficient referral and reference in the field.
- 25% increase in profitability through monitoring patient length of stay while maintaining quality of care.
- Selected to conduct pilot record reviews for development of Quality tool to ensure compliance with NCQA standards.

PUBLIC RELATIONS AND NETWORK MANAGEMENT

Planned, organized and managed the overall public relations and network activities for various facilities which included: researching and resolving compliance issues; communicating network gaps with public relations and contracting areas; and identifying potential customer sensitive issues.

Facilities: Physicians Office, Aetna, PPLC

- 20% increase in new members through developing a results-oriented marketing approach.
- 100% increase in quality assurance through developing a system to facilitate compliance with established healthcare guidelines.
- 10% increase in organization's visibility through promoting educational programs on preventive healthcare procedures.
- 92% increase in productivity through establishing a results-oriented purchasing process and vendor information system.

CLINICAL NURSING

Planned, organized and managed the overall patient care activities in private practice and health care facilities which included assessing patient needs, implementing action plans and ensuring all goals and objectives were met.

- Recognized for outstanding patient care for providing Hospice service.
- Recognized for outstanding performance for preventing serious patient complications through proactive management.

EXPERIENCE

Aetna Health Plans Orlando, FL	Network Management Coordinator/Case Manager On-Site Concurrent Review Nurse	Oct 1995 - Present
Contract Nursing Orlando, FL	Nursing, Special Projects	Oct 1993 - Sep 1995
Gastroenterology Associates Miami, FL	Office Nurse	Feb 1988 - Oct 1993
St. Francis Hospital New York, NY	Primary Care Nurse Cardiac	May 1984 - Jan 1988

EDUCATION

- **B.S. DEGREE IN NURSING**
  State University of New York, Binghamton, New York
- Certified Case Manager
- **Continuing Education:**
  60 current credit hours: Case Management, Utilization Review, D/C Planning, Quality Improvement/Risk Management, Workers Compensation

---

CAMERON CROMWELL, RN, BSN, CCM

CHARLES R. DARLING

424 Peach Avenue • Atlanta, GA 54701 • (715) 835-9828

Qualified for:

• Speech Pathology •

PROFESSIONAL PROFILE

- Results-oriented professional with more than 15 years of accomplishments in the speech pathology and medical services.
- Team contributor, with proven interpersonal and relationship-building strengths.
- Diverse achiever, able to interpret task directions and provide solutions in a timely manner.
- Enthusiastic, confident and dependable, with premium communication and customer service skills.
- Motivated self-starter, exhibiting high ethics, hard work, dedication, competence and confidence, underscored by a personal commitment to outstanding professional performance.

AREAS OF EXPERTISE

- Program Development
- PACE/MIT/VAT
- Alzheimer's
- Laryngectomy
- Occupational Therapy
- Physical Therapy
- Physician/Medical Liaison
- Team Leader
- Clinical Components
- Quality Assurance
- Community Involvement
- Patient Relations
- CVA
- TBI/CHI
- Dysphagia
- Insurance Contracts
- Patient Advocate
- Problem Solving
- Medical/Surgical
- HMO/PPO/Medicare
- Education & Training
- Provider Liaison
- Speech-Language Pathology
- Dementia
- Voice
- Barium Swallow Studies
- Negotiations
- Physiology
- Ventilatories/Tracheostomies
- Rehabilitation
- Evaluation & Diagnosis
- In-Service Training
- Inpatient/Outpatient

PROFESSIONAL BACKGROUND

SPEECH-LANGUAGE PATHOLOGY

Plan, organize and execute the overall speech-language pathology functions for healthcare practices which included: evaluating and diagnosing patients; developing patient treatment plans; and monitoring patients to comply with goals, objectives and healthcare standards.

- 100% compliance with Speech-Language Pathology and overall healthcare standards through developing a specific plan of action.
- Selected to administer new research programs including modified barium swallow studies.
- 60% increase in physician referrals by in-servicing new programs to physicians while demonstrating a complete dedication to quality and service.
- 100% increase in seminar/in-service attendance by promoting and presenting innovative educational seminars for healthcare professionals.
- 50% increase in efficiency by streamlining paper-flow, prioritizing & planning projects, and creating an effective time management system.
- Recognized by physicians and healthcare professionals for creating tailored in-service training programs and presenting dynamic educational seminars.

EXPERIENCE

- Peachtree Medical
  Atlanta, GA
  Speech & Language Pathologist — Jan 1996 - Present
  Projects: Home Health, Skilled Nursing Facilities & Hospitals.
  Patients: Acute Care Inpatient & Outpatient.
  Responsibilities: Patient Relations, Evaluation & Diagnosis, Scheduling Therapy Administration & Physician Liaison.

- Florida Hospital
  Orlando, FL
  Speech & Language Pathologist — Nov 1994 - Dec 1995
  Patients: Acute Care Inpatient & Outpatient.
  Research Project: Barium Swallow Studies.
  Responsibilities: Patient Relations, Evaluation & Diagnosis, Developing Treatment Plans, Therapy Administration, Physician Liaison, Program Development, & In-Service Training.

- MaxiCare, Inc.
  Orlando, FL
  Speech & Language Pathologist — May 1992 - Nov 1994
  Responsibilities: Patient Relations, Physician Liaison, Evaluation, Diagnosis, Group Program Development & In-Service Training.

- Florida Heart Group
  Orlando, FL
  Program Director, Cardiac Rehabilitation/Wellness Center — Apr 1983 - Jan 1989
  Responsibilities: Overall Operations, Marketing, Public Relations, Budgeting, Forecasting, Client Relations, Recruiting, In-Service Training & Seminars.

EDUCATION

- **Master of Science in Speech-Language Pathology** - GPA: 3.8
  University of Wisconsin - Stevens Point
  Clinical Settings:
  - St. Michael's Hospital, Acute Care Facility - Stevens Point, WI
  - Sand Lake Hospital, Brain Injury Rehab Center - Orlando, FL

- **BS in Cardiopulmonary Physiology** - GPA: 4.0
  University of Central Florida - Orlando

CHARLES R. DARLING

LISA MARIE GLASS

936 Del Sol Boulevard • Haines City, Florida, 33844 • (941) 439-0866

Qualified in

• Social Work •

PROFESSIONAL PROFILE

- Results-oriented professional employing more than 15 years of progressive accomplishments in health care and social work services.
- Flexible and dependable, always willing to help out wherever needed.
- Goal-oriented self-starter, with effective organizational skills and attention to detail.
- Motivated team player, able to plan, organize and complete projects on time.
- Eager to learn, meet new challenges and assimilate new concepts and ideas quickly.

AREAS OF EXPERTISE

- Patient Relations
- Education
- Home Care
- Nursing Homes
- Medical Records
- Scheduling
- Geriatrics
- PC: IBM
- Counseling
- Research
- Policies & Procedures
- Presentations
- Planning
- Product Research
- Special Events
- Microsoft Word
- MS Windows
- Case Management
- Training
- Manual Development
- Problem Solving
- Organization
- Patient Care
- Psychosocial Assessment
- WordPerfect

PROFESSIONAL BACKGROUND

SOCIAL WORK

Plan, organize and manage the overall assigned activities for clients which included assessing client needs; developing treatment programs and coordinating facilities required; and representing client in court if required. Companies/Organizations: Nursing homes, home health care, hospitals and social service agencies

- Received "Whatever It Takes" Award for Outstanding Professional Performance - September 1996.
- 100% accomplishment of all assigned goals and objectives through developing a plan of action.
- 100% compliance with charting requirements through developing a system to ensure quality.
- 95% increase in client satisfaction through designing a client plan of care for activities of daily living which maximized their quality of life.
- 100% compliance with project specifications in producing outcome studies.
- Recognized for "Outstanding Performance" in developing liaisons with appropriate agencies and organizations to ensure compliance with state and federal guidelines.

SUPERVISION AND TRAINING

Planned, organized and managed the overall activities for special projects in nursing homes which included: supervising and training staff; developing curriculum requirements; and ensuring students would meet state guidelines for
certification.

- 100% compliance with corporate objectives in designing an orientation program and job descriptions.
- 300% increase in productivity through establishing an orientation program to ensure continuity in the delivery of client services.
- 80% increase in productivity through standardizing scheduling system.
- 99% student achievement of state certification for Certified Nursing Assistant as a result of attending results-oriented training program.
- 75% increase in productivity through designing a problem resolution system.

EXPERIENCE

• SunBelt Living Centers	**Social Services Director**	Jul 1996 - Dec 1996
	Social Services Assistant	Mar 1996 - Jul 1996

EXPERIENCE WHILE WORKING WAY THROUGH SCHOOL

• Seniors First	**Case Manager**	Jul 1995 - Sep 1995
• Senior Rights & Advocacy	**Case Manager**	Jan 1995 - Jun 1995
• Youngstown State University	Secretary Bookstore	Mar 1994 - Dec 1994
• Scripps Gerontology Miami University	**Research Assistant**	Feb 1994 - Sep 1994
• Martin Family	**Private Duty Nurse**	Feb 1990 - Mar 1993
• Wilmington House	**Supervisor/Instructor** Nursing Assistants	Dec 1985 - Nov 1987
• IBM	**Market Research Intern**	Jun 1985 - Nov 1985

EDUCATION

- **Major: Graduate Work in Social Work,**
  University of Central Florida, Orlando, Florida - GPA - 3.57
- **BA in Social Work**
  Youngstown State University, Youngstown, Ohio - GPA 3.56 - June 1995

SONYA CARPENTER

444 Myles Lane • Orlando, Florida 34746 • (407) 888-8888

Job Objective:

- **Receptionist**
- **Office Support**

PROFESSIONAL PROFILE

- Motivated employee, with experience in customer service and administrative support.
- Eager to learn and meet new challenges.
- Flexible, always willing to help out wherever needed.
- Focused on meeting goals and objectives.
- Loyal and dedicated team player.
- Dedicated to excellence in service and relationships.

AREAS OF EXPERTISE

- Customer Service
- Appointment Setting
- PC:IBM/DOS
- Typing: 55 wpm
- Spanish
- Billing
- Special Projects
- Filing
- Office Equipment
- Hospitality
- Telephone Reception
- Problem Solving
- Office Procedures

PROFESSIONAL BACKGROUND

ADMINISTRATIVE SUPPORT AND CUSTOMER SERVICE

Planned, organized and coordinated assigned activities for customer service/office support which included: assessing client/project needs; providing support and timely solutions; and following client/project from inception to completion to ensure compliance with assigned goals and objectives.

- 100% accomplishment of all assigned projects and tasks through developing a plan of action to ensure the job gets done on time.
- Recognized for excellent customer service by customers and supervisor.

EXPERIENCE:

- Marriott Orlando World Center **Customer Service Attendant** Dec 1997 - Present
  Orlando, FL

EDUCATION

- **Valencia Community College,** Orlando, Florida
  Major: Business Administration & Radiology

SARAH GOODING

428 Ralston Place • Winter Park, Florida 32765 • (407) 485-3029

Qualified for:

• Office Administrator •

PROFESSIONAL PROFILE

- Dynamic professional with more than 15 years of progressive accomplishments in office management and executive support.
- Motivated team player, demonstrating effective communication skills in working with people at all levels and from various backgrounds.
- Diverse achiever able to interpret task directions and provide solutions in a timely manner.
- Personable and hard working team leader, exhibiting results-oriented organizational skills and attention to detail.
- Focused self-starter, able to analyze, plan, organize and complete projects on time and within budget.
- Proven leader providing the momentum required to unite diverse groups towards a common goal.

AREAS OF EXPERTISE

- Customer Service
- Interviewing
- Scheduling
- Recruiting/Hiring
- Customer Relations
- Training
- Written Communications
- Logistics Planning
- Word Processing
- Planning & Organization
- MS Office
- Office Management
- Problem Solving
- Office Layout/Moves
- Management Support
- Team Leader
- Presentations
- Multi-Task Management
- WPM: 75
- Purchasing
- Oral Communications
- Meeting/Travel Arrangements

PROFESSIONAL BACKGROUND

OFFICE SUPPORT AND ADMINISTRATION

Plan, organize and manage the overall office/administrative support functions for various companies which include: hiring, training and supervising support staff; identifying management needs/concerns and providing support/solutions; and ensuring compliance with departmental/corporate goals and objectives.

Companies: DPT, Shell, Westinghouse, MasterCard International, FCB/Leber Katz Advertising, New York Telephone

- 40% increase in productivity through developing a cross-training program to ensure the job gets done on time and within budget.
- 125% increase in productivity through establishing a streamlined workflow process in supporting management and coordinating internal operations.
- 250% increase in productivity through reorganizing the Medical Office at Westinghouse and computerizing system.
- Recognized for "Excellence in Customer Service" at MasterCard International documented by management and clients; represented management on assigned projects with clients.
- 20% in cost savings through developing an "as needed" expendable supply system for the department.
- 100% accomplishment of assigned projects on time and within budget through developing time lined plans of action.
- 95% retention of support staff through developing an employee-oriented communications system resulting in increased productivity.

EXPERIENCE:

- DPT, Maitland, FL — **Administrative Assistant to Senior VP** — Jan 1996 - Present
  Administrative/Management Support to 6 Managers, 2 Buyers & Training Manager. Purchasing, Time Cards, Travel/Meeting Arrangements, Expense Reports, Presentations. Support Domestic & International Special Projects.

- Shell Systems, Orlando, FL — **Office Manager, Assistant to Branch Manager & Service Manager** — Dec 1995 - Dec 1996, Company Restructured
  Administrative/Supervisory Support for 6 Salespeople, 7 Service Techs & 1 Receptionist. Managed Master Schedule, Commissions/Payroll, Secretarial Support, Proposal/Reports Development, Logistics Support; Corporate Liaison.

- Westinghouse, Orlando, FL — **Human Resources - Senior Administrative Associate** — Jan 1995 - Dec 1995
  Research/Investigation Potential Staff; Office Management & Reorganization; Computerized Filing System.

- MasterCard International, New York, NY — **Executive Secretary/Administrative Assistant to Sr. VP of Sales** — Jul 1992 - Dec 1994
  Coordinated/Scheduled National Sales Staff. Travel/Meeting Scheduling & Arrangements. Liaison with Clients & Banks. Coordinated Special Promotions: World Cup, Telephone Campaigns, New Products & Others.

- FCB/Lybrand El Partners, New York, NY — **Executive Secretary/Administrative Assistant to Senior VP of Sales Promotions & Special Events Specialist** — Sep 1987 - Jul 1992
  Managed Key Executive Projects & Organized Monthly Agendas, Travel Arrangements, Client Invoicing, Advertising Mechanicals & Problem Solving. Supervised Clerical Staff. Coordinated Special Events/Festivals in Boston, Dallas & Atlanta.

- New York Telephone, New York, NY — **District Secretary to Vice Present** — Feb 1983 - Aug 1987
  Community Liaison, Special Events Coordinator, Grants, Monthly Agendas. Support 6 Officers & Supervised Clerical Staff.

  Acting Business Office Supervisor — Jan 1980 - Jan 1982
  Supervised & Trained Clerical/Support Staff.

EDUCATION

- **Bergen Community College**, Bergen County, New Jersey
  Major: Business Administration & Marketing

- **MC University,** New York, New York
  - Banking
  - MS Power Point, Persuasion
  - Management, Customer Service, Interpersonal Relations and Others

RACHEL COSBY

3488 Crysal Lane • Orlando, Florida 32839 • (407) 855-9327

Qualified:

- LEGAL SECRETARY/ASSISTANT

PROFESSIONAL PROFILE

- Proficient professional employing more than 15 years of progressive accomplishments in executive level administrative support.
- Creative and open-minded, completing projects on time and within budget.
- Dependable and dedicated achiever employing strong communication skills in working with diverse populations.
- Flexible, always willing to help out where needed.
- Hard working and goal-oriented team player exhibiting strong organizational skills and attention to detail.
- Loyal and level-headed individual, respectful of others.

AREAS OF EXPERTISE

- Customer Service
- Loan Administration
- WordPerfect
- MS Word
- Accounts Payable
- Dictation
- Paralegal
- Timeslips Billing
- Team Leader
- PC: IBM/Mac
- Lotus 1-2-3
- E-Mail
- Planning & Organization
- Meetings/Conferences
- Problem Solving
- Oral Communications
- Accounts Receivable
- MS Windows
- Interpersonal Relations
- Volunteer
- Office Management
- Special Projects
- Multi-Task Management

PROFESSIONAL BACKGROUND

LEGAL ADMINISTRATIVE SUPPORT

Plan, organize and manage the overall legal administrative support activities which include: evaluating department requirements for resources, manpower and materials; interacting with clients, vendors and other departments; and ensuring all required support activities were completed in accordance with corporate standards.

Companies: Sun Trust, David Rhett Baker, P.A., Southern Legal Staffing, Inc., and others

- 10% increase in client retention through developing a detailed client relations program.
- Awarded "Woman of the Year" by the American Business Womens Association for "outstanding service".
- 100% compliance with assigned special projects through developing a targeted plan of action.
- 200% increase in productivity through developing specific organizational procedures.

EXPERIENCE:

•	Southern Legal Staffing, Inc./ Legal Couriers/Special Orlando, FL	**Legal Assistant/Courier** Legal Documents: Mediations; Short-Term Projects, Scheduling, Marketing, Reporting, Typing, Phone Support, Copying & Filing.	Jul 1996 - Present Seeking Full-Time Permanent Position
•	Rhett Butler, P.A. Orlando, FL	**Legal Assistant** Legal Documents: Benefits/401K Modifications; Special Projects, Typing, Dictation, Internet Liaison, Phone Support, Accounts Payable/Receivable, Copying, Filing, Mailing	Jan 1996 - Jul 1996 Office Relocated
•	SunTrust, N.A. Orlando, FL	**Loan Administrator** Legal Documents: Satisfaction of Mortgages, Partial Releases and Notes; Borrower/Bank Liaison; Commercial/ Residential Loans; Training; Ledger Accounts; Typing; Scheduling; Reporting; Phone Support; Filing.	May 1991 - Nov 1995 Advancement
		Assistant Auditor Territory: Florida Borrower/Bank Liaison; Scheduling Verifications; Problem Solving; Reporting; Government Regulations	Aug 1980 - May 1991 Promotion

EDUCATION

- **B.S. in Paralegal, Orlando College,** Orlando, Florida
- **B.A. in Management, Rollins College,** Winter Park, Florida

CONTINUING EDUCATION

- **Executrain,** Maitland, Florida (WordPerfect & Lotus 1-2-3)

CATHERINE DRUMMOND

498 Howell Drive • Altamonte Springs, Florida 32714 • (407) 767-8907

Qualified for:

• Office Management • Accounting/Bookkeeping

PROFESSIONAL PROFILE

- Dedicated professional employing more than 10 years of progressive accomplishments in accounting and bookkeeping.
- Dependable, always gets the job done on-time.
- Disciplined self-starter with the unique ability to comprehend complex and unrelated information and organize it into workable terms.
- Highly motivated individual with premium communication skills in diverse settings.
- Proven leader, providing the momentum required to unite diverse groups toward a common goal.
- Loyal and dedicated team player, demonstrating integrity in achieving all goals and objectives.

AREAS OF EXPERTISE

- Business Operations
- Quality Assurance
- Business Plans
- Non-Profit Sector
- Policies & Procedures
- Accounts Receivable
- Multi-Faceted Tasks
- Client Relations
- MS Windows
- Taxes
- Staffing/Interviewing
- Team Building
- Cost Reduction
- Advertising Strategies
- Scheduling
- Accounts Payable
- Budgeting
- Time Management
- MS Word
- Word Perfect
- Payroll
- Reconciliations
- Office Management
- Strategic Planning
- Oral Communications
- Inventory Control
- Problem Solving
- Purchasing
- Special Events
- Lotus 1-2-3
- Accounting/Bookkeeping
- Financial Reporting
- Medical Terminology

PROFESSIONAL BACKGROUND

OFFICE MANAGEMENT& SUPPORT SERVICES

Plan, organize and manage the overall business activities which include: evaluating customer/office/project requirements; developing creative strategies and cost-efficient procedures; and monitoring activities to ensure compliance with targeted goals and objectives while enhancing quality service.

Industries: Medical, Education, Non-Profit Organizations, Retail/Consumer and Others.

- 25% increase in revenues through developing creative weekly promotions.
- 13% increase in productivity and cost savings through streamlining manpower requirements and refining office procedures.
- 300% increase in client base through building client relations and a results-oriented referral process.
- Recognized for "Outstanding Leadership and Organization" for successfully developing new location resulting in increased profitability.

EXPERIENCE

- Biltmore Academy
  Miami, FL

  Office Manager/Bookkeeper — Sep 1991 - Aug 1997
  Staff: 6; Clients: 350 Students.
  Special Projects: Holiday Parties, Parents Night, Plays, Parades, Graduation.
  Reported Directly to President.
  Office Operations, Bookkeeping, Scheduling, Payroll, AP/AR, Invoicing, Special Events, Financial Statements, Hiring & Training.

- Dynamics, Inc.
  Miami, FL

  Executive Assistant/Bookkeeper — Dec 1987 - Sep 1991
  Staff: 5; Facilities: 2.
  Reported Directly to Agency Director.
  Special Projects: Volunteering (Acclimating Prisoners to Society).
  Office Management, Confidential Projects, Administration Liaison, Bookkeeping, Payroll, AP/AR, Hiring & Training.

- BAC Center
  Coral Gables, FL

  Business Manager — Oct 1981 - Jul 1987
  Staff: 5 Direct, 35 Indirect; Facilities: 3.
  Reported Directly to Owner.
  Special Projects: Weekly Promotions, Location Start-Up, Advertising.
  Overall Operations, Bookkeeping, Financial Statements, Inventory Control, Staffing, Training, Purchasing, Quarterly Taxes, Cash Accountability & Customer Relations.

EDUCATION

- **Associate of Arts in Accounting,** Miami Dade Community College, Miami, Florida
- **Continuing Education:** Management Training Certificate, Lindsay Hopkins School

Carlos Z. Romero

1234 Willow Road Lane • Little Ferry • New Jersey 493332 • (685) 886-8654

Career Objective:

- Pharmaceutical Representative

PROFESSIONAL PROFILE

- Goal-directed graduate with over 4 years of progressive accomplishments in customer service and sales.
- Hard working team player, with strong organizational skills and attention to detail.
- Ethical leader exhibiting the ability to motivate individuals/groups towards achieving a common goal.
- Resourceful and creative in pursuing unique methods to attain goals and objectives.
- Energetic self-starter, able to plan, organize and complete projects on time and within budget.
- Results-oriented organizer possessing analytical acumen, perception, judgement and energy.

AREAS OF EXPERTISE

- Spanish Fluent
- Client Relations
- Strategic Planning
- New Accounts
- Financial Analysis
- WordPerfect
- MS Excel
- Interpersonal Relations
- Creative Strategies
- Sales
- Telephone Sales Strategies
- Accounting
- Lotus 1-2-3
- Travel
- Customer Service
- Contract Negotiations
- Target Marketing
- Problem Solving
- Multi-Task Management
- Planning & Organization
- MS Widows
- Communications
- Negotiations

PROFESSIONAL BACKGROUND

SALES & CUSTOMER SERVICE

Plan, organize and manage assigned sales and marketing activities for various companies which included: evaluating market and assessing client needs; developing and negotiating contracts; and promoting add-on sales and on-going customer service in compliance with corporate standards.

Clients: Corporate, Finance, Commercial, Public Services - Government, Industrial

- 70% closing ratio developed through a targeted system of relational sales.
- Recognized for "Excellence in Sales and Customer Service" for consistently exceeding quotas.
- 25% increase in revenues through developing a client referral system to increase market penetration.
- 80% client retention through developing a client-centered education and service program.

EDUCATION

- **BS in Business Administration** -University of Central Florida - **December 1998**
  Orlando, Florida
  Emphasis: Marketing & Finance

EXPERIENCE WHILE WORKING WAY THROUGH SCHOOL:

•	UPS Little Ferry, NJ	**Courier - Part-Time** Territory: NE New Jersey Customer Service, Customer Relations, Problem Solving, Territory Management, Cash Handling, Scheduling, Product Management, Sales & Marketing. 115% Goal Achievement.	Jul 1998 - Present
		Cargo Handler Customer Service, Problem Solving.	Jun 1997 - Jul 1998
•	World Gym Fitness Center Little Ferry, NJ	**Account Executive** Corporate Sales Clients: Banks, Businesses, Retail Operations, Technical Facilities. 160%Quota Achievement.	Jun 1996 - Jun 1997
•	JohnstonCorporation Maryville, NJ	**Loss Prevention Officer** Customer Relations, Safety, Security, Surveillance, Liaison: Law Enforcement.	Aug 1995 - May 1996
•	Able Brothers Inc. Winchester, VA	**Data Entry Clerk** Statistical Data Entry & Reports.	May 1995 - Aug 1995
•	Telecon Telecenters Maitland, FL	**Telephone Sales** Clients: Financial/Commercial Companies.	Feb 1995 - May 1995

- Other experience includes working in various positions in sales and customer service.

JAMES HICKS, II

340 Lincoln Trail • Knoxville, Tennessee 37804 • (423) 984-2223

Qualified for:

• **Production/Operations Manager** •

PROFESSIONAL PROFILE

- Disciplined professional with more than 5 years of progressive accomplishments in operations management.
- Dependable team leader, employing strong communication skills with diverse groups.
- Enthusiastic self-starter, able to get the job done on-time and within budget.
- Hard-working and goal-oriented achiever, employing strong organizational skills and attention to detail.
- Highly energetic and open-minded, offering outstanding growth potential.
- Loyal and dedicated team player, demonstrating integrity in achieving all goals and objectives.

AREAS OF EXPERTISE

- Team Leader
- Risk Management
- Customer Relations
- Word Perfect
- Team Building
- Environmental Issues
- Safety/OSHA/HAZMAT
- Public Relations
- Planning & Organization
- Scheduling
- Multi-Task Management
- Trouble Shooting
- Supervision
- Training
- Project Management
- Liaison
- Operations Management
- Security Clearance
- MS Office
- Office Management
- Quality Assurance
- Interpersonal Relations
- Policies & Procedures
- Staff Development

PROFESSIONAL BACKGROUND

OPERATIONS MANAGEMENT

Plan, organize and manage the overall operational activities which include: identifying client/project needs; developing strategies and coordinating projects; and monitoring projects to ensure targeted goals and objectives are achieved on-time and within budget.

- 400% increase in productivity through developing active training courses to increase staff efficiency.
- 10% increase above targeted on-time delivery goals through developing a strategic plan of action for staff empowerment.
- 100% compliance with safety regulations, corporate policies and standard operational procedures.
- Awarded #1 Team Leader through developing individualized team building/training programs resulting in increased productivity.
- Consistently awarded for "Outstanding Leadership, Dedication and Hard Work" by managers and staff members.

EXPERIENCE

- US Army, Orlando, FL

  Operations Manager — Apr 1996 - Present
  Direct Staff: 5; Trained: 325;
  Budget: $260K Annually;
  Overall Operations; Planning & Organization;
  Policies & Procedures; New Program Development;
  Curriculum Development; Team Building; Liaison;
  Training; Evaluations; Special Projects.

  Ft. Campbell, KY

  Personnel/Administration Manager — Mar 1995 - Mar 1996
  Direct Staff: 12; Indirect Staff: 670;
  Staff Development; Public Affairs; Operations;
  Legal Issues; Personnel; Finance; Team Building;
  Promotions; Publications; Employee Awards;
  Mail Center; Evaluations; Planning; Research;
  Problem Solving; Morale/Family Support Group.

  Supervisor — Dec 1994 - Mar 1995
  Direct Staff: 14; Equipment: $2MM;
  Operations; Professional Development; Planning
  & Organization; Crime Prevention & Security.

  Team Leader — Jan 1992 - Dec 1994
  Direct Staff: 39;
  Planning; Operations Management;
  Advising/Counseling; International Readiness
  Preparations; Emergency Relief; Safety.

EDUCATION

- **Bachelor of Arts Degree in Criminal Justice,**
  University of Tennessee, Knoxville, Tennessee

- **Continuing Education:** Leadership and Supervisory Management Courses

JAMES HICKS, II

ROBERT M. HANSON

3452 Masters Avenue • Sciotoville, Ohio 45662 • (740) 776-9472 • Email: robertmh@ncr.net

Qualified for:

- **Quality Auditor**
- **Instrumentation & Control Systems Specialist**

PROFESSIONAL PROFILE

- Results-oriented professional employing more than 15 years of progressive accomplishments in auditing, instrumentation and control systems.
- Disciplined, self-starter with the unique ability to comprehend complex, unrelated information and digest it into workable terms.
- Loyal and dedicated team player, demonstrating integrity in achieving all goals and objectives.
- Motivated achiever, able to implement workable solutions to diverse situations.
- Motivated self-starter, exhibiting high ethics, hard work, competence and confidence, underscored by a personal commitment to outstanding professional performance.
- Eager to learn, meet new challenges and assimilate new concepts and ideas quickly.

AREAS OF EXPERTISE

- Quality Assurance
- ISO 9000
- Written Communications
- TQM
- MS Office Professional
- Technical Writing
- Technical Consulting
- Troubleshooting
- Internal Auditing
- Self-Assessments
- Policies & Procedures
- Training
- WordPerfect Suite
- Trend Analysis
- OSHA/Safety
- Planning & Scheduling
- Supervision
- External Auditing
- Oral Communications
- Problem Solving
- PC: IBM/Mac
- DOS/Windows/Win 95
- Tests & Measurements
- Team Leader
- Team Building

PROFESSIONAL BACKGROUND

AUDITING, INSTRUMENTATION AND CONTROL SYSTEMS

Plan, organize and manage assigned auditing, instrumentation and control systems which include: reviewing regulatory and procedure requirements; testing and monitoring of systems and processes; and reporting compliance with established standards to management.

- 100% achievement of audit projects on time and within budget through developing a time-lined plan of action.
- $300K increase in revenues through combining technical expertise and marketing strategies into a "client-centered" presentation.
- 200% increase in technical procedure accuracy through researching and analyzing current procedures, compliance regulations and technical and formatting standards.
- 100% increase in productivity through developing and implementing a planning and scheduling system used by supervisors and technicians.
- 200% increase in availability of support systems through developing and implementing a preventative maintenance program.
- Increase in audit productivity through standardizing the methods used in performing system and process audits to determine effectiveness of implementation.
- Awarded "Outstanding Service" by Lockheed-Martin for demonstrated efforts as a lead auditor.

EXPERIENCE

- Lockheed Martin
  Piketon, Ohio

Quality System Specialist III Oct 1992 - Present
Supervise: 1-5 Auditors.
Lead Auditor for: Compliance, Quality, Process & Management Assessments.
Duties: Auditing, Presentations, Recommendations, Audit Scheduling, Staff Selection/Development, Management Interface & Reporting.

Procedure Development Section Mgr. Jun 1990 - Oct 1992
Supervise: 10-12 Writers & Clerical Staff.
Procedures: Safety Systems & Administrative.
Duties: Procedure Development Supervision, Document Control/Distribution, Records Management & Writer Training/Development.

- Quadrex Energy Services
  Corapolis, PA

Supervisory Service Engineer Feb 1984 - Jun 1990
Site Manager (Various Contracts)
Staff: 10-30 Engineers, Technical Writers, QA, Safety Analysis & Administrative.
Duties: Coordinated Daily Activities for Corporate Contracts & Technical Writing.

- Nuclear Energy Inc.
  Newtown, PA

Level III Instrument Technician Supv. Aug 1982 - Jul 1984
Supervised: 12-15 Technicians.
Duties: Support Field Engineers for System Startup & Security, Procedure Development, Technical Procedure Review, System Analysis.

Level II Instrument Technician
Duties: Hands-On System Testing.

- Goodyear AEC
  Piketon, OH

lst Class Instrument Mechanic Jan 1980 - Jul 1982
Instrumentation & Control: Pneumatic, Hydraulic & Analog Electronics.
Duties: System Maintenance & Trouble Shooting.

EDUCATION

- **Shawnee State University,** Portsmouth, Ohio
  - **Bachelors Degree Program (Social Sciences)**
  - **Associates Degree (Plant Maintenance Engineering Technology)**
- ISO 9000 Auditor/Lead Auditor of Quality Systems - #24059717
- Lead Auditor, Lockheed-Martin/ASQ
- Kepner-Tregoe, Decision Making & Problem Solving
- TAP Root (Root Cause) Analysis

ROBERT M. HANSON

Ronald A. Masey, CPM

706 Kensey Avenue, • Altamonte Springs, Florida 32701 • (407) 323-1372 • Office (407) 331-0145
• Fax (407) 331-3378 • Email RAM1234@aol.com

Qualified:

• Manager, Real Estate Management •

PROFESSIONAL PROFILE

- Dynamic professional employing more than 20 years of progressive accomplishments in promoting and managing real estate activities and properties.
- Visionary leader, able to empower others and motivate diverse groups towards a common goal.
- Results-oriented planner possessing analytical acumen, perception, judgement and energy.
- Effective achiever, able to meet all goals while staying within budgetary constraints.
- Motivated self-starter, exhibiting high ethics, dedication, competence and confidence underscored by a personal commitment to outstanding professional performance.
- Hard working and goal-oriented communicator employing strong organizational skills and attention to detail.

AREAS OF EXPERTISE

• Property Management	• Real Estate	• Negotiations
• Client Relations	• Government Relations	• Community Development
• Presentations	• Land Acquisitions	• Leasing
• Special Events	• Problem Solving	• Contracts
• Land Appraisals	• Eminent Domain	• Planning & Organization
• Communications	• Multi-Family	• Multi-task Management
• Construction	• Commercial/Residential	• Turnarounds
• Court Appointed Receiver	• Government Housing	• Sales & Marketing

PROFESSIONAL BACKGROUND

REAL ESTATE MANAGEMENT

Planned, organized and managed the overall activities for diverse real estate programs budgeted in excess of $12 million with sales/brokerage of $22 million annually which included: property management and leasing, due diligence and acquisition, contract negotiations and ensuring compliance with appropriate state and local regulations.

Properties: Apartments, Offices, Strip Centers, Warehouses, Condominiums, Land Development, Single Family Homes, Hotels, Mobile Home Parks and others.

- Recognized for "Exceeding Goals and Objectives" annually through developing innovative approaches for property development while maintaining compliance with all governing regulatory bodies.
- Increased profitability through developing marketing strategies.
- 100% achievement of client's goals and objectives through managing successful turnaround of properties.
- 40% increase in productivity through establishing an organization-wide communications system for 85 employees at three locations.
- Recognized for "Excellence in Implementing Long-Range Plans and the Development of Policies and Standards" documented by clients and corporate management.

EXPERIENCE:

- SMInc
  Orlando, FL
  Senior Vice President Sep 1990 - Present
  Staff: 85; Locations: 3.
  Property Acquisition, Asset Management, Leasing.
  Properties: 500+M square feet Office Space; 500M square foot Strip Center.
  New Business Development: Renovated/Developed 12 Properties; 3600 Apartment Units.

- Marketing & Management, Inc.
  Miami, FL
  Vice President/ Director of Management Sep 1985 - Sep 1990
  Marketing, Sales, Property Management, Acquisitions, Financing, Project Manager.
  Properties: 4,400 New Condominiums, 1,050 Apartments Converted to Condominiums, 55 Projects, 4100 Rental Units.

- Seay & Thomas, Inc.
  Chicago, Illinois
  Regional Manager May 1984 - Sep 1985
  Commercial, Multi-Family Units.
  Leasing & Marketing in Florida.
  Feasibility Analysis & Due Diligence.

- T.G. Masters Company
  Boston, Massachusetts
  Area Manager Sep 1982 - May 1984
  Properties: 100 M square foot Strip Centers - Mixed Use - Retail/Office; 1200 Units; 6 Properties.

EDUCATION

- **BS in Business Administration,** Florida International University, Miami, Florida

PROFESSIONAL AFFILIATIONS AND LICENSES

- Certified Property Manager (CPM)
- Member Institute of Real Estate Management (IREM)
- Registered Real Estate Broker - Florida & Massachusetts
- Member Building Owners & Managers Association (BOMA)
- Florida Community Association Managers License
- Member National Association of Realtors
- Member Community Association Institute (CAI)
- Member Central Florida Chapter of IREM

BERTRAM BARTELL

684 Winston Commons Place • London, UK • (XXX) XXX-XXXX • bbartell@worldnet.att.net

Qualified For:

• **Real Estate - Property Development** •

PROFESSIONAL PROFILE

- Resourceful professional with more than 15 years of accomplishments in real estate development.
- Innovative, diverse and open-minded.
- Highly motivated self-starter, with strong communication skills in diverse settings.
- Personable, with outstanding analytical skills and attention to detail.
- Creative and hardworking in pursuing unique methods to attain goals and objectives.

AREAS OF EXPERTISE

- Client Relations
- Sales & Marketing
- Brokering
- Acquisitions
- Office/Business Space
- Subcontractors/Owners/ Financial
- Presentations
- Project Management
- Construction
- Market Research

- Real Estate
- Property Assets
- Appraisals
- Leasing & Renewals
- Contract Negotiations
- Strategic Planning
- Computer Proficient
- Site Selection
- Phase Development
- Leisure/Entertainment Property

- New Business Development
- Property/Land Development
- Consulting
- Liaison: Architect/ Developers/
- Start-Up Operations
- Retail/Hotel Properties
- Governmental Regulations
- Power Centers
- Industrial Parks
- Financial/Investment Analysis

PROFESSIONAL BACKGROUND

REAL ESTATE DEVELOPMENT

Plan, organize and manage the overall real estate development activities which include: determining client/ project needs; marketing, developing and managing properties; and monitoring clients/projects to ensure client satisfaction and compliance with goals and regulations.

- 98% increase in projected revenues through actively penetrating the local real estate market and developing solid relationships with financial/construction/development contacts.
- 20% increase in departmental revenues through strategically planning and coordinating the appraisal process for a publicly listed company who owns 56 major UK sea ports.
- 10% increase in client base through developing creative marketing strategies, enhancing advertising promotions and improving/modernizing communication methods.
- 100% accomplishment of project goals for a new company start-up operation by researching the market and creating a need for real estate consulting services.
- 22% increase in office productivity through utilizing existing exmployees to create a new business area offering add-on services: results - 30% increase in profitability.
- Recognized for "Outstanding Performance" for successfully researching, marketing and developing domestic and international properties.

EXPERIENCE

- EuroAsia Ventures
  Thailand

  Associate Director, Retail Development Jan 1997 - Present
  Property Range: $10K - 30MM+ Annually.
  Retail Properties: Free Standing Strip Malls & Shopping Centers.
  Clients: European Retailers (Newly Introduced to Asian Markets) & Asian Retailers.
  Duties: Development Consulting, Liaising, Project Management & Sales & Marketing.

- AsianCorp
  Thailand & Vietnam

  Director, Property Development Feb 1995 - Jan 1997
  Property Range: $500K - 250MM.
  Properties: Residential, Commercial (Office) & Hotels/Resorts.
  Liaison: Architects, Subcontractors, Financial Institutions, Land Owners & Designers.
  Duties: Coordinating Property Development, Liaison, Project Management & Financial Analysis.

- Manpower International
  United Kingdom

  Director, Real Estate Staffing Mar 1992 - Feb 1995
  Recruited Construction/Professional Staff For: Building & Mechanical Service Companies.

- John Lawrence Intl.
  United Kingdom

  Property Manager Jan 1989 - Feb 1992
  Property Range: $500K - 40MM.
  Properties: Office/Business Space.
  Clients: British Telecom, Prudential Insurance, Shell Oil, The Rank Organization & Grant Thornton.

- Haltey & Billings International
  United Kingdom

  Property/Asset Manager Apr 1986 - Jan 1989
  Clients: Associated British Ports (All major UK Ports), British Coal, British Shoe Co., Scottish Amicable & Other Major Institutions.
  Duties: Property Appraisals, Staff Management (3 Brokers) & Project Management.

EDUCATION & PROFESSIONAL DESIGNATIONS

- **Bachelors in Real Estate Management & Appraisal Diploma**
  University of South West England, United Kingdom

- Real Estate Broker's License

- FSVA-Fellow (10 Year Status) of the Incorporated Society of Valuers (Appraisers) & Auctioneers, UK

BERTRAM BARTELL

FREDRICK FROST

9380 Wymore Boulevard • Winter Springs, Florida 32712 • (407) 678-2305

Qualified for:

• Restaurant Manager •

PROFESSIONAL PROFILE

- Dynamic professional employing more than 15 years of progressive accomplishments in banquet coordination and food/beverage management.
- Motivated self-starter, exhibiting high ethics, hard work, dedication, competence and confidence, underscored by a personal commitment to outstanding professional performance.
- Dependable and dedicated team player, employing strong communication skills with diverse groups.
- Hard-working and goal-oriented achiever employing strong organizational skills and attention to detail.
- Poised innovator with strong people skills and leadership ability.
- Resourceful in pursuing unique methods to attain goals and objectives on-time and within budget.

AREAS OF EXPERTISE

- Leadership
- Menu Planning
- Theme Parties
- Training Manuals
- Team Leader
- Inventory Control
- Weddings
- Florist Coordination
- Banquet Planning
- Policies & Procedures
- Planning & Organizing
- Staff Development
- Budgeting
- Cost Reduction
- Advertising
- Special Events
- Creative Promotions
- Pricing
- Scheduling
- Purchasing
- Quality Assurance
- Entertainment Liaison
- Conventions

PROFESSIONAL BACKGROUND

BANQUET COORDINATION & FOOD/BEVERAGE MANAGEMENT

Plan, organize and manage the overall food & beverage/banquet operations for various companies which include: evaluating project/client requirements; developing budgets, strategies and creative menus; and monitoring to ensure compliance with targeted goals while enhancing quality service.

- 55% increase in banquet sales through developing creative advertising and special promotions.
- 34% increase in annual sales through achieving quality food service and customer satisfaction.
- Maintained 36% food cost and 22% liquor cost through training and employee awareness programs and incentives.
- 75% of employees have increased sales averages 10-15% through weekly sales training on "Service That Sells".
- 113% increase to bottom line profitability in a five year period through strategic menu planning, pricing, special promotions, culinary expertise, employee performance, and quality customer service.
- Doubled banquet business within three years by researching and targeting wedding/convention markets.

EDUCATION

- **Bachelor of Science in Business Administration**, Duquesne University, Pittsburgh, PA
  (Major: Accounting; Minor: Tax and Law)
- **Certified Professional Food Manager,** State of Florida

EXPERIENCE

- Hilton Lakes & Villas
  Orlando, FL

  Restaurant Manager &
  Guest Services Coordinator — Aug 1997 - Present
  Sales Volume: $1.8MM Annually;
  Staff: 65; Seats: 250;
  Theme: Casual Island Steak & Seafood;
  Key Projects: International Intern Training Program Development & Implementation, Designing New Wine List & Menu, Booking/Selling/Coordinating Parties/Banquets.

- Nascar Raceway Cafe
  Daytona, FL

  Restaurant Manager — Jan 1996 - Aug 1997
  Sales Volume: $1.1MM Annually;
  Staff: 35; Seats: 175; Theme: Racing;
  Special Events: Antique/Racing Car Shows;
  Duties: Operations; Staffing; Training; Food/Beverage/Memorabilia Purchasing; Special Promotions; Advertising; Scheduling; Cost Controls; Policies & Procedures; Floor Plans/Layouts; Inventory Control; Private Parties.

- Aladin's at Ocean Resort
  Ft. Pierce, FL

  Restaurant Manager — Aug 1992 - Dec 1995
  Sales Volume: $1.2MM Annually;
  Staff: 40; Seats: 300+; Theme: Rustic Ocean Dining;
  Special Events: Banquets; Weddings; Private Parties; Holiday Events; Business Meetings;
  Duties: Operations; Menu Planning; Budgeting; Training; Policy & Procedures; Food/Liquor/Labor Cost Reporting; Forecasting; Cost Controls; Entertainment Booking; Florist Liaison; Suggestive Selling; Special Promotions; TV/Radio/Newspaper Advertising; Staffing; Customer Service.

- Fairways at Ocean Dunes
  Country Club
  Jensen Beach, FL

  Restaurant Manager — Feb 1990 - Jul 1992
  Sales Volume: $1.6MM Annually;
  Staff: 50; Seats; 250; Theme: Country Club Dining;
  Special Events; Conventions; Weddings; Parties; Banquets; Golf Outings; Business Meetings;
  Duties: Operations; Policies & Procedures; Training; Team Building; Employee Performance Tracking; Incentives; Menu Planning; Pricing; Guest Relations; Banquet Development/Organization; Entertainment/ Linen/Florist Liaison.

THOMAS PHILLIPS

789 Wymore Road • Altamonte Springs, Florida 32714 • (407) 767-8832

Qualified for:

• Food & Beverage Management •

PROFESSIONAL PROFILE

- Dynamic professional with more than 6 years of progressive accomplishments in sales, restaurant and club management.
- Results-oriented team leader employing strong organizational skills and attention to detail.
- Motivated self-starter exhibiting high ethics, dedication, competence and confidence, underscored by a personal commitment to outstanding professional performance..
- Resourceful and creative team player demonstrating the ability to pursue unique methods for attaining goals on time and within budget.
- Open-minded and logical organizer, able to work independently and in a group setting.

AREAS OF EXPERTISE

- Customer Service
- Planning & Organization
- Recruiting
- Inventory Control
- MS Windows
- Food Service
- Supervision
- Customer Relations
- Purchasing
- Cost Reduction
- Scheduling
- Training
- Special Events
- Counseling
- Sanitation
- Sales
- Staffing
- Problem Solving
- Lotus 1-2-3
- Night Clubs/Show Rooms & Restaurants
- OSHA/Safety
- Payroll

PROFESSIONAL BACKGROUND

FOOD AND BEVERAGE MANAGEMENT

Plan, organize and manage food and beverage activities for Church Street Station (Restaurants, Clubs and Showrooms) which include: evaluating operational and customer requirements (staff, resources, equipment); providing services and solutions; and ensuring quality customer service in compliance with corporate goals and objectives.

- Recognized for excellence in service in managing Rosie O'Gradys, Apple Annies, Phineas Phogg's and the Cuban Cafe.
- 60% increase in revenues for Phineas Phogg's through developing special promotions, sales incentives and relational sales; increased profits through minimizing operating costs.
- 6 points increase in profit margin at Rosie O'Gradys through increasing employee morale, sales incentives and beverage control.
- Recognized for "Outstanding Contributions" for revamping training and establishing state-of-the-art standards for the Bar School.

EXPERIENCE

• Church Street Station Orlando, FL	**Food & Beverage Manager/ Training Coordinator**	Sep 1996 - Present
Rosie O'Grady's	**Lead Bartender**	May 1995 - Sep 1996
Apple Annies	**Senior Bartender**	May 1994 - May 1995
Cheyenne Saloon	**Senior Bartender**	Apr 1992 - May 1994

JOHN M. KIRBY

533 West Monroe Street • Orlando, Florida 32806 • (407) 343-4211

Qualified For:

• Restaurant Management •

PROFESSIONAL PROFILE

- Dynamic professional employing more than 15 years of progressive accomplishments in restaurant management.
- Dependable and dedicated team player, employing strong communication skills with diverse populations.
- Effective achiever, able to meet all goals while staying within budgetary constraints.
- Motivated self-starter, exhibiting high ethics, hard work, dedication, competence and confidence, underscored by a personal commitment to outstanding professional performance.
- Positive motivator with accelerated skills in organization and planning.
- Respected team builder, able to empower others to achieve common goals.

AREAS OF EXPERTISE

- Customer Service
- Oral Communications
- Staff Development
- Public Relations
- Team Building
- Scheduling
- Risk Management
- Menu Planning
- Special Events
- Policies & Procedures
- Purchasing
- Written Communications
- Operations Management
- Time Management
- Recruiting
- Target Marketing
- Travel
- Pricing
- Banquets/Parties
- Planning & Organization
- Inventory Control
- Marketing Strategies
- Cost Reduction
- Creative Strategies
- Presentations
- Guest Relations
- Trouble Shooting
- Cost Control
- New Restaurant Openings

PROFESSIONAL BACKGROUND

RESTAURANT MANAGEMENT

Plan, organize and manage the overall restaurant operations for various companies which include: evaluating restaurant/equipment/employee/client requirements; developing budgets, marketing strategies and creative menus; and monitoring to ensure compliance with goals and objectives while enhancing quality service.

Restaurants: Houlihans; Sbarro's; Club Med; Bennigans; Howard Johnson; and Others.

- 20% increase in sales through researching and surveying market and creating a "guest-centered" menu/buffet.
- 500% increase in productivity through streamlining food service procedures and refining guest line formation resulting in a 33% increase in sales.
- 60% increase in sales through developing and marketing special promotion activities.
- Ranked in the "Top Ten Managers of the Year" (Nationwide) for "Increasing Profitability and Successful Team Building".
- Awarded #2 Full-Service Restaurant (of 35) based on sales, secret shopper reports, cleanliness and guest relations.
- Recognized for "Outstanding Planning and Creative Innovation" for successfully organizing an 850 seat banquet resulting in increased sales, public relations, and banquet bookings.

EXPERIENCE

- Houlihans Restaurant & Bar, New York, NY — **General Manager** — Mar 1996 - May 1997
  Sales Volume: $3.5MM Annually.
  Staff: 100 (70 Full-time, 30 Part-time); Seats: 480.
  Theme: Casual American Dining.
  Special Events: Election Parties, Meals on Wheels, Singles Parties, Anniversary/Birthday Parties.
  Total Operations: Inventory Control, Scheduling, Purchasing, Receiving, Staffing, Training, Cost Control, & Marketing.

- Sbarro's Restaurant, East Coast, US — **General Manager/Trouble Shooter** — Mar 1990 - Feb 1996
  Sales Volume: $400K - 1.5MM Annually.
  Territory: Upper East Coast US (NY, NJ, PA, DE, VA).
  Staff: 25; Seats: Mall Food Courts.
  Theme: Casual Italian Food.
  Total Operations, Trouble Shooting, Problem Solving, Target Marketing, Costing, Policies & Procedures, Purchasing, Scheduling, Staffing, Re-Training, New Restaurant Openings.

- Club Med, New York, NY — **Restaurant Manager** — Nov 1988 - Mar 1990
  Staff: 25; Seats: 500-600.
  Theme: All-Inclusive Resort Menus.
  Scheduling, Planning, Guest Relations, Training.

- Bennigans Restaurant, Florham Park, NJ — **General Manager** — Aug 1985 - Oct 1988
  Sales Volume: $5MM Annually.
  Staff: 120; Seats: 240.
  Theme: Casual American Dining & Disco Bar.
  Total Operations - See Above.

- Howard Johnson Company, Clark, NJ — **Food & Beverage Manager** — Sep 1983 - Aug 1985
  Sales Volume: $1.6MM Annually.
  Staff: 70; Seats: 140.
  Total Restaurant Operations - See Above.

- Snuffy's Restaurant, Scotch Plains, NJ — **Banquet Beverage Director** — Jan 1980 - Aug 1983
  Banquet Rooms: 6 (Seats: 150 - 500 Each).
  Banquet Coordination, Special Events.
  Assistant Bar Manager
  Bartender

EDUCATION

- **Western Illinois University**, Macomb, Illinois
  Major: Business Management
- **Continuing Education:** Problem Solving, Communications, Interpersonal Management, Time/Action Planning, Sales Development, Guest Relations, and Others.

Bryce Montero

449 White Spruce Lane • Lake Mary, Florida 34746 • (407) 302-5972

Qualified for:

• **Sales & Marketing** •

PROFESSIONAL PROFILE

- Results-oriented professional employing more than 15 years of progressive accomplishments in business operations and sales.
- Dedicated to excellence in service and relationships.
- Eager to learn, meet new challenges and assimilate new concepts and ideas quickly.
- Motivated self-starter, exhibiting high ethics, hard work, dedication, competence and confidence, underscored by a personal commitment to outstanding professional performance.
- Personable, with the ability to make clients happy.
- Resourceful problem-solver, able to gather, comprehend and convey information.

AREAS OF EXPERTISE

- Inside/Outside Sales
- Prospecting
- Business Operations
- Estimates/Bids
- Advertising Strategies
- Problem Solving
- Agency/Client Liaison
- Key Account Sales
- Technical Consulting
- Strong Follow-Up
- Print Production
- Planning & Organization
- Graphics
- Promotional Materials
- Multi-Faceted Tasks
- Client Education
- Project Management
- Vendor Relations
- New Business
- Scheduling
- Marketing Strategies
- Client Relations
- PC: IBM/Mac

PROFESSIONAL BACKGROUND

SALES

Plan, organize and manage the overall business/sales operations for various companies which include: evaluating project/client needs; providing creative strategies and support services; and monitoring process to ensure compliance with targeted goals and objectives.

Clients: Motorola, Universal Studios, Scholastic Book Fairs, Florida Hospital, Higgins & Heath, Global Travel International, and Others.

- 60% increase in company sales through finding and developing niche markets.
- 450% increase in key product sales through researching and implementing creative pricing structures while maintaining quality business relationships.
- 85% client retention and 32% increase in customer base through developing a customer-centered sales and service approach.
- Increased revenues through coordinating a large-scale print promotion project.

EXPERIENCE

- Thompson Printing Company
  Orlando, FL
  Technical Sales Representative Jun 1996 - Present
  Sales Volume: $360K Annually.
  Products: Marketing Print Materials.
  Clients: Florida Hospital, Universal Studios, Valencia Community College, Scholastic Book Fairs, Global Travel, Higgins & Heath, Florida Nurse Association & Others.
  Sales, Technical Consulting, Prospecting, Consumer Education, Market Research, Account Development & Business Partnering.

- Printcolor
  Colorado Springs, CO
  Technical Sales Representative Jan 1990 - May 1996
  Sales Volume: $290K Annually.
  Products: Marketing Print Materials.
  Clients: Olympic Sport Venue Accounts, Medical Accounts, Software Developers, Advertising Agencies, Manufacturers, Attractions & Others.

- BR Graphics
  Colorado Springs, CO
  Sales & Operations Manager Jan 1987 - Dec 1989
  Services: Design & Typesetting.
  Clients: Printing Companies.
  Account Sales & Development, Print Production, Creative Design & Client Liaison.

- Unijax, Inc.
  Ft. Lauderdale, FL
  Store Manager Oct 1983 - Dec 1986
  Locations: 2 (Paper Etc. - Paper Retail Outlet).
  Store Volume: $1MM+ Annually; Staff: 4.
  Products: Fine Printing Paper Products.
  Clients: Printing Companies, Corporate Offices & End Users.
  Sales, Inventory Management, Purchasing, Merchandising, Customer Service, Advertising, Training & New Store Development.

- All Printing, Inc.
  Ft. Lauderdale, FL
  Sales Representative Jun 1981 - Sep 1983
  Key Accounts: Motorola & Government.

EDUCATION

- **BA Program in Accounting & Business Management,** Montana State College, Bozeman, MT
- **Graphic Design & Layout,** Art Institute of Pittsburgh, Pittsburgh, PA
- **Continuing Education:** Business Management & Graphic Arts Seminars

---

BRYCE MONTERO

Steven Northman

1907 Stanley Street • Chicago, IL 60630 • (912) 928-0748

Qualified for:

• **Store Manager** •

PROFESSIONAL PROFILE

- Results-oriented professional employing more than 15 years of progressive accomplishments in retail operations management.
- Creative promoter, able to work independently and in a group setting.
- Highly energetic and open-minded; offers outstanding growth potential in any capacity.
- Motivated self-starter, exhibiting high ethics, hard work, dedication, competence and confidence, underscored by a personal commitment to outstanding professional performance.
- Personable individual, with outstanding analytical skills and attention to detail.
- Eager to learn, meet new challenges and assimilate new concepts and ideas quickly.

AREAS OF EXPERTISE

- Retail Management
- Training
- Problem Solving
- Policies & Procedures
- Customer Service
- Target Marketing
- Negotiations
- Visual Merchandising
- Budgeting
- Scheduling
- Presentations
- MS Excel
- Multi-Task Management
- Planning & Organization
- Business Operations
- Staff Development
- Sales
- P & L
- MS Word
- Interface/Liaison
- Human Resources

PROFESSIONAL BACKGROUND

RETAIL MANAGEMENT

Plan, organize and direct the overall activities for store operations which included: merchandising, human resources (staffing, training and team building) and operations management.

Stores: Dillards, Byrons, Maison-Blanche/Robinsons

- 100% achievement of project requirements for opening prototype store on time and within budget through developing a specific plan of action.
- 400% increase in productivity by developing an information resource base for problem resolution.
- 25% increase in sales by developing a merchandise tracking system to ensure availability of hot items.
- Named "Manager of the Quarter" three times out of a field of 12 stores for exceeding goals in sales, club cards, credit card solicitations and cost of selling.
- 15% increase in sales over plan through creative merchandising, maintaining basic stocks and motivation and training of sales associates and managers.
- 300% increase in employee morale and 95% retention through structuring a career ladder promotional program.

EXPERIENCE

- Dillards
  Chicago, IL

  Operations Manager Apr 1997 - Present
  90 associates
  80,000 sq. ft.
  $30MM budget
  8% increase in profit margin
  200% increase in customer satisfaction

- Byrons/Uptons
  Altamonte Springs, FL

  Store Manager Oct 1989 - Apr 1997
  38 associates
  60,000 sq. ft.
  $7MM budget
  135% achievement of sales goals
  20% increase in cost savings

- Robinson's/Maison Blanche
  Orlando, FL

  Divisional Sales Manager Apr 1988 - Oct 1989
  250 associates
  3 stores
  175,000 sq. ft. (each)
  $12MM budget
  30% increase in regional sales

  Operations Manager Jul 1983 - Apr 1988
  75 associates
  8 departments
  15% decrease in shrink
  128% achievement of sales goals

EDUCATION

- **Bachelor of Science Degree in Marketing**,
  University of Central Florida - Orlando, Florida

SADDASH VINCES

333 Randave Drive • Orlando, Florida 32837 • (407) 6321-7820

Qualified in:

- Sculpting
- Fine Art
- Model Making
- Automotive Finishes
- Scale Models
- Creative Design
- Scenic Art

PROFESSIONAL PROFILE

- Creative professional employing more than 9 years of progressive accomplishments in sculpting and creative design.
- Diverse achiever, able to interpret task directions and provide solutions in a timely manner.
- Effective team builder, exhibiting the ability to motivate diverse groups to achieve a targeted goal.
- Enthusiastic, eager to learn, meet new challenges and assimilate new concepts and ideas quickly.
- Motivated self-starter, exhibiting high ethics, competence and confidence underscored by a personal commitment to outstanding professional performance.
- Dependable and dedicated team leader, who thinks logically, values creativity and always gets the job done on time and within budget.

AREAS OF EXPERTISE

- Problem Solving
- Creative Design
- Theme Park Projects
- Industrial Molds
- Life Castings
- Sculpting
- 3D/2D Art
- Troubleshooting
- Cost Containment
- Scenic Painting
- Automotive Finishes
- Injection Molding
- Team Leader
- Carving
- Planning & Organization
- Scheduling
- Entertainment Construction
- European Finishes
- Roto Molding
- Cement/Plaster/Foam/ Wood/Stone/Clay/Epoxy

PROFESSIONAL BACKGROUND

SCULPTING AND CREATIVE DESIGN

Plan, organize and manage special sculpting and design projects for various companies/projects which include: evaluating project requirements (materials, manpower); developing proposals and obtaining approvals; and following process from inception to completion to ensure compliance with project goals and objectives.

Key Projects: Tree of Life, Branch Assembly, Show & Pre-Show Sculpting, Swiss Family Robinson Rehab. & Many Others.

- Recognized for "Creativity and Productivity" resulting in selection for participation in continuous Animal Kingdom projects.
- 100% accomplishment of assigned projects on time and within budget through developing a time-lined plan of action.

EDUCATION

- **Art Institute of Pittsburgh**, Pittsburgh, Pennsylvania
  BA in Specialized Technology Degree in Industrial Design

EXPERIENCE

• Master Design Walt Disney Imagineering Buena Vista, FL	**Field Supervisor/Sculptor** Presently Quality Control/Field Art Direction at All Star Resort Phase III for Shot Crete & Plaster Icons. Animal Kingdom Projects: Field Art Direction, Tiger Wall, Asia Project, Tree of Life, Branch Assembly, Motion Sensor Housing, Show & Pre-Show Sculpting, Cattle Gate Enclosures & DinoLand Bone Yard & Savana Overlook. Magic Kingdom Project: Assistant Art Director for Swiss Family Robinson (1997 - 1998 Rehab). Crew Supervision & Design.	Sep 1996 - Present
• Universal Studios Orlando, FL	**Scenic Artist/Sculptor** Projects: Television, Theme Park, TV Land, You-Pick-Nick. Crew Supervision/Field Management. 1000 Projects: Entertainment Construction - Movies, TV, Theme Parks, Theatre, 3D Billboards, Kiosk, Museums. Managed Field Operations Crew of 12. Clients: Pepsi, Walt Disney World, Universal Studios & Others.	Mar 1993 - Sep 1996
• Adventure Design Orlando, FL	**Sculptor/Designer** Architectural/Industrial Molds, Mold Design - Fiberglass & Urethane. Managed 3 Man Team Operations. Clients: Walt Disney World & Others.	Dec 1990 - Mar 1993
• International Design Orlando, FL/Italy	**Sculptor/Instructor** Entertainment Construction/Animatronics. Taught Sculpting/Mold Making in Italy.	May1989 - Nov 1990 Special Project
• Exquisite Engineering, Inc. Orlando, FL	**Designer/Manufacturer** Designed Sales/Marketing Kiosks. Clients: Universal Studios, Barney's Coffee & Team & Others.	Oct1987 - May 1989
• Artistry Sculpturing Pittsburgh, PA	**Sculptor/Scenic Artist** Entertainment Construction. Architectural & Engineering Models.	May 1985 - Oct 1987

KAREN M. LIGHT

798 Swan Lake Road • Lake Mary, Florida 32744 • (407) 332-8888

Qualified for:

• Teacher •

PROFESSIONAL PROFILE

- Dedicated professional with more than 10 years of progressive accomplishments in education.
- Committed to excellence in service and relationships.
- Effective communicator, demonstrating strong interpersonal skills with diverse populations.
- Motivated self-starter, eager to learn, meet new challenges and assimilate new concepts quickly.
- Levelheaded team player, respectful of others and able to work with all types of people.

AREAS OF EXPERTISE

- Special Education
- Student Development
- Assessments
- Motivation
- Interpersonal Relations
- Computer Proficient
- Organization
- Annual Reviews
- Scheduling
- Parent/Admin. Liaison
- Diagnosing
- Behavior Modification
- Consulting
- Multi-Task Management
- IEP's
- Academics
- Planning
- Teaching & Mentoring
- Remediating
- Problem Solving
- Team Work/Collaborator
- Supervising
- Progress Reports
- Social Skills

PROFESSIONAL BACKGROUND

SPECIAL EDUCATION

Plan, organize and manage assigned special education activities for various schools which include: evaluating student needs; providing academic and social skills instruction; and following students to ensure maximum progress in learning focused on being successfully mainstreamed.

- 100% accomplishment of required special education-related documentation on time and in accordance with state regulations.
- Achieved "Tenure" and recognized for "Excellence in Student Motivation" Scott M. Ellis Elementary School.
- "Ernest E. Bell Memorial Award", (given annually in the Greenville Central School District) for greatest skills/behavior improvement was awarded to one of my students for five consecutive years.
- Recognized for "Outstanding Performance in Parent/Student/Staff Relations" documented by parents and administration.
- 150% increase in productivity in lesson plan developing and instruction through standardizing process while enhancing quality.

EDUCATION

- **MS in Education**, College of Saint Mary, New York, New York - GPA 3.9
  Focus: Learning Disabilities
- **BS in Animal Science,** Columbia College, New York, New York - GPA 3.62
  Focus: Equine Studies

EXPERIENCE

•	Sylvan Learning Center Glen Burnie, MD	**Teacher** Administered Assessments, K - Adults & Recorded Progress.	Oct 1997 - Jun 1998 Relocated to Florida
•	Anne Arundel County Public Schools, Annapolis, MD	**Special Education Teacher** Grades 1-5: Students with Varying Exceptionalities. Scheduling, Teaching, Planning & Consulting with Classroom Teachers.	Jul 1996 - Sep 1997
		Substitute Teacher Assistant Taught Autistic Child. Academic & Social Skills in a Mainstream Classroom.	May 1996 - Jun 1996
•	Relocation to MD	Masters Internship	Sep 1995 - Apr 1996 Completed Masters
•	Greenville Central School District Greenville, NY	**Primary Basic Skills/Resource Room/Teacher** Teaching K-6 Academic & Social Skills, Scheduling, Assessing, IEP's, Remediating, Consulting, Teacher Aides Supervision, Progress Reports, Annual Reviews, Special Education Committee Meetings, Parent Conferences. Received Tenure.	Sep 1989 - Aug 1995
•	Riding Instructor	Able Bodied & Disabled Students. Therapeutic Teaching	1985 - 1990 (Part-Time)

CONTINUING EDUCATION

- Another Door to Learning: Certificate - Assessment Workshop, Reading Institute and Learning Fair
- Columbia-Greene Community College: Certificate - Coursework/Training in Identification and Reporting Child Abuse
- Crossroads Farm: Certificate - Therapeutic Riding Instructor's Course

STEVEN HALPRIN

428 Laurel Avenue • Orlando, Florida 32888 • (407) 247-2267 • sthalprin@aol.com

Qualified for:

• TV & FILM PRODUCTION •

PROFESSIONAL PROFILE

- Dynamic professional with more than 15 years of progressive accomplishments in entertainment production and operations.
- Creative promoter, able to work independently and in a group setting.
- Dependable self-starter, always gets the job done.
- Loyal and dedicated individual demonstrating integrity in achieving all goals and objectives.
- Poised innovator with strong people skills and leadership ability.
- Eager to learn, meet new challenges and assimilate new concepts and ideas quickly.

AREAS OF EXPERTISE

- Customer Service
- Customer Relations
- Theme Park Industry
- International Marketing
- Liaison: Community & Clients
- WordPerfect
- Live Satellite Up-Links
- Staffing
- Scheduling
- TV Production
- Product Promotions
- Media Relations
- Team Leader
- Lotus 1-2-3/Excel
- MS Windows
- Travel
- TV Specials
- Special Events
- Product Research
- PC: IBM
- Budgeting
- Multi-Task Management
- Project Coordination

PROFESSIONAL BACKGROUND

MARKETING & TV/FILM PRODUCTION

Plan, organize and manage the assigned marketing and TV/film production activities which include: researching creative materials, concepts and ideas for program development; developing and presenting proposals to appropriate authorities and obtaining approvals; and following process from inception to completion to comply with goals.

Projects: Walt Disney World Inside Out Show, Christmas Parade, 25th Press Event, ABC 25th Special, Notable Commercials, Euro-Disney, Music Venues & Imagineering Projects (Honey I Shrunk the Kids, Muppets and Ninja Turtles).

- Recognized for "Excellence in Program Production and Coordination" documented by clients and management.
- 50% increase in productivity through computerizing standard documents for show sponsorships. (Delta, Kraft, American Express, Kodak, Nestles, Coca Cola, General Motors and others.)
- 100% accomplishment of special project for coordinating Euro-Disney's media positioning, coverage and production of a grand opening and press event.
- 60% increase in project productivity through developing positive liaisons with all Disney Parks and Resorts through working in positions ranging from entertaining, training, creative production and representing Disney with outside and corporate affiliates.

EXPERIENCE

• **Walt Disney World Co.** Lake Buena Vista, FL	**Note: Overlapping dates due to selection for each project.**	**Feb 1990 - Present**
Television Productions	**Associate Producer/Unit Manager** WDW TV Shows: Long Term Strategic Production Planning & Reporting; Budgeting, Scheduling, Manpower, Booking Crews & Facilities; Post Production Coordination; Liaison: Directors & Producers; & Other Administrative Support. Recent Projects: WDW 25th Press Event, Christmas Parade, ABC 25th Special and Others.	Aug 1995 - Present
International/Regional Marketing	**Unit Manager/Production Coordinator** Coordinated Radio, TV, Film Media Events; Press Event Preparations; Domestic Markets Research & Other Marketing Projects/Support.	Nov 1992 - Aug 1995
Production Operations Disney-MGM Studios	**Unit Manager, Talent Coordinator, Production Assistant** Coordinated & Produced Multiple Media Events, TV Creative, Radio Remotes, WDW Special Events Including Budgets & Schedules.	May 1990 - Apr 1994
Disneyland Paris, France	**Unit Manager, Grand Opening Task Force** Coordinated European TV Productions, Celebrity Interviews, Equipment, Facilities, Live Satellite Up-Links, Pre-Post Production.	Feb 1992 - May 1992
Grand Floridian	**Guest Services Trainer** Training, Program Planning, Liaison with WDW Departments & Corporate Affiliates.	May 1992 - Oct 1992
Disney-MGM Studios	**Hostess Trainer/Lead**	Feb 1990 - May 1993
• Theater/Commercials	**Actor, Set Designer, PA Coordinator**	May 1985 - Jan 1990

EDUCATION

- **University of Florida**, Gainesville, Florida
  Concentration: Theater Arts & Video Production
  Major: Theater & Commercial Acting
  Minor: Television

STEVEN HALPRIN

Power Resume Builder Forms

You will love these forms! They will make your resume fall into place easily and will market you well.

1. **Introducing the Power Resume Builder Forms**

1 A	**Header** (Name, address, phone, fax, email)
1 B	**Career Objective** (Should be exact job title)
1 C	**Professional Profile** (Who you are)
2	**Areas of Expertise** (What you can do for the company)
3	**Professional Background** (What you have done during your entire world of work in one sentence focused according to what the company wants
4	**Accomplishments** (How well you have performed in previous positions focused according to what the company wants)
5A-C	**Work History/Experience** (Where you have worked, what you have done, and how it translates to the new company)
6A-B	**Education**
7A	**Affiliations/Memberships**
7A	**Certification/Licensure**
7B	**Publications/Articles**
7B	**Projects**
7C	**References**

2. Review the forms.

3. Introducing →. As you proceed through the chapters, whenever you see →, this indicates action. Follow the directions and begin to complete the Power Resume Builder Forms. Before you know it, your resume will be done!

Power Resume Builder Form 1

Sample

Section

Sam Lender

FIRST NAME MIDDLE INITIAL LAST NAME
(24-30pt.font, large & small capitals, right justified, ref. p.___)

A

Street Address • City, State Zip • (xxx) xxx-xxxx • Fax (xxx) xxx-xxxx • Pager (xxx) xxx-xxxx • Email ABC@xxx.com
(10 pts, right justified Ref. p.____)

300 North Way Avenue • Orlando, Florida 35555 • Fax (407) 555-5555 • Email slender@xxx.net

Objective/Qualified for:

B

- **Operations Manager**

(Write in EXACT Job Title from ad, lead, internet, etc.)

PROFESSIONAL PROFILE

C

- **Results-oriented** professional with more than **15** years of progressive accomplishments in **operations management.**
- **A loyal and dedicated professional committed to high ethical standards and attention to detail.**
- **Goal-directed team player able to manage and motivate staff to meet goals and objectives.**
- **Proactive achiever able to negotiate proposals and manage multiple projects in a competitive environment.**
-
-

Express Power Quick Tips

In the PROFESSIONAL PROFILE:

1. This section represents *who you are/your personality.*
2. There should be no more than 6 lines listed.
3. The first line should always contain the copy presented above which focuses on what you *have done* as it applies to *what you want to do.*
4. Do not go over **15** years, unless you are an independent consultant.
5. Each line should start with a descriptive word.
6. The remaining 5 statements should represent your personality–at home, work and play.
7. Sample profile statements can be found on page 38-39.

Power Resume Builder Form 1

Section

FIRST NAME MIDDLE INITIAL LAST NAME
(24-30pt.font, large & small capitals, right justified, ref. p___) — A

Street Address • City, State Zip • (xxx) xxx-xxxx • Fax (xxx) xxx-xxxx • Pager (xxx) xxx-xxxx • Email ABC@xxx.com
(10 pts, right justified Ref. p.____)

Objective/Qualified for: — B

• ______________________________________
(Write in EXACT Job Title from ad, lead, internet, etc.)

PROFESSIONAL PROFILE — C

- ____________________professional with more than _____years of progressive accomplishments in ____
____
- ____
____
- ____
____
- ____
____
- ____
____
- ____
____

Express Power Quick Tips

In the PROFESSIONAL PROFILE:

1. This section represents *who you are/your personality.*
2. There should be no more than 6 lines listed.
3. The first line should always contain the copy presented above which focuses on what you *have done* as it applies to *what you want to do.*
4. Do not go over **15** years, unless you are an independent consultant.
5. Each line should start with a descriptive word.
6. The remaining 5 statements should represent your personality–at home, work and play.
7. Sample profile statements can be found on page 38-39.

Power Resume Builder Form 2

AREAS OF EXPERTISE

• Project Management	• Quality Control	• Budgeting
• Proposal Preparation	• Planning & Forecasting	• Cost Estimates
• Bid Soliciting	• Construction Admin.	• Contracts
• Team Building	• Purchasing	• Petroleum Pipelines
• ______	• ______	• ______
• ______	• ______	• ______
• ______	• ______	• ______
• ______	• ______	• ______
• ______	• ______	• ______
• ______	• ______	• ______
• ______	• ______	• ______

Express Power Quick Tips

In the AREA OF EXPERTISE/SKILLS/KNOWLEDGE:

1. This section represents *what you can do for a company*.
2. There should be no more than 33 items listed.
3. Items listed should represent your skills and knowledge.
4. Include the skills *that you have* and that match the skills identified in the classified ad, job posting or other information collected. See page 24, "Keys to Targeting Your Resume."
5. You may put all related items in a particular column if you wish. This is not necessary, however. Whatever the reviewer is looking for will jump out and say "here is what you are looking for–I am a match!"
6. No more than one or two words should be used to represent a skill area.
7. Sample Areas of Expertise words (according to profession) can be found on pages 42 to 61.

Areas of Expertise Exhibit

Power Resume Builder Form 2

AREAS OF EXPERTISE

• ______________	• ______________	• ______________
• ______________	• ______________	• ______________
• ______________	• ______________	• ______________
• ______________	• ______________	• ______________
• ______________	• ______________	• ______________
• ______________	• ______________	• ______________
• ______________	• ______________	• ______________
• ______________	• ______________	• ______________
• ______________	• ______________	• ______________
• ______________	• ______________	• ______________
• ______________	• ______________	• ______________

Express Power Quick Tips

In the AREA OF EXPERTISE/SKILLS/KNOWLEDGE:

1. This section represents *what you can do for a company*.
2. There should be no more than 33 items listed.
3. Items listed should represent your skills and knowledge.
4. Include the skills *that you have* and that match the skills identified in the classified ad, job posting or other information collected. See page 24, "Keys to Targeting Your Resume."
5. You may put all related items in a particular column if you wish. This is not necessary, however. Whatever the reviewer is looking for will jump out and say "here is what you are looking for–I am a match!"
6. No more than one or two words should be used to represent a skill area.
7. Sample Areas of Expertise words (according to profession) can be found on pages 42 to 61.

Power Resume Builder Form 3

PROFESSIONAL BACKGROUND

NEW BUSINESS DEVELOPMENT ________ (All caps & bold.)
(Focus your resume on what the company wants based upon what you can do. Reference p. __)

(Verb) **Plan** ________, (Verb) **organize** ________ and

manage ________ overall/assigned activities of

client retention and new business development activities for various companies ________ which included:

(verbing) **evaluating client/project scope/requirements;**

(verbing) **coordinating professional consultants;**

and (verbing) **and following projects from inception to completion to ensure quality service and client retention.**

Insert Name Droppers. Ref. pg.70 **Universal, Disney, MGM, Home Depot, Heilig Meyers, Orion Pictures, Bob Carr, First Union, Nations Bank, Massey Services, and others.**

Express Power Quick Tips

In the PROFESSIONAL BACKGROUND, the statement should:

1. The statement should represent *what you have done during your entire world of work in one sentence focused on what the company wants.*
2. Only use one sentence.
3. Follow the rule of three: Verb, Verb and Verb. (Reference page 65)
4. Ensure the background *that you have* that match those identified in the classified ad, job posting or other available information collected are included under this heading. See page 24, "Keys to Targeting Your Resume."
5. Sample statements according to profession can be found on pages 66 to 67.
6. Use "Name Droppers" when applicable. (Reference page 70)

Power Resume Builder Form 3

PROFESSIONAL BACKGROUND

______________________________ (All caps & bold.)
(Focus your resume on what the company wants based upon what you can do. Reference p. __)

(Verb)______________________, (Verb)______________________ and ____

______________________ overall/assigned activities of

____

____ which included:

(verbing)____

____

(verbing)____

____

and (verbing) ____

____

____

Insert Name Droppers. Ref. pg.___ __________________________________

____

Express Power Quick Tips

In the PROFESSIONAL BACKGROUND, the statement should:

1. The statement should represent *what you have done during your entire world of work in one sentence focused on what the company wants.*
2. Only use one sentence.
3. Follow the rule of three: Verb, Verb and Verb. (Reference page 65)
4. Ensure the background *that you have* that match those identified in the classified ad, job posting or other available information collected are included under this heading. See page 24, "Keys to Targeting Your Resume."
5. Sample statements according to profession can be found on pages 66 to 67.
6. Use "Name Droppers" when applicable. (Reference page 70)

Power Resume Builder Form 4

ACCOMPLISHMENTS (Note: This word does not appear on your resume. The accomplishments speak for themselves in presentation. All of the following may not apply to you. Use what works best!)

- **20%** % increase in profitability/(revenues)/sales through **targeting high-end markets and streamlining expenses while ensuring quality.**

- **200** % increase in productivity through **reengineering workflow process and automating payroll function**

- 100% compliance with **OSHA/HAZMAT and other governing standards** through **developing a results-oriented training program and monitoring waste disposal process.**

- Recognized for "Excellence in **Customer Service**" through **documented surveys, peer reports and management evaluations.**

- 100% achievement of **targeted goals and objectives** through **developing a strategic plan of action.**

Express Power Quick Tips

The ACCOMPLISHMENTS section:

1. Represents *how well you have performed in your previous positions (focused on what the new company wants).*
2. Presents what you have done for the bottom line—increase productivity, sales, profitability, clients, quality, employee retention, cost savings, revenues, etc.
3. Quantify your results, preferably with a percentage. (Reference page 71-85)
4. Always begin your statement with the percent or number–they are great attention-getters!
5. Identify awards, recognition and other commendations.
6. ONLY list the most notable accomplishments that will support the job for which you are applying and that would be of interest to the new company.

Accomplishments Exhibit

Power Resume Builder Form 4

ACCOMPLISHMENTS (Note: This word does not appear on your resume. The accomplishments speak for themselves in presentation. All of the following may not apply to you. Use what works best!)

- ________% increase in profitability/revenues/sales through ________________________
  ____
  ____
  ____
- ________% increase in productivity through ________________________________
  ____
  ____
  ____
- 100% compliance with ____
  through ____
  ____
  ____
- Recognized for "Excellence in ________________________________" through
  ____
  ____
  ____
- 100% achievement of ________________________________ through
  ____
  ____
  ____

Express Power Quick Tips

The ACCOMPLISHMENTS section:

1. Represents *how well you have performed in your previous positions (focused on what the new company wants).*
2. Presents what you have done for the bottom line—increase productivity, sales, profitability, clients, quality, employee retention, cost savings, revenues, etc.
3. Quantify your results, preferably with a percentage. (Reference page 71-85)
4. Always begin your statement with the percent or number–they are great attention-getters!
5. Identify awards, recognition and other commendations.
6. ONLY list the most notable accomplishments that will support the job for which you are applying and that would be of interest to the new company.

Power Resume Builder Form 5

WORK HISTORY

Express Power Quick Tips

The WORK HISTORY section:

1. Represents *where you have worked, what you have done and how it translates to the new company.*
2. Include all jobs you have had—but, do not exceed the last 15 years or 7 companies.
3. Include both the month and year (start and end dates) for each position you have held.
4. Use sub-headings as appropriate under the Job Title section: Sales Volume, Staff, Gross Margin, Net Profit, Revenues, Special Projects, Products, Clients, Industries, Services, etc. (See page 91, Work History Focus Points).
5. Identify and include one or two select awards or outstanding accomplishments.
6. Use a capital letter at the beginning of each word listed under the Job Title Section. People are more inclined to read *titles* than *paragraphs.*
7. Keep your text in the three-column format.
8. Refer to Work History, Exhibit 7-1 to 7-4.
9. Review resume samples presented in this book.

Company City, ST (Most recent job)	**Job Title** (Responsibilities / Accomplishments, Reference page 71)	(Use 3 letters for month, e.g., Jan) MON 19XX-MON19XX
Commercial Contractors **Orlando, FL**	**Business Development Manager** **Key Accounts: Datametrix, Taurus Investments, Smith Hale & Associates & Others** **Project Ranges: $500K - $5M** **Manage Two Divisions: Marketing & Collateral Administration Support; Business Development.** **Key Projects: Disney World, Universal Studios, National Parks & Others.** **12% Net Profit.**	**Oct** 19__ **Present** 20

Work History Exhibit
Form 5

Power Resume Builder Form 5

WORK HISTORY

Express Power Quick Tips

The WORK HISTORY section:

1. Represents *where you have worked, what you have done and how it translates to the new company.*
2. Include all jobs you have had—but, do not exceed the last 15 years or 7 companies.
3. Include both the month and year (start and end dates) for each position you have held.
4. Use sub-headings as appropriate under the Job Title section: Sales Volume, Staff, Gross Margin, Net Profit, Revenues, Special Projects, Products, Clients, Industries, Services, etc. (See page 91, Work History Focus Points).
5. Identify and include one or two select awards or outstanding accomplishments.
6. Use a capital letter at the beginning of each word listed under the Job Title Section. People are more inclined to read *titles* than *paragraphs*.
7. Keep your text in the three-column format.
8. Refer to Work History, Exhibit 7-1 to 7-4.
9. Review resume samples presented in this book.

(Use 3 letters for month, e.g., Jan)

Company City, ST (Most recent job)	**Job Title** (Responsibilities/Accomplishments, Reference page 71)	MON 19XX-MON19XX
____________________	____________________	_____ 19__ - ___ 20__
____________________	____________________	
	____________________	
	____________________	
	____________________	
	____________________	
	____________________	
	____________________	
	____________________	
	____________________	
	____________________	

Company City, ST	**Job Title**	Mon 19XX - Mon 19XX

(Job 2)

_____ 19__ - ___ 19__

(Job 3)

_____ 19__ - ___ 19__

(Job 4)

_____ 19__ - ___ 19__

Company City, ST	**Job Title**	Mon 19XX - Mon 19XX
(Job 5)		_____ 19__ - ___ 19__
(Job 6)		_____ 19__ - ___ 19__
(Job 7)		_____ 19__ - ___ 19__

Company
City, ST
(Job 8)

Job Title

Mon 19XX - Mon 19XX

_____ 19__ - ___ 19__

(Job 9)

_____ 19__ - ___ 19__

(Job 10)

_____ 19__ - ___ 19__

Company City, ST	**Job Title**	Mon 19XX - Mon 19XX
(Job 11)		
______________	______________	____ 19__ - ___ 19__
______________	______________	
(Job 12)		
______________	______________	____ 19__ - ___ 19__
______________	______________	
(Job 13)		
______________	______________	____ 19__ - ___ 19__
______________	______________	

Power Resume Builder Form 6

Express Power Quick Tips

The EDUCATION section:

1. Represents your educational background as it supports the job for which you are applying.
2. Only use your GPA *if you are a recent graduate* and it is above 3.3.
3. Include significant events, scholarships and awards *if you are a recent graduate*.
4. Include dates of graduation *only if you are a recent graduate*.
5. Include continuing education courses that support the focus of your resume.
6. Don't overwhelm them with every educational program you have ever attended beginning with high school.
7. Don't use anything that can be used against you.
8. Don't include your AS/AA, high school, vocational/trade school credentials, etc. if you have a bachelor's degree, unless it is critical to meeting the job requirements for the position for which you are applying.
9. Don't include the fact that you are not a high school graduate. Leave it out.
10. Refer to Step 8 in Power Resume Builder for a more detailed explanation.

EDUCATION

Highest Degree
(Select one: BA/BS/MA/MS/PhD/MD,/DDS, etc.) (if appropriate)

BA in (your major) **Business Administration** - GPA **3.9**

(Name of School) **University of Maryland**

(City) **Rockville,** (State) **MD**

Other Degree
(Select one: BA/BS/MA/MS/PhD/MD/DDS, etc.) (if appropriate)

MA in (your major) **Finance** - GPA **4.0**

(Name of School) **Georgetown University**

(City) **Washington** (State) **D.C.**

Education Exhibit
Form 6

Power Resume Builder Form 6

Express Power Quick Tips

The EDUCATION section:

1. Represents your educational background as it supports the job for which you are applying.
2. Only use your GPA *if you are a recent graduate* and it is above 3.3.
3. Include significant events, scholarships and awards *if you are a recent graduate*.
4. Include dates of graduation *only if you are a recent graduate*.
5. Include continuing education courses that support the focus of your resume.
6. Don't overwhelm them with every educational program you have ever attended beginning with high school.
7. Don't use anything that can be used against you.
8. Don't include your AS/AA, high school, vocational/trade school credentials, etc. if you have a bachelor's degree, unless it is critical to meeting the job requirements for the position for which you are applying.
9. Don't include the fact that you are not a high school graduate. Leave it out.
10. Refer to Step 8 in Power Resume Builder for a more detailed explanation.

EDUCATION

Highest Degree
(Select one: BA/BS/MA/MS/PhD/MD,/DDS, etc.) (if appropriate)

________________in (your major) ______________________________________- GPA__________

(Name of School)____

(City)____(State)__________________________

Other Degree
(Select one: BA/BS/MA/MS/PhD/MD/DDS, etc.) (if appropriate)

________________in (your major) ______________________________________- GPA__________

(Name of School)____

(City)____(State)__________________________

EDUCATION

If you have gone to a college or university but did not get a degree

(List the school first)	(City)	(State)
University of Maryland	Rockville	MD

Major: Business Administration

If you have gone to a vocational/trade school and received a diploma or certificate

(List the school first)	(City)	(State)
Orlando Tech.	Orlando	FL

Diploma/Certificate: Electrical Technician

If you are a high school graduate (See pages ___ and ___ for when to include on your resume.)

(List the school first)	(City)	(State)
Mount Vernon High School	Alexandria	VA

(List significant honors or leadership experience if you are a recent graduate only)

- National Honor Society, President
- Student Government, Secretary
- Football Team, Captain
- Yearbook Club, Editor

CONTINUING EDUCATION (List the course first, followed by the institution you attended.)

- First Aid/CPR, Belfour Hospital
- Automotive Engineering, GMC
- Stress Management, Dynamic Consultants
- Sales Training, Dale Carnegie
- Microsoft Certification, New Horizons
-
-
-
-
-

Education Exhibit
(Form 6 cont'd)

EDUCATION

If you have gone to a college or university but did not get a degree
(List the school first) (City) (State)

- ____

Major:______________________________

If you have gone to a vocational/trade school and received a diploma or certificate
(List the school first) (City) (State)

- ____

Diploma/Certificate:______________________________

If you are a high school graduate (See pages ___ and ___ for when to include on your resume.)
(List the school first) (City) (State)

- ____

(List significant honors or leadership experience if you are a recent graduate only)

- ____
- ____
- ____
- ____

CONTINUING EDUCATION (List the course first, followed by the institution you attended.)

- ____
- ____
- ____
- ____
- ____
- ____
- ____
- ____
- ____
- ____

Education Exhibit
(Form 6 cont'd)

Power Resume Builder Form 7A

Express Power Quick Tips

The AFFILIATIONS, MEMBERSHIPS, CERTIFICATION & LICENSURE sections:

1. Represents your professional associations, certification and licenses in relation to the position for which you are applying.
2. Only include those sections that directly support your targeted job.
3. Always include the license/certification first, then the organization.
4. Refer to step 9, page 99 and to sample resumes.

AFFILIATIONS/MEMBERSHIPS

(State Membership office, then association.)

- Member at Large, American Medical Association
- Secretary, Association of Clinical Pathologists
- Chairman, American Board of Certified Accountants
-
-

CERTIFICATION/LICENSURE

(State Certification/License, then certifying/licensing body. Include license number if appropriate.)

- Registered Nurse #2987503, Florida Board of Nursing
- Certified: Auto Engineering Technician
- Licensed Contractor #2222, South Carolina
- Certified Public Accountant, State of Georgia
-

Affiliations, Memberships, Certification, Licensure Exhibit
Form 7A

Power Resume Builder Form 7A

Express Power Quick Tips

The AFFILIATIONS, MEMBERSHIPS, CERTIFICATION & LICENSURE sections:

1. Represents your professional associations, certification and licenses in relation to the position for which you are applying.
2. Only include those sections that directly support your targeted job.
3. Always include the license/certification first, then the organization.
4. Refer Step 9, page 99 and to sample resumes.

AFFILIATIONS/MEMBERSHIPS

(State Membership office, then association.)

- ______________________________
- ______________________________
- ______________________________
- ______________________________
- ______________________________

CERTIFICATION/LICENSURE

(State Certification/License, then certifying/licensing body. Include license number if appropriate.)

- ______________________________
- ______________________________
- ______________________________
- ______________________________
- ______________________________

Power Resume Builder Form 7B

Sample

PUBLICATIONS/ARTICLES

(State Title, published by, date)

- The Dynamics of Combustion, Environmental Issues, January 1988
- 40 Minute Power Resume, Renaissance Ink Press, January 2000
- Public Relations and the Press, Marketing Image Magazine, July 1999
-
-
-
-
-
-
-

PROJECTS

Project Title	Description	Accomplishment
Seven Corners Mall	500 Store Fronts on 42 Acres	On time 10% Cost Savings
The Entrepreneur	1.5 Hour Film Promoting Business	$2M raised in Venture Capital
Power Resume Software Package Development	How to do a resume in as little as 15 mintues	On Time Within Budget

Power Resume Builder Form 7B

PUBLICATIONS/ARTICLES

(State Title, published by, date)

- ____________________
- ____________________
- ____________________
- ____________________
- ____________________
- ____________________
- ____________________
- ____________________
- ____________________
- ____________________

PROJECTS

Project Title	Description	Accomplishment

Power Resume Builder Form 7C

Sample

REFERENCES

(Never send references with your resume. Only send when requested. When requested, notify references and educate them about the job for which you are being considered. Include 3 professional and 3 personal references. All should be professional people.)

Name George Washington Hall
Job Title President
Company Hall & Associates
Address 333 West Street
City, State, Zip Alexandria, VA 44444
Home Phone (555) 444-4444
Work Phone (555) 444-3333
Email GWHall@yyy.com

Name ____
Job Title ____
Company ____
Address ____
City, State, Zip ____
Home Phone (____) ____
Work Phone (____) ____
Email ____

Name ____
Job Title ____
Company ____
Address ____
City, State, Zip ____
Home Phone (____) ____
Work Phone (____) ____
Email ____

Name ____
Job Title ____
Company ____
Address ____
City, State, Zip ____
Home Phone (____) ____
Work Phone (____) ____
Email ____

Name ____
Job Title ____
Company ____
Address ____
City, State, Zip ____
Home Phone (____) ____
Work Phone (____) ____
Email ____

Name ____
Job Title ____
Company ____
Address ____
City, State, Zip ____
Home Phone (____) ____
Work Phone (____) ____
Email ____

References Exhibit
Form 7C

Power Resume Builder Form 7C

REFERENCES

(Never send references with your resume. Only send when requested. When requested, notify references and educate them about the job for which you are being considered. Include 3 professional and 3 personal references. All should be professional people.)

Name ______________________________

Job Title ______________________________

Company ______________________________

Address ______________________________

City, State, Zip ______________________________

Home Phone (_____) ______________________

Work Phone (_____) ______________________

Email ______________________________

Name ______________________________

Job Title ______________________________

Company ______________________________

Address ______________________________

City, State, Zip ______________________________

Home Phone (_____) ______________________

Work Phone (_____) ______________________

Email ______________________________

Name ______________________________

Job Title ______________________________

Company ______________________________

Address ______________________________

City, State, Zip ______________________________

Home Phone (_____) ______________________

Work Phone (_____) ______________________

Email ______________________________

Name ______________________________

Job Title ______________________________

Company ______________________________

Address ______________________________

City, State, Zip ______________________________

Home Phone (_____) ______________________

Work Phone (_____) ______________________

Email ______________________________

Name ______________________________

Job Title ______________________________

Company ______________________________

Address ______________________________

City, State, Zip ______________________________

Home Phone (_____) ______________________

Work Phone (_____) ______________________

Email ______________________________

Name ______________________________

Job Title ______________________________

Company ______________________________

Address ______________________________

City, State, Zip ______________________________

Home Phone (_____) ______________________

Work Phone (_____) ______________________

Email ______________________________

References Exhibit
Form 7C

Index

I

J

L

M

N

O

P

Q

R

S

T

W